Healing Secular Life

CONTEMPORARY ETHNOGRAPHY

SERIES EDITORS
Kirin Narayan
Alma Gottlieb

A complete list of books in the series
is available from the publisher.

Healing
Secular Life

Loss and Devotion
in Modern Turkey

Christopher Dole

PENN

UNIVERSITY OF PENNSYLVANIA PRESS

PHILADELPHIA

Published by
University of Pennsylvania Press
Philadelphia, Pennsylvania 19104-4112
www.upenn.edu/pennpress

Printed in the United States of America
on acid-free paper
10 9 8 7 6 5 4 3 2 1

Library of Congress Cataloging-in-Publication Data

Dole, Christopher.
   Healing secular life : loss and devotion in modern
Turkey / Christopher Dole — 1st ed.
      p.   cm. — (Contemporary ethnography)
   Includes bibliographical references and index.
   ISBN 978-0-8122-4416-8 (hardcover; alk. paper)
      1. Spiritual healing—Political aspects—Turkey.
2. Healers—Legal status, laws, etc.—Turkey.   3. Secularism—
Turkey.   I. Titl.   II. Series: Contemporary ethnography
HN656.5.Z9:D65   2012
615.8′5209561—dc23   2012008451

For Joy

Contents

Healing Secular Life

Introduction

Venerating Death

Speeding through the streets of Ankara in his new Passat, Zöhre Ana's son-in-law incessantly looked into the rearview mirror for the trailing cars. Behind me, in the back seat, sat Gülay, Gülay's husband, and their freshly circumcised eight-year-old son. I had not recognized Gülay initially. More than five years had passed since I had last seen her, while she was on a visit from the Netherlands, and even then we had exchanged only brief introductions. I knew Gülay's father well, though, as someone who figured among the most passionate followers of Zöhre Ana, a woman whose ability to perform miracles—especially for the sick and dying—had attracted a modest following, as well as the title of *evliya*, or "saint." Years earlier, when I lived in a nearby squatter neighborhood and visited Zöhre Ana's compound regularly, Gülay's father, Ümit, seemed always to be there and willing to talk with me. We had become quite close. His passion was infectious. When I asked after her father, Gülay's face darkened. Ümit no longer accepted Zöhre Ana's authority, and this rejection had precipitated a division in the family, pitting the mother and children against the father. He was now living across the city, alone, having moved out of the apartment the family had bought at great expense and with great excitement five years earlier to be closer to Zöhre Ana.

Behind us, in the caravan of five additional cars, sat five more recently circumcised children and their families. I assumed we were heading to the tomb of a holy person—where, as was common practice, prayers would be offered and food distributed to guests. In the case of circumcisions, visits to tombs are typically festive and brief, unlike the pleadings of and for the severely ill. As we streamed across the city—through outer squatter neighborhoods, new yet rapidly decaying industrial districts, blocks of upscale apartments—I learned that this would be not a typical tomb visitation but a trip to Anıt-Kabir, the final resting place of the great revolutionary leader of the republic Mustafa Kemal Atatürk.

Atatürk endures as an emblematic figure in Turkey's pitched battle over the place of religious authority in political institutions, as well as the proper place of religious expression in public life. In the secularization reforms ushered in under his leadership in the 1920s and 1930s, as a dimension of the state's Kemalist ideology, the Ottoman Sultanate and Islamic Caliphate were abolished to make way for a political order organized around secular democratic principles. The state simultaneously took over directorship of mosques and actively sought to limit religion's authority to the private sphere, such that religion would become strictly a matter of personal sentiment. Along with its efforts to loosen the influence of religious authority on political institutions, the state would also work to forcibly close the influential networks of religious orders and lodges, many organized around the tombs of holy persons, that were a prominent presence in the religio-political landscape of the Ottoman Empire.

The irony of our impending visit to Anıt-Kabir was inescapable.

Gülay, her husband, and the others in the caravan regarded Zöhre Ana, the *evliya*, as the inheritor of Atatürk's spirit (*ruh*) and a person through whom Atatürk was once again able to speak. As such, the form that their devotion to Atatürk assumed drew intense animosity from neighbors, reporters, and police alike. The excited accounts of Zöhre Ana's repeated arrests that I had listened to on so many previous occasions began to take a more ominous cast as we approached Atatürk's tomb. Zöhre Ana and her followers not only embodied a formation of religious life at odds with the nation's founding secularist ideals—a form of religious organization that had been expressly targeted for suppression to make way for the current secular political order—but the object of their devotion is generally recognized as the principal agent of this history of religious suppression. And here we were, poised to enter the site of his burial, a site where his death figures so prominently, and with such raw intensity, into the staging of a nation's origins and wonder.

We crossed the vast open plaza of Anıt-Kabir, with its nationalistic juxtaposition of mythologized Hittite symbolism and sobering modernist monumentality (Figure 1), and gathered on the steps ascending to the mausoleum. After taking pictures, we passed between two soldiers flanking the door, posing immobile in the late summer heat, and entered the

Figure 1. Anıt-Kabir. Sibel Bozdoğan rightly describes "monumentality, national symbolism, and power" as constituting the primary preoccupations of Anıt-Kabir's architectural discourse (2001:290). Photograph by author.

mausoleum's central room—a grand, marble affair at the far end of which stood the marker for Atatürk's tomb below. Tourists—Turkish and foreign—made the circular clockwise movement to the left side of the room, passing in front of Atatürk's tomb, and exiting along the right. We moved forward, as would any unassuming group of tourists. As we passed in front of the tomb marker, the group suddenly took formation, with circumcised children in front and others lined up behind, their palms turned upward in prayer. Tourists in line looked on in frustration, the Turkish among them visibly aghast at the spectacle.

Security guards appeared immediately. Descending from the rear, they ordered the group to move forward. The saint's followers asserted their freedom to worship as they pleased. The guards, enraged, insisted that this was no place for "worship." The argument continued to escalate as guards began to push men in the group. Eventually, Zöhre Ana's followers relented and moved on. We filed back out onto the plaza, where the head guard approached us and began reprimanding Zöhre Ana's son-in-law. The guard spoke of Zöhre Ana knowingly, as if he was accustomed to such visits. Aware that his power in this situation was quite limited and that arrests would draw media attention (and perhaps attract more followers), the guard struggled to contain his anger.

We moved yet again to the outer steps leading down from the central plaza, into the shade. A member of the party soon appeared with plastic trays of bottled water and prepackaged pastries purchased from the nearby gift shop. He slowly made his way from person to person, ceremoniously offering food and water. Moments later, guards were again surrounding us. Such behavior was not permitted here. Some offered feeble protests, pointing to others snacking nearby. The guards waved them off. Others were certainly snacking in a less threatening manner. He ordered us to immediately desist. Zöhre Ana's son-in-law apologized and we returned to our cars, and back across the city to the saint's compound to continue celebrating their boys' circumcisions.

*   *   *

From praying before a burial site to the ceremonial distribution of food, our visit to Anıt-Kabir assumed the basic form of a shrine visitation. Although visits to shrines and tombs do not typically unfold amid such hostility, our destination proved unsettling to the tomb's caretakers. That is, in the appeals of a living saint for help from a deceased Atatürk, our visit touched on a nerve exposed since Atatürk's passing in 1938. How is one to venerate the death of the person who ushered in a new nation established on principles that fundamentally rejected the possibility of the founder's sanctity and the state's sacredness as a legitimate basis of sovereignty? For the caretakers of his tomb, Atatürk was a secular political and military leader to be memorialized, not a saint or miracle worker to be worshiped. The projects of secular modernity and societal reform he inspired—which aimed to liberate the nation from both imperialism and what was seen as the crippling mental effects of an older, corrupt order—sought precisely to end such behavior and the forms of desire inspiring it. "It is a disgrace," after all, as Atatürk once venomously remarked, "for a civilized society to appeal for help from the dead."[1]

Despite the fleeting and seemingly exceptional character of these events, I had a sense that something larger was at stake in this confrontation between the followers of a saint who gives voice to the nation's dead founder and government officials laboring to regulate how the state and its past are to be venerated. In time, I came to understand the confrontation as publicly staging what I had been hearing with urgency in the stories of suffering and loss I encountered over the course of my research. Namely, to recount one's experiences of healing and being healed—especially among those seeking the assistance of healers and forms of care outside the country's network of state-authorized health clinics and hospitals—was not only to reflect on one's experiences of personal and familial loss, but simultaneously to engage a series of interlocking struggles over the status of death, loss, and devotion in relation to state power. Such a recognition would set the course of this book.

While the open veneration of Atatürk as a saint is undoubtedly rare in Turkey, figures such as Zöhre Ana index a broader complex of "marginal" or "popular" religious practices that are, in varying ways, concerned with healing and recovery—from Qur'anic healers who treat those being afflicted by *cins* (spirits) to *evliya*s who offer the hope of miraculous recovery, from those who address the effects of malevolent gazes (*nazar*, or "evil eye") to those who have inherited healing gifts from grandmothers, on to innumerable curative sites scattered across the country. This project began amid such figures and sites, as a study of the practice and utilization of ritual and religious forms of healing within two working class neighborhoods located in Turkey's second largest and capital city, Ankara. At the time, I was specifically interested in the subjective and embodied experience of healing and personal transformation that such ritual practices make possible (Csordas 1994; Desjarlais 1992; Csordas and Kleinman 1996).

The project resulted, however, in an attempt to make sense of the contentious debates that surrounded these practices, the processes through which they were and continued to be forcibly excluded from Turkey's project of secular modernity, and the forms of therapeutic and religious authority that they (as a discordant collection of people, practices, and ideas that only come together through their exclusion) were able to sustain within inhospitable discursive and material conditions. Why were religious healers despised with such abandon—as exploiters of the sick and vulnerable, as swindling profiteers, as heretical distortions of a true Islam, and as superstitious holdovers from a surmounted era? And why, despite this animosity, did all sorts of people—not just the desperately ill—continue to seek them out? What forms of desire did their continuing allure engender?

Given the enmity they attracted and the limited scale of their practices (the healers I met rarely treated more than a handful of patients in any given week, most from the surrounding neighborhood), the religious healer would seem to be far removed from, if not altogether irrelevant to, conventional conversations about religion and politics in Turkey. Even in the rare instance when a healer did attract a small following, my concern with experiences of suffering and recovery revealed the vast majority of relationships that formed around such figures to be particularly transient, as individuals episodically consulted healers to address specific problems. These forms of religiosity and religious practice did not, in other words, constitute any sort of organized religious or political "movement." In the accepted political script of "Islamists" and "Secularists" struggling for state control—a script being dutifully studied by experts the world over in the hopes of discovering in Turkey a viable model for secular democratic rule in the Muslim world, as well as clues to imagining the future of a new Europe—the religious healer would appear to have no discernible role.

Nevertheless, it would become ever more clear over the course of my research that the figure of the religious healer was deeply embedded in the larger drama that this script was trying to capture. That is, it would become clear that efforts to cultivate small-scale forms of religious and therapeutic authority condensed as they took part in large-scale projects of world making, especially those aligned with the political and religious management of collective and individual life in conditions of secular modernity.[2] If, as I ask, we regard healing as the remaking of worlds (as opposed to simply a return to "normalcy"), how do healers of different sorts participate in and reformulate competing projects of world and subject making, whether they be religious, political, or scientific? If one regards words and speech as potentially curative, how is it that certain forms of speech are listened to, held to be true, and experienced as containing a material force, while others are regarded as empty, treacherous, or even criminal? As these questions begin to indicate, this book is organized around the vital entanglement of therapeutic power and political rule.[3]

Aesthetics and the Healing of Secular Life

You are researching faith healers, for example, an interesting topic to study. A very, very interesting topic to study. But we psychiatrists aren't really permitted to do such work. We have to base our scientific grounds on secularity [*laiklik*]. That's it. (Turkish psychiatrist discussing the political constraints of her therapy)

The stories of affliction and recovery I gathered over the course of research turned with unanticipated consistency to the theme of secularism. With an initial focus on the subjective and embodied experience of therapeutic processes, I pushed these references to secularism aside—secondary concerns born, I presumed, of misunderstanding. If secularism was a political doctrine that aimed to either establish a separation between political and religious institutions or regulate religion's public expression, the relevance of secularism to the intimacy of recovery and healing would appear distant. Moreover, considering the intense animosity that religious healers attracted, especially from self-described "secularists," one would assume that talking about one would necessarily exclude the other, or that they would only coincide in oppositional terms. Yet the continued repetition of the theme of secularism in stories of healing and being healed seemed to indicate a labor whose value was escaping me. Considerable time would be required for me to learn how to listen to such stories.

Among other lessons, I would have to learn how these stories were registering the extent to which healing and secularism were mutually indebted. Doing so would necessitate that I rethink not only my understanding of those therapeutic processes associated with healing, but also the meaning of secularism in these settings. The concept of "secularity" to which the psychiatrist above refers, for instance, certainly meant something other than secularism's formulation as a political principle regarding the organization of political and religious authority within state institutions. It also spoke toward something other than conventional accounts of secularization—that with secularization comes the differentiation of society into discrete spheres (e.g., politics as separate from religion as separate from the economy as separate from science, and so forth), the "privatization" of religion into the domestic sphere, and the declining significance of religion as a social force (see Casanova 1994). For this psychiatrist, "secularism" was less a political doctrine than a normative discourse concerning one's proper conduct as both a citizen and a psychiatrist. As with others, it was less a legal principle than an encompassing way of life.[4]

This vision of secularism as a normative way of life brings into view, I argue, an irreducibly aesthetic dimension of Turkey's project of secular modernity. By this I mean not that secularism is merely an example of politics as a form of art (that secular political discourse relies on a reservoir of persuasive images, symbols, and narrative conventions), but that a critical element of Turkey's project of secularism works to shape the horizons of the sensible, in terms of both what is available to perception and what is deemed possible in a given set of conditions. In other words, I approach secularism not simply as a political doctrine regarding the relationship between religious and political authority, but as a social force concerned with the organization of sensibilities, sentiment, and possibilities. In contrast to studies of secularism that work along the well-worn path of political doctrines and religio-political movements, I am concerned with secularism as an assemblage of interdependent ideas, practices, institutions, and processes that organize relationships between seeing and being seen, speaking and listening, the limits of perception and possibility, and the distribution of abilities, sensibilities, and people in space.

With my interest in conceiving of healing and secularism as overlapping projects of world and subject making, I am particularly concerned with the way that both share a common investment in the "distribution of the sensible," in the sense Jacques Rancière has given this phrase in his conceptualization of a politics of aesthetics (2004). For Rancière, aesthetics involves not simply the valuation of sense perception or the effects of perceptible phenomena on the perceiver. Rather, aesthetics additionally concerns the processes and practices through which particular phenomena become visible, speakable, or thinkable—how they become, that is, sensible—in a specific set of conditions. As compared to typical aesthetic inquiries into the effects of images, words, or performances on viewers, readers, or audiences, this formulation insists on a different line of questioning: How are we to understand the ways that particular and contingent aesthetic relations—between perception and the imperceptible, modes of visibility and seeing, sound and hearing, doing and making—become articulated with specific forms of meaning and thought in a given set of material, discursive, and historical conditions?

Rancière's notion of the "distribution of the sensible" is critical for conceptualizing these aesthetic relationships, as well as the forms of community they suggest. In a discussion of the relationship between literarity and historicity, Rancière characterizes these distributions of the sensible as organizing "material rearrangements of signs and images, relationships between what is seen and what is said, between what is done and what can be done. . . . They define models of speech or action but also regimes of sensible intensity. They draft maps of the visible, trajectories between the visible and the sayable, relationships between modes of being, modes of saying, and modes of doing and making. They define variations of sensible intensities, perceptions, and the abilities of bodies" (2004: 39). The study of aesthetics, in this regard, thus involves an examination of the processes and conditions within and through which phenomena become available to sense perception, how they become thinkable and speakable in a particular way in particular settings, and how they participate in as well as reflect the delimiting of horizons of possibility (i.e., that which is "sensible").

Approached in these terms, the aesthetic, social, and political are inescapably intertwined. For Rancière, the commonality on which community is founded turns not on a shared claim of territory but on a shared partition of the sensible—or "common sense"—that provides community with its perceptual coordinates. The implications of such a commonality of sense extend beyond mere sense perception and shared sensibilities. As the partitioning of the sensible structures relationships between perception, thought, and speech, it simultaneously organizes the distribution of abilities and possibilities for participating in a common world, which is at once the distribution of bodies in space—the separating of those who are seen from those who are invisible, those who are heard from those without a voice, those who are able to take part from those who are excluded. The aesthetic and political are thus intimately bound, for the aesthetic is precisely what is at stake in all political arrangements—the organization of the sensible, the delimitation of spaces and times, the distribution of bodies in space, the apportioning of occupations and domains of activity, and the parceling out of possibilities (Rancière 1999, 2004). "Politics," as Rancière explains, "revolves around what is seen and what can be said about it, around who has the ability to see and the talent to speak, around the properties of spaces and the possibilities of time" (2004: 13).[5]

While we will need to complicate Rancière's formulation of a singular structuring of the sensible—for the communities where I worked were constituted by a multiplicity of forces, certainly not always working collaboratively—it nonetheless begins to offer a language for thinking about the intersection of the aesthetic and political at the entanglement of therapeutic power and political rule. Moreover, it offers us a language for conceptualizing this entanglement that neither exaggerates the political significance of therapeutic encounters (as if the entire political order were at stake in the meeting of a patient and a healer) nor reduces secularism to a coherent totality that preexists the social fields that, in our case, healers and their patients move through. In particular, as I argue in this book, that which is at stake in Turkey's project of secular modernity—to reframe Rancière's observation—is precisely what is at stake in healing: the organization of the sensible, the ordering of social relations, and the building of alternate constellations of past limits and future possibilities.

Framing our therapeutic concerns in terms of a politics of aesthetics also puts before us a set of questions to be unraveled in the chapters to come. What forms of saintly speech are able to gather an audience today,[6] and what does this tell us about the conditions of speaking and being heard in contemporary Turkey? How does the criminalized voice of the religious healer—which is understood to possess curative powers—interact with other, permitted types of religious, political, and medical speech? In patients' desire for such forms of religious and therapeutic authority, how do they rework the ideals of reason, scientific progress, and individual freedom that are central to Turkey's project of secular modern development? As I will illustrate in the chapters to come, it is because of the unique ability of marginalized forms of religious and therapeutic authority to challenge dominant regimes of perception and sensibility—as they labor to find voices that can be heard, words that can touch and heal, visions and forms of visibility that can reorder relationships between past limits and future possibilities—that I speak of the healing of secular life.[7]

Secularism and Recovery

In Turkey, the concept of secularism, or *laiklik*,[8] occupies a fundamental position in the nation's vision of its own past, the limits of the present, and the possibilities of political futures. At least in the versions of Turkish nationalism that took root in the late Ottoman period and have prevailed since the nation's founding in 1923, Turkey's projects of modernization and secularization have remained closely aligned. Throughout this period, secularization has been broadly construed in normative terms: in order to be "modern," the state had to be "secular." Accordingly, the state's secularization campaigns of the early and mid-twentieth century were principal sites for the reformist revision and modernization of society. In thinking through the legacy of this history, and the significance of secularism to my interest in contemporary stories of loss and healing, it will be imperative to keep in mind the specificity of Turkey's project of secular modern development.

Unlike common accounts of political secularism, Turkey's history of secular reform was as much about structural differentiation (of religious from political institutions) as it was about control and regulation. As a new nation emerged from the remnants of an Ottoman state organized around interdependent political and religious institutions, secular reformers sought to remove religious institutional influence from state structures, regulate public forms of religious expression, subordinate Islam's role as a binding force of the polity to Turkish nationalism, and restrict religion to a matter of personal or private concern. Through these reforms, the removal of religious influence from within the state was to be achieved by subordinating religion to the state, rather than simply their separation. In time, and as we will consider in significantly more depth in the following chapter, no dimension of life—religious or otherwise—would remain untouched by the reforms secularism inspired. Today, the idea of secularism persists as a core value of the nation's political imaginary, continuing to organize discourse in an array of institutional and noninstitutional settings.

Over the course of research for this book, I would come to recognize the extent to which the stories of suffering and loss I was hearing were deeply indebted to this history of secular reform. In fact, it seemed impossible to talk about healing without talking, in some way, about secularism. Conversations about religious healing insistently escaped the therapeutic, reliably becoming stages for larger social commentaries—where a desire for recovery would raise questions about the proper place of religious authority in the ordering of both state power and community life, where the powers of the religious healer would bring into the open an anxious sense that the present secular order was under threat by the return of a past age of theocratic Islamic rule, or where complaints about physicians in the local clinic and the financially exploitative practices of healers would give voice to a legacy of ideologies of scientific progress and economic development at the center of Turkey's project of secular modern reform. In each, it seemed that conversations about what it meant to be a good patient were invariably discussions of what it means to be a good citizen. Put otherwise, much as our visit to Anıt-Kabir was an instance of government officials endeavoring to manage how the state's power was imagined and its reality performed into existence—in a space where so many fantasies of political unity and freedom take flight—I would continually encounter in everyday intimacies of therapeutic desire traces of a political order similarly laboring to make and remake the grounds of its own authority.

As the above begins to suggest, this book's engagement with secularism is not an interrogation of the "problem" of religion in politics—as is implicitly the case in the vast majority of considerations of secularism, especially those situated in the Muslim world. Rather, and following Talal Asad, my concern is with secularism as a dynamic assemblage of ideas, policies, and institutional practices that work to establish particular configurations of religion, politics, and ethics (2003). More precisely, I am interested in exploring secularism's multifaceted capacity to reorder social life, as well as the ordering of social life that sustains accompanying regimes of sensibility, intelligibility, and possibility. In this regard, the chapters to follow take part in a larger set of scholarly conversations about secularism that seek to examine secularism as a productive historical, social, and ethical force (rather than merely the subtraction of religion from the public sphere), problematize assumptions about the oppositionality of the theological and political (or religion and the secular), and de-center conventional histories of secularism that locate its origins within a specifically European narrative of democratic emancipation (rather than a history of colonial regulation and subjugation).[9]

Appreciating secularism's politics of aesthetics will invite us to approach the topic otherwise than through state-centered politics (which, in Turkey, would mean framing secularist politics as a struggle between "Islamists" and "Secularists" for control of state institutions, which would in turn be situated in a history of political parties and electoral politics). In our case, this will entail attending to the divergent ways secularism works to organize the forms of speech and truth that are to be granted credibility in a given set of conditions, the forms of sociability and subjectivity that are at once the objects and subjects of such truth, the types of (Islamic) visibility acceptable in spaces delimited as "public," the (gendered) distribution of bodies in such an apportioning of space, and the general horizons of intelligibility and possibility for acting on the world. Toward this end, the following chapters trace multiple efforts to cultivate religious and therapeutic authority within a world that has been dramatically remade by a state's project of secular modern world making. By exploring the ways these efforts both bear witness to the historical exclusion of particular forms of practice, truth, and ability from the order of the nation in the name of secular modernity and also work to transform intimate spheres of bodily and subjective experience, I argue that religious healing offers a privileged location for examining the constituting force of sociopolitical systems within everyday life.

While secularism is assuredly not the only means available for examining a state's politics of aesthetics, and while the state itself is of course neither a unified entity nor the sole player in secular reform,[10] I suggest that by examining closely the processes associated with the fashioning and recognition of therapeutic authority in a given set of conditions we confront a set of shared heritages, if not genealogies, that join the transformations of subjectivity constituting healing with those techniques employed for the governance of collective life and production of governable subjects within secular modern conditions (Foucault 1986; see also Rose 1999). Put differently, where some may assert that experiences of healing and recovery reveal something fundamental about the nature of being human, my argument contends that healing instead tells us more about the character of being governed in conditions born of secular modern political imaginaries.

This is not to suggest that the stories of healing and loss recounted in this book are simply veiled accounts of political control. Rather, by approaching the entanglement of therapeutic power and secular political rule through the formulation of aesthetics we have set for ourselves, and by locating this inquiry in the interstices of state and religious law where the religious healer labors, we enter into a setting wherein the state's hold on the subject is tenuous and, as Das and Poole have argued, "the state is constantly refounding its modes of order and lawmaking" (2004: 8). This approach will not only introduce us to the everyday ways that large-scale political structures are continually being built and rebuilt in the course of social life, but also help us appreciate the remarkable diversity of religious sensibilities one encounters in a setting such as Turkey.

Exilic Forms of Religious Life / Islam Without Movement

Had I not visited Anıt-Kabir with Zöhre Ana's followers that afternoon, I suspect that the ensuing events would never have moved much farther than their original stage. Beyond idle chat over tea between security guards, or perhaps a minor contribution to an existent sense of Zöhre Ana's unwarranted repudiation by the state among her followers, this confrontation between Zöhre Ana's followers and the guardians of Atatürk's tomb would have left few remains. For those committed to the state's vision of secular political rule, such an event should not have occurred. To acknowledge it officially would be to suggest an unproductive disunity within the nation. Nor was this a type of religious conduct supported by dominant forms of Islamic orthodoxy in Turkey. Even for scholars of the social sciences, especially those dedicated to the study of political Islam, this visit to Atatürk's mausoleum assuredly did not fit into accepted models of political contestation. Such encounters, in other words, are too peripheral to "real" politics, too distant from "true" Islam, too oblique and disordered to fit into fashionable debates over "Islamists" and "Secularists," "Radicals" and "Moderates."[11] For each, these fleeting moments of devotion are either exceptions to the general order of things or superficial symptoms that, at best, point toward something else, more solid, underlying them.

In taking these sorts of moments seriously, however, I am struggling to bring together two scholarly conversations that rarely meet. This book emerges from a sense that the longstanding interest in ritual and religious healing within anthropology, medical anthropology in particular, has something important to contribute to more recent anthropological efforts to rethink secularism, especially as these efforts are being worked out in the context of the Middle East. In the first instance, I approach the therapeutic practices that concern me in this book as generative sites of self and world (re)making—as involving the transformation of the constraints and affordances of human action and subjectivity, the elaboration of alternative constellations of social relatedness, the reworking of configurations of sensibility and bodily experience, and the building of possibilities for alternate futures and re-imagined pasts.[12] In the second instance, the stories of healing and being healed that I attempt to retell here traverse at multiple angles a series of ongoing scholarly debates about the relationship between Islam, modernity, and subjectivity.

Whether writing against a conception of modernity that is singular and prototypical (Hefner 1998; Deeb 2006; Çınar 2005; Özyürek 2006), or against formulations of subjectivity bound to liberal models of agency, autonomy, and freedom (Asad 1993, 2003; Mahmood 2005; Hirschkind 2006; Silverstein 2008, 2011), scholars engaged in these debates have attempted to (1) develop an analytic lens that recognizes the force of European models of governmentality in the shaping of political and religious realities outside of Europe without (2) presuming the status of the subject or modernity as either replicating or defined exclusively in opposition to Western models of secular modernity. In addition to complicating singular models of modernity and subjectivity, these works have offered much-needed ethnographic interrogations of the complex interplay of religious and political experience within secular modern conditions. They thus represent a critical counterpoint to the narrow and anemic rendering of religious experience found in conventional studies of Islam, especially those based on textual and doctrinal sources.[13]

Despite these important contributions, this small but influential literature's focus on juridical or authorized forms of Islamic orthodoxy and its accompanying emphasis on the pious religious subject nonetheless present a circumscribed conceptualization of the interweaving of Islam, modernity, and subjectivities. In particular, this body of work runs the risk of offering but a more refined articulation of a wider set of problematic debates concerning the uneasy position of orthodox Islam in modernity—the "problem," that is, of Islam in secular modernity. While this intersection of Islam and politics takes many forms and appears under many labels ("political Islam," "Islamism," "radical Islam," "Islamic conservatism," or some other variant that emphasizes an orthodox religiosity of political concern), the questions posed in its name are by now familiar. Are Islamist activists working within or against the state? What is the proper place of religion in democratic state structures? Can Islam (spoken impossibly in the singular) coexist with liberal democracy? In Turkey, a country situated at the center of debates surrounding secularism and liberal democracy within predominantly Muslim nations, such questions are particularly consuming—whether they concern the ascendance of Islamist-inspired political parties, the political influence of religious leaders, or the political fate of religious minorities.[14]

While there is a justified urgency to these questions, in Turkey as throughout the Muslim world, looking for responses by exclusively attending to the intersection of authorized forms of Islamic orthodoxy and state politics is to take what is most visible as the limit of what can be said. When approached this way, for instance, Islam tends to be conceived in the form of a social movement—with organized sets of actors who are self-described representatives (or "defenders") of a "true" Islam and who ground their theological-political claims in their expertise with scriptural and juridical sources seeking to cultivate a distinctly "religious" voice in relation to state structures (as a voice of opposition, a claim for inclusion, or an expressed desire to be left alone). While such an approach, which is the study of religion as a social movement and, more precisely, the study of social movements through idioms inherited from the analysis of identity-based politics, enriches our understanding of the possibilities for alternative, or even "enchanted" models of secular modernity (Deeb 2006), it simultaneously hollows out our appreciation of the complexity and abundance of religious life. Moreover, because the study of Islam in the model of social-political movement works from within the state—because it takes shape through terms and in spaces designated by the state—one is left with depictions of Islam grounded in concepts and divisions amenable to state-sponsored ways of defining the social field it seeks to govern (e.g., "Islamists" versus "Secularists," "Extremists" versus "Moderates").[15] Put in terms that will be of use later in our discussion, this reflects a conceptualization of religion bound within the limits of a discourse of reason and (political) utility (Bataille 1989).

Beyond this dominant concern with orthodox Islamic practice is the vast, dispersed, and heterogeneous topography of less formal yet deeply intimate and constitutively local forms of Islamic practice—those religious figures, practices, and sites that flourish with particular vigor around illness, suffering, and misfortune. Missing from this discussion, in other words, are the forms of Islamic practice that have been cast out of orthodoxy and dismissed as corrupted forms of Islam—such as divine utterances of saintly figures, ritual responses to malevolent gazes, "heretical" techniques for commanding armies of spirits, ritualized procedures for promoting fertility, exuberant forms of religious passion that thrive around holy sites, and countless everyday acts of personal devotion.[16] These are the sorts of practices, figures, and settings that will provide the setting for our inquiry into the relationship between Islam, modernity, and subjectivity.

While taking innumerable forms, this book considers the four major traditions of religious healing practiced in the two neighborhoods of Ankara where my research was conducted. As a preface to the discussion to come, I want to briefly outline these traditions by introducing their representative practitioners. The *kurşuncu* is a healer who specializes in treating people who have been struck by the *nazar*, or "evil eye." The ritual practice at the center of this technique consists of pouring molten lead (*kurşun dökme*,[17] hence *kurşuncu*) into a basin of water and reading the resulting solidified piece of lead to discern the *nazar*'s origin. The *ocaklı*, which for some would also include the *kurşuncu*, is a person who (or, at times, a place that) has special powers to heal based on one's descent from an ancestor to whom miraculous powers have been attributed. The *cinci hoca* or *üfürükçü* (or Qur'anic healer, as they occasionally appear in the anthropological literature) treats individuals being struck, harassed, or possessed by spirits (*cins*, or *jinn* in Arabic transliteration) with a combination of curative amulets (*muska*), Qur'anic verses (*ayet*), and ritual prescriptions. Lastly, the *evliya* is a person acknowledged as possessing extraordinary spiritual powers based on the possession of *keramet*, the God-given ability to perform miracles.[17]

Although these forms of healing were widespread, their presence was assuredly not celebrated. To present a categorization of religious and therapeutic practice, as I have just done, to someone in the neighborhood where I lived would be to invite an argument. To give such figures a place in an analytic order was to grant them an authority that was insistently denied. It certainly did not help matters that I resisted explaining my research in the less threatening language of "folklore," a term that evoked a comfortable traditionality of a national past to be found surviving amid home remedies, aging bonesetters, and assorted *kocakarı ilaçları* (literally, and coarsely, "old woman" remedies). These healers were bitterly criticized by most as exploitative swindlers of the vulnerable who betray the promises of a modern world. For those who considered themselves to be conservative or pious Muslims, these practices were additionally rejected for being impermissible under religious law. The transgression of these healers was thus twofold: to practice religious healing and treat serious injury without a license was to transgress the state's law, and attract accusations of criminality; to promise miraculous cures by interceding with God was to transgress religious law, and attract accusations of heresy. Working between these prohibitions (of state and religious law), such persons were not representatives of community (understood in terms of neighborhood, nation, and religion), but exceptions to its ethical order. Consequently, and unlike scholars concerned with Islam in the public sphere,[18] we are dealing here with a set of decidedly un-public (yet not exactly private) religious dispositions, sensibilities, and practices.

A difficult ethnographic problem follows from these observations. What happens when your topic of research is what a community defines itself against? What is to be done, and learned, when a significant aspect of how a community makes and remakes itself is through the rejection of such forms of religious and therapeutic authority? Ultimately, it was precisely in the intensity and thoroughness of their exclusion—from authorized forms of religiosity, from state-sponsored medical practice, from an ethics of community—that I found these figures and practices to be so generative. In other words, thinking through their exceptionality—which was engaged with particular passion by my interlocutors, as opposed to the superficiality of general conversations about "religion and politics"—brought to light the ways that the forcible exclusion of religious healing from modernity played a constitutive role in Turkey's staging of the secular modern.[19] It is with this sense of being at once excluded from yet included within secular modernity that I am interested in informal and dispersed forms of religious life flourishing outside social movements and formal institutions (of state, medicine, and religion) as exilic formations of religious life.

Here we enter onto the unstable terrain of Islam without movements—where coherently articulated philosophies, established doctrines, and stable frameworks of interpretation are in short supply. One cannot presume that these practices offer a clear direction of religious development (other than, perhaps, freedom *from* affliction) or any sort of teleology of political liberation (other than, perhaps, a unique capacity to disrupt governing distributions of the sensible). These formations of religious life and Islamic practice fall outside the frameworks of social movements, identity politics, and battles between "Islamists" and "Secularists." Yet they are impossible to talk about without invoking these frames. The exilic, in this sense, suggests the remoteness of something being cast out and placed at a distance, as well as an intimacy of something being held close and continuing, however obliquely, to organize events.

Resistances / Building at Night

> For Plato, writing and painting were equivalent surfaces of mute signs, deprived of the breath that animates and transports living speech. Flat surfaces, in this logic, are not opposed to depth in the sense of three-dimensional surfaces. They are opposed to the "living." (Rancière 2004: 15)

Research for this book took shape through countless resistances. In many respects, ethnography is itself an accumulation of resistances, where expectations are continually turned back as they encounter lives differently organized. A distinct power of ethnography, in this respect, resides in the mutually generative resistance of lived lives and theoretical elaboration. By paying close attention to what is at stake in people's lives (Kleinman 1995, 2006), constantly scanning for difference, comparison, and multiple voices (Fischer 2003), the ethnographer is pushed to reformulate conceptual frameworks and persistent habits of scholarly practice. Veena Das eloquently frames this as a matter of love and a willingness to be marked: "For me the love of anthropology has turned out to be an affair in which when I reach bedrock I do not break through the resistance of the other, but in this gesture of waiting I allow the knowledge of the other to mark me" (2007: 17). Resistances encountered during fieldwork—a recurrent sense of being turned back—are precisely what carried this project from being about the phenomenology of therapeutic experience to the politics and aesthetics of religious healing. Among the many resistances (both personal and social), one that I found particularly challenging to unravel, and one worth briefly addressing here, was the way many of my interlocutors' conversations precisely articulated the sorts of academic arguments against which my research was critically defined. Recurrently, "local" resistance took the (naively) unexpected form of familiar theoretical elaboration. The following example illustrates the sort of mark such returns (of knowledge) left, as it also provides an opportunity to further introduce important dimensions of the social dynamics and historical context of research.

One afternoon late in my fieldwork, stopping by to visit the owner of a small photocopy and typing shop in downtown Ankara, I entered, as I had before, through the building's unassuming steel door and climbed the narrow cement staircase to what had once been a small flat. Situated midway between "old" and "new" Ankara, the shop was filled with aging computers, a single photocopier, and a cluster of bookbinding equipment in the back. With its steady stream of students from the nearby university and an unshakable smell of stale smoke, it was a common place—both typical and communal. As always, I felt incredibly, if undeservedly, welcome. On this afternoon, I was introduced to another visitor, an older gentleman who had lost an eye—as I would later be told—in an automobile accident.

When the shop's owner explained my research interests, the other visitor turned to me, cocked his head back, and examined me from head to toe, with his remaining eye. With his eye fixed on me with grim intensity—an eye so enlarged that its socket seemed barely able to contain it—he leaned forward and, through a loose assortment of tar-stained and rotting teeth, warned me: "Yours is a dangerous profession. These healers, especially the *cinci hoca*, are not people to play around with. Many work on the side of the devil. . . . You must be able to discern which are good and which are bad. For this, you must either have knowledge or a pure heart. These ones that do Satan's work, they may seem good, but they are really evil." As he leaned back in his chair, he concluded: "If you aren't careful, they will surely bring harm to you."

I left later feeling not a little disconcerted, as well as confused by the seemingly formulaic predictability of the episode. The encounter overflowed with so many ethnographically archetypal figures and warnings that it was hard not to be compelled by its prohibitions and drawn into the events as a larger, unfolding drama: the ethnographer, encountering the monstrous "Other" and shaken by ominous warnings, proceeds to appropriate the accompanying abjection so as to usher in a radical cultural difference and open, as a tale of personal threat, a space for self-reflection. Yet I could not help but feel that this gentleman was also aware of his own role in this larger drama. It seemed as if the genre was familiar to him, and that he was playing up this position of cultural difference in his desire to mark me.

On the long bus ride home, I remained consumed by the episode. Admittedly, I felt that the exchange bordered on the comical, if not absurd. I also felt that there was an obligation to listen to him. Questions perhaps common to the inexperienced anthropologist multiplied on the trip home: Was my refusal to take his words seriously some sort of ethnographic—or personal—failure, of not being sufficiently compelled by his speech, drawn into his discourse? Was this evidence of an unwillingness on my part to listen openly, to break through the distance that separated us? Or, in more scholarly terms, was this distance itself a vestige of anthropology's enlightenment legacy and its radical partitioning of subjects and objects, belief and knowledge, the natural and supernatural?[20] And what, then, of this fear I was supposed to feel, that was being demanded by the genre? What form was it to take and what was meant to be its object? How could I be certain that such fear was not simply a reflection of my own assumptions and the sorts of social worlds that I moved through?[21]

I stepped off the bus at the neighborhood where I lived and immediately, as many times before, entered into a conversation with a group of men and women congregated at the foot of the road. My research again came up, and again the angry "debate" ensued—really a series of didactic monologues that derided such "superstition" as ignorant, unscientific, and useless. "These are the ways of the past, before science and medicine." "That is what ignorant and uneducated people did." "We've moved beyond it." While my comments had certainly set off this exchange, our conversation could not be fully reduced to speakers positioning themselves in relation to some sort of presumed modernity or (male) "Western" gaze that I might stand in for (see Pigg 1996; Ewing 1997). I had lived there long enough, talked to enough people, and witnessed such reactions in enough settings to know that this was not merely for my benefit, and also that it was a widely shared sentiment.[22]

So much for the generalizability of the remarks from the gentleman with one eye. For these neighbors and friends gathered at the bus stop, the religious healer was not to be feared but eradicated. Indeed, after a year and a half of listening to and recording people's opinions about religious healing, talking with patients and healers about their healing sessions, arguing with physicians and government officials over the validity of religious healing as a topic of research, visiting shrines and subjugating myself before healers, weathering sweeping dismissals of healers as swindlers and profiteers, and defending myself in arguments with neighbors over "this kind of crap," I had grown accustomed to such contempt. I had come to recognize these conversations as rituals in their own right. They were not merely opportunities to express opinions, but enunciative sites for producing communities and iterating realities.[23] Yet, again, what sort of ethnographic listening was required here?

For I rejected their critiques. I was critical of and frustrated with their unbending condemnation of these healers, but not because I embraced some sort of vision of "complementary medicine" that was more "holistic" or "tolerant." Rather, what troubled me were the traces of rigidly construed and authoritarian models of modernization and nationalism that were so apparent in their strident denunciations. It was as if their disdain for these healers fed from the same sources as the state's suppression of political dissent and its brutal repression of Kurds in eastern Turkey—knowing well that those in front of me strongly disagreed with these practices. At the same time, I was overcome by the thoroughly modernist quality of their arguments—their irrepressible devotion to progress and commitment to the power of reason, technology, and capital to make such progress inevitable, regardless of the alternatives that had to be discarded along the way.

Even though it has become no longer viable to formulate cultures as texts to be analyzed, it was difficult not to imagine these arguments as taking textual form—as, indeed, textbook examples of the much-maligned master narrative of "modernization theory." As James Ferguson described his fieldwork in Zambia, I was enmeshed in a situation where social scientific metanarratives of modernization theory had become "local tongue" (1999: 84). In this case, the models of development and modernity that Europe and North America promoted for so long as an ideal had become a powerful social and moral discourse in marginalized communities at their peripheries. And here I was rejecting it. In those moments of particular exasperation, I was tempted to turn such discourses of modernity back onto the speaker and argue, as a public health official had with me, that they were not being "modern enough" because of their singular commitment to biomedical models of healing. To be "modern" today, after all, was to be at least open to and tolerant of "alternative" therapies. If they were to dismiss my research by invoking textbook modernization theory, I found myself being drawn toward a well-worn colonial discourse in response— that they were certainly being modern, but not quite modern.[24] Such is the ever-receding horizon of an ideal modernity.

As this begins to suggest, speaking about social life in Turkey can be a perilous endeavor, given both the history of fantasy the region has accumulated and Turkey's incessant depiction as the gathering place of threatening alterities—where East meets West, where the Muslim world menaces Christian Europe, where the traditional threatens the modern. Turkey, in the end, seems to be caught between them all—alterities that confirm, once again, the persistence of what Edward Said identified long ago as those insidious ontological and epistemological distinctions on which elaborate theories are constructed and institutions of colonial domination fabricated (1979). While even a casual glance at Turkey's history problematizes such distinctions—if for no other reason than that this history shows us the impossibility of disaggregating Turkish and European modernities[25]—my neighbors and friends gathered at the bus stop nonetheless understood themselves and envisioned the world through these precise distinctions. In the context of my research, where the figure of the religious healer spoke toward all that was "traditional," "ignorant," and of the past, the figure of the physician exemplified the "modern," the technological, and the future.

In order to appreciate the social forces organizing my neighbors' strident rejection of religious healing, there are, of course, many histories that need to be recounted—about nationalist projects of civilizational change and societal regeneration promoted by early leaders of the Turkish republic;

the struggle to consolidate a binding historical consciousness that would render the nation's founding as a radical historical break; efforts to consolidate a form of Islam that was both meaningful to citizens and amenable to state regulation; and the coinciding suppression of cultural traditions and institutions deemed antithetical to national development, such as the extensive networks of saintly figures, shrines, and religious orders spread across the country. Not only was this conversation at the bus stop deeply indebted to these histories, it is not lost on me that my interest in "religious healing" implicates a concept itself indebted to the very divisions of religious, ethical, and therapeutic knowledge and expertise that grew out of a history of secular reform, and within which most of my interlocutors grew up. But this is getting us ahead of ourselves.

Because the intensity of my neighbors' reaction at the bus stop—as well as the very presence of a bus stop—speaks in important ways to the specific role that residents of such neighborhoods played in Turkey's history of nation-building, a few additional remarks are in order concerning the setting of our exchange. Although research for this book carried me all over the city, and at times far from the city, fieldwork took place primarily in two neighborhoods on the outskirts of Ankara, a city of approximately four million residents.[26] The neighborhoods are generally characterized, by residents and scholars alike, as "squatter settlements" or "shanty towns" (*gecekondu semtleri*). The term *gecekondu*, literally "built or settled at night or overnight," refers to homes that have been quickly constructed without legal permission, frequently on land that had been originally expropriated from the state. The result of massive internal labor migrations, *gecekondus* constitute sprawling neighborhoods of single-story, densely clustered homes that remain the predominant form of available housing in Turkey's major urban centers. While these neighborhoods are not home to the forms of visible misery commonly associated with unregulated housing at urban peripheries, they are nevertheless settings of widespread poverty that house staggering numbers of the unemployed and working poor. By most estimates, well over half Ankara's population live in *gecekondus* (Keleş 1996; Demirtaş 2009).

These neighborhoods have long been looked upon as privileged sites for social, economic, and religious reform. The migrants who settled these neighborhoods, as well as their parents, had been, as rural farmers, idealized as a particularly malleable raw material for the production of a citizenry intensely committed to an emerging nation. Today, these neighborhoods

embody the history of innumerable campaigns and initiatives introduced
in an effort to manufacture the social basis of a new nation-state, a history
whose discourses of modernity have come to assume a powerful role in
mediating how residents envision themselves individually and collectively.
Although we will have more to say about this in the chapters to come, this
is the sort of history that must be kept in mind as we listen to my neighbors
complain bitterly about the continued presence of religious healers in contemporary Turkey.

While the two neighborhoods where I worked were strikingly similar—
residents had a common history of migration and resettlement, were born
in and departed from the same provinces, held similar jobs, ate similar
foods, spoke a similar Turkish, and shared innumerable common habits
and tastes—they also diverged sharply along religious and political lines.
The neighborhood where I lived and conducted the bulk of my research
was principally an Alevi community whose residents regarded themselves
as politically leftist and who had a long history of commitment to Kemalist
models of secular democratic reform. Although we will consider Alevism
in more depth later, I simply note here that Alevis comprise approximately
15–20 percent of Turkey's population and are commonly regarded (by
scholars, but not by all Alevi) as a Shi'i religious minority. In contrast, the
majority of residents in the second neighborhood were Sunni Muslims who
regarded themselves as observant, pious Muslims and widely supported the
pro-Islamist political party that came to power during the course of my
fieldwork. Given the distinctive character of these two neighborhoods,
the research for this book thus took shape across some of Turkey's most
prominent lines of social, political, and religious difference (Sunni/Alevi,
Islamist/Secularist, Left/Right), divisions that reverberate throughout the
Muslim world. As the discussion to come will demonstrate, appreciating
the aesthetic entanglements of secularism and therapeutic power will offer
us an important lesson on the social force of these divisions, and how
they are produced and reproduced within the interpersonal flow of the
everyday.

Text and Deferral

This book traces the experiences of religious healers and their patients in
settings of urban poverty as they seek new future possibilities outside the

law of both the state and Islam. It is an attempt to locate an array of marginalized or subjugated forms of Islamic authority and practice in relation to political struggles over the forms of religious and scientific practice regarded as appropriate for a modern, secular nation. In this respect, I am particularly concerned with relationships among forms of speech, visibility, sentiment, sociability, and truth made possible by Turkey's project of secular modern world making, as well as the forms of historical consciousness that both precipitate out of and sustain accompanying distributions of the sensible. Toward such an end, the chapters to follow begin with an extended consideration of the historical, material, and discursive conditions within which these forms of healing live. This opening attention to the conditions of therapeutic experience is also intended to reflect the unfolding nature of the research, such that—with few exceptions—the competing stories, recollections, and commentaries about healers long preceded the opportunity for healers to speak for themselves. As with the research itself, the actual presence and voice of healers will be deferred for some time. The danger of organizing the text in this way is that the voices of patients and healers arrive later than one might desire, at a point at which they may seem impossible to sustain.

Because a significant amount of the material explored in the opening chapters revolves around the figure of the *cinci hoca*, an expanded introduction to the practices of the *cinci hoca* may be of use to the reader at this point. In contrast to *evliya*s like Zöhre Ana—whose powers are understood to be an expression of the divine gift of *keramet*—the therapeutic abilities of *cinci hoca*s are generally associated with their expert religious knowledge and ritual proficiency. In treating patients, *cinci hoca*s rely on an assortment of ritual formulas and techniques for the fabrication of ritual objects that can, when properly utilized, exert an influence on the world of spirits, or *cin*s, so as to address a range of problems. Unlike the *evliya*, *cinci hoca*s do not tend to attract followers and they are typically consulted sporadically to address specific ailments or problems. While I will repeatedly refer to people as *cinci hoca*s or *üfürükçü*s (terms that can be used interchangeably), it should be understood that the title is a shorthand reference to people who have gained proficiency in the ritual practices associated with the *cinci hoca* or *üfürükçü*.

With the exception of the *evliya*, people practicing the forms of healing described in this book are individuals who, like others, assume a variety of social positions—neighbor, shop owner, relative, acquaintance—but who have also acquired a body of specialized knowledge that has earned them the reputation of being religious and ritual specialists. They are not, in other words, charismatic leaders of religious sects. Nor does there appear to be any sort of revival of interest in such practices in Turkey. People seeking the assistance of these healers come from a variety of backgrounds (men and women, young and old, educated and not, some with careers, some with jobs, others with neither) and appeal to healers for a wide assortment of problems—such as marital and familial conflict, physical disabilities, seizures, nightmares, daytime fears, depression, skin rashes, sleeping difficulties, alcoholism, infertility, a host of "incurable" or *çaresiz* diseases (e.g., lung cancer, leukemia, cirrhosis), and any number of everyday aches and concerns. As this list begins to suggest, the reasons that bring people to such healers are multiple: for the treatment of problems not defined as treatable in clinical settings, in instances where one has no access to or cannot afford biomedical treatment, or, most commonly, alongside biomedical treatments seen as overly impersonal and fraught with divisions of class and authority. From this perspective, going to the sorts of healers I describe here is neither necessarily an act of devotion nor a conscious act of resistance (against the state, medicine, or the rich), but a decision driven by the desire to receive appropriate and effective care.

In my effort to make sense of the forms of animosity and possibility that gathered around the figure of the religious healer, I found myself continually raising questions of a historical nature. For this reason, Chapter 1 begins our discussion by tracing the historical consolidation of the image of the religious healer as a dangerous symbol of backwardness and a threat to the order and progress of the nation. Based primarily on archival research, this chapter examines the development of Turkey's health care system and campaigns of medical literacy introduced during the early years of the republic as prominent sites for the articulation of the state's broader project of secular modern development, a project defined in opposition to a set of practices and modes of religio-political authority represented in the figure of the religious healer. In the state's campaign against practitioners of religious forms of healing, we will encounter the distinct ways in which bodies and populations became administrative problems for an emerging nation, as well as sites where newly imagined relationships between biological life and national health could be productively united. It is here where we will also find the figure of the religious healer being marked in advance as a site of future political struggle.

Turning to the ethnographic settings of research, Chapter 2 traces competing visions of secular order and disorder that course through everyday conversations about religious healing in the two neighborhoods where my research was conducted. Of particular interest will be the ways the topic of religious healing allows one to speak of community difference and, simultaneously, the ways that difference becomes speakable in talking about religious healing. In this chapter, I will suggest that conversations—and frequently arguments—about religious healing not only provide a discursive setting for speakers to narrate their inclusion in an imagined ideal of secular modern development, but also work to demarcate the limits of moral communities as thresholds of reason, sense, and the sensible. In listening closely to these commentaries on religious healing, we will also encounter a series of competing visions of community loss and societal decay, which will identify in the religious healer's voice the seeds of an obscured force that, if allowed to flourish, threatens the future viability of secular political rule.

The subsequent chapters turn our attention to the forms of religious and therapeutic authority that are able to find a home within such inhospitable conditions. These chapters read against the grain of much contemporary scholarship that looks for the persuasiveness of language in the performativity of speech events, here framed in therapeutic terms—where the therapeutic encounter (between patient and healer) is recurrently construed as the persuasive core of healing. Put otherwise, I make a case in these chapters for approaching therapeutic and religious experience otherwise than through a model of command and event. In this regard, while instances of radical transformation could certainly be found among the stories of healing and being healed that I listened to over the course of research, they were rare and fleeting moments made possible by both the slow, sprawling work of constituting authority and the continued enactments of relatedness that trailed long behind. Chapters 3 and 4 begin to take up these concerns as they examine the work of different healers who struggle to cultivate an authoritative presence in conditions that are organized against such capacities and possibilities.

Chapter 3 explores the exilic religious universe that has formed around the *evliya* whose followers we met earlier. This chapter asks: What formations of religious speech and truth are possible within the discursive conditions incited by Turkey's ongoing project of secular modernity? What sorts of saintly speech are capable of drawing and holding an audience today, as they hold out the possibility for re-imagined futures? Addressing these questions will return us again to Atatürk and the traces of his voice that erupt from this saint, as one of the many deceased *evliya* who periodically speak through her. My aim in this chapter is to consider the language of the saint—and the distinct ways it is understood to assume material and spatial form—as a means of examining secularism as a politics of aesthetics, and the possibilities of speaking and listening within community life that it depends on. Here I am particularly interested in the ways that the voice of this saint, as a disqualified and illicit form of speech, comes to represent an important site of return—where an unresolved violence of secularism's origins is staged and the entanglement of therapeutic power and political rule becomes particularly intense. It is here, as well, where we will find the regimes of discursive practice authorized in the name of secular modernity conjuring an aesthetics that transgresses itself, a secularist aesthetics that will be repurposed as a resource to sustain exilic formations of religious life.

Chapter 4 takes us to the most controversial form of religious healing, that of the *cinci hoca*. Whereas Chapter 3 explores the *evliya*'s gift for drawing into the open a series of political assumptions and sensibilities embedded within Turkey's project of secular modernity, this chapter introduces the distinctively economic and ethical entanglements of therapeutic power and secular political rule. In particular, it traces the unexpected ways market forces and pious ethics fold into one another within the therapeutic intimacies of the *cinci hoca*'s ritual practices. By considering the ways these healers bring together idioms of economic rationality and ascendant models of Islamic piety—the ways, that is, that they conjugate markets and ethics—this discussion will bring into view the emergent arrangements of ethics, markets, and value that I see being worked out in the folds of social life in which the *cinci hoca* labors.

This discussion sets the stage for the final two chapters of the book, chapters that move across different healing traditions and engage more directly the experiences of those seeking the assistance of healers. Whereas Chapters 3 and 4 examine the varied ways in which healers struggle to cultivate religious authority in inhospitable social, economic, and political milieus, the final two chapters raise complementary questions regarding the possibilities of listening and desire that take shape in relation to such forms of religious authority, language, practice, and truth. Toward this end, Chapter 5 traces the complexity, density, and indeterminacy of lives that move through the presence of healers. Building on the questions posed in the preceding chapters, it asks: How are we to conceptualize experiences of suffering and recovery in relation to the idioms and forms of secularism's politics of aesthetics? Here, I engage the ways patients emphasized the distributive and transactional qualities of therapeutic experience in order to shift attention away from discrete therapeutic encounters and toward the indeterminate complexities of social ties and intersubjective relations that constitute everyday lives. To understand patients' experiences of suffering and healing, I argue in this chapter, we must understand these relationships as distributions of possibility and new becoming, relationships that can just as ably heal as they can wound.

Chapter 6 turns our focus to stories of failed therapeutic possibility. Structured around multiple accounts of foreclosure—patients unable to find relief, healers who give up their practice, devotees who come to reject the authority they so intensely desired, and patients who doubt the possibility of healing—this chapter introduces a persistent sense of loss that haunted the intensity of therapeutic desires. I will argue that accounts of the faltering therapeutic power of healers not only capture a feeling that the ability of healers to convene and bind audiences is fragile, but also bring into view a more pervasive structure of loss embedded within and enabled by secularism's politics of aesthetics. Here, as well, we will discover an unexpected affinity between the therapeutic desires of patients and the scholarly labors of early secularist historians of the republic, as they both struggle to recover the past to make new futures imaginable.

*   *   *

While the confrontation between the followers of an *evliya* and the caretakers of Atatürk's tomb may have few chances of rising to the occasion of an historical event, I want to hold onto this scene for a moment longer. For in it, as noted at the outset, I would come to recognize an unfolding allegory on the commerce between death, healing, and political power that was similarly circulating through the stories of loss and healing I had been listening to over the course of my research. Before we can fully appreciate such configurations of sentiment and story, however, we first need to understand the sorts of processes and conditions that can give rise to the civilizational disgrace these healers evoke, the forms of panic before the future they give life to, and the irony that was our visit to Atatürk's burial site. In our case, this means we need to track the historical diversion of particular formations of religious life to the outside of a national order, an exiling that would require an alliance between science and secularism that medicine could make possible. For it would be the traces of this past of medical and secular modern world marking that I would time and again encounter as people both maligned and sought out the forms of religious and therapeutic possibility embodied by the figure of the religious healer. And it would be in these traces, which had prepared in advance experiences of injury, affliction, and suffering as sites of new struggle, where I would similarly struggle to recognize stories of healing and being healed as sites of social, political, and subjective becoming.

Chapter 1

Medicine and the Will to Civilization

In . . . disqualified, popular knowledge there lay the memory of hostile encounters which even up to this day have been confined to the margins of knowledge.

> —Michel Foucault, on subjugated knowledges, "Two Lectures"

[I]n traditional societies, opinions on disease and health were born as a part of folk culture. For this reason, practices related to this issue are the realm of anthropology, ethnology and sociology, while technical analysis falls under the disciplines of medicine and pharmacology.

> —Ministry of Culture, Republic of Turkey

The Landing

On May 19, 1919, as history textbooks eagerly recount, Mustafa Kemal disembarked from a ship anchored off the Black Sea town of Samsun and, as the new Inspector of the Ninth Army, was rowed ashore to one of the port's wooden jetties. This is the moment, the story goes, when the history of modern Turkey begins. Nurturing a long-incubating plan for a new nation, and set into motion by a recent Greek invasion of Anatolia and the Ottoman Empire's reassignment of him to the hinterlands, Kemal splashed toward the port's shallow quay not as the great war hero of Gallipoli that he was but simply as the new Inspector.

Ashore, he cast his eyes—"those pale blue eyes" that his biographer Lord Patrick Kinross would describe as "gleam[ing] with a cold steady challenging light, forever fixing, observing, reflecting, appraising"[1]—across a teetering Ottoman Empire. And his presence—that "latent . . . extra dimension, of a singularity of tempo and rhythm . . . that strangely, for all his slightness of frame, [made him seem] bigger"—threw a long shadow across a newly forming homeland as it climbed 4,000 feet to the great Anatolian plateau, reaching from Mount Ararat and the frontiers of Persia and Russia in the east a thousand miles westward to the Marmara and Aegean seas. This was the same shadow that would later be discerned across hillsides and within clouds as otherworldly apparitions of the great Atatürk, the father of the Turks.

From here, the story continues, he set out in his open car to the Anatolian plateau, thus beginning his campaign to mobilize the nationalist underground and organize local village forces of Anatolia against foreign invasion. As with most stories of this nature, however, singular figures condense, conflate, and overshadow other characters entangled—some willingly, others not—in the culmination of the story's ever-happy ending. It was through sheer force of personality, this story relentlessly asserts, that the Republic of Turkey was wrested from the grip of invading imperialists. Yet, at that mythologized moment of landing, with all its images of conquest, heroism, and liberation, Mustafa Kemal was not alone. In the curious play of light fostered by the mythologization of a past, a perhaps darker—and ever-darkening—shadow stretches away from the Anatolian plateau and toward the rocky coast of the Black Sea, a shadow in which other figures barely discernible were plotting with Kemal for the future of a new nation.

For my story, at least one figure in these shadows is significant—Dr. Refik Saydam. On graduating from a military medical academy in 1905 and receiving further medical training in Germany, Dr. Saydam returned to Turkey to join the underground nationalist movement. Here, on May 19, 1919, he similarly splashed to Samsun's quay and gazed across a newly forming homeland. Like Atatürk, he climbed toward the Anatolian plateau in the long march toward national liberation.

Why, at the very moment Turkey's history is said to begin, was a doctor present? With his expertise in discerning the truth of disease buried deep in the body's interior, what sorts of political possibilities was Dr. Saydam able to envision? Can we discern a deeper significance to Dr. Saydam's presence, beyond his rank as a medical officer?

Dr. Saydam would be Atatürk's personal physician and close companion throughout the War of Independence. In time, his medical authority over bodies would extend across the body politic. Twenty years later, in 1939, Dr. Refik Saydam would become the fourth prime minister of the Republic of Turkey.[2]

*   *   *

When one raises questions about the possibilities of constituting therapeutic authority in conditions of secular modernity, one invariably comes on the figure of the physician. As an entry into our concern with the intersection of therapeutic power and political rule, I want to begin with a consideration of the transforming authority of the physician over misfortune that came with the founding of the republic, a history of medical expansion that is deeply embedded within the development of secularism in Turkey. It is here that we will find the religious healer, along with other discredited modalities of religious and therapeutic authority, becoming entangled in an emergent politics of truth and, in turn, exiled from the order of the nation—as a specter of Turkey's to-be-forgotten past, a dangerous symbol of backwardness, and a threat to both national liberation and personal freedom. If we are to understand the sorts of stories of healing and being healed I listened to over the course of research, as I argue in this chapter, we must take into account this history.

In an effort to capture the sense of revolutionary fervor that coincided with the expansion of Turkey's biomedically oriented healthcare system, and the way the figure of the religious healer was captured in this history of institutional and discursive expansion, this chapter examines the activities of a network of state-sponsored "cultural centers" (*Halkevleri* and *Halkodaları*) that were charged with promoting political reforms in the years following the republic's founding. I am particularly interested in the series of popularly oriented journals these centers published in their effort to promote medical and scientific literacy, and especially the ways the discourse of medicine they promoted served to articulate new relations between state and citizen, as well as the proper relationship of citizens to themselves. In both instances, we will see how the health of individual bodies and the health of the body politic would emerge during this period as interdependent problems of governance. It is here, as well, where the larger implications of Dr. Saydam's presence at the site of Turkey's political birth will become apparent. Setting the stage for this discussion, however, I first offer a brief introduction to the history of secular reform during the early years of the republic and its relationship to the expanding importance of biomedically based healthcare institutions in the state's transition from Ottoman Empire to Turkish Republic.

Medicine and Civilization in Turkish Nationalist Thought

The nationalist thematic that took hold after the founding of the Republic of Turkey in 1923—one of several vying to bind a new political community following the dissolution of the Ottoman Empire—presumed that the emergence of a Turkish nation would require a "total civilizational switch," to borrow Bozdoğan's felicitous phrase (2001: 57). Toward such civilizational ends, early reformers, especially those inspired by influential nationalist thinker Ziya Gökalp,[3] distinguished "civilization" (a rational, universal system of knowledge, science, and technology) from "culture" (the set of values and habits current within a community) in order to argue that the regeneration of Turkey was to be achieved through replacing its medieval Islamic-Byzantine civilization with a European civilization, while promoting the nation's distinctively Turkish cultural traditions. Reflecting the technical-sociological imagination of the time, this basic framework would become the foundation for the all but official state ideology of the republic, Kemalism.[4]

Rather than the earlier Ottoman emphasis on progress for the sake of order—modernization to maintain political authority—Kemalism rendered central the notion of order (through political control) for the sake of progress (Kadıoğlu 1998; see also Sayyid 1997). With Kemalism as a flexible yet never fully coherent or comprehensive ideology (Zürcher 1997), the young Turkish state under the influential leadership of Mustafa Kemal (hence Kemalism) began a sweeping campaign of state secularization and social reform. In 1924, for instance, the Islamic Caliphate was abolished, the position of Şeyhülislâm (Shaykh al-Islam, chief religious official of the Ottoman Empire) was dissolved, the Islamic law courts were dismantled, religious schools were closed, and the administration of pious foundations (vakıf) was taken over by the state. In 1925, the fez, along with other religious clothing, became illegal, and religious shrines (türbe) and dervish lodges (tekke) were forcibly closed. By 1926 the Swiss civil code and the penal code of (Mussolini's) Italy would be adopted. Within the ensuing decade, a modified Latin alphabet replaced the Arabic alphabet; women received the right to vote; Western weights and measures became official standards, as did the European clock and calendar; adoption of surnames became mandatory; and a campaign of language purification began in an attempt to nationalize an "authentic" Turkish language.

In what Ayşe Kadıoğlu (1998) and Fuat Keyman (1995) describe as a vast, top-down, and imposed "will to civilization," the Kemalist elite sought to engineer a democratically organized society constituted by modern, rational citizens—a society no longer impeded by corrupted forms of religio-political authority, especially as embodied in the figure of the sultan and the sorts of religious leadership able to flourish under Ottoman rule. In this civilizational project of political and social regeneration, secularism was to play a decisive role. For the Kemalist leadership, secularism was promoted as both a foundational political principle and an encompassing philosophy of life. It was not only to function as the cornerstone of national sovereignty and offer an integrative framework for binding an ethnically, linguistically, and religiously fragmented society; it was also to serve as the basis of individual and collective liberation.

The secularization reforms of the early republic did not aim simply to separate religious and political institutional structures. These reformers sought, rather, to subordinate religious to political authority within state institutions and, at the same time, to confine and regulate religious expression within the population. A decisive dynamic of this subordination was the state's desire not only to eliminate religious institutions deemed threatening to the state, but also to submit the remaining religious institutions to government regulation under the General Directorate of Religious Affairs (Diyanet İşleri Reisliği, later to become the Diyanet İşleri Başkanlığı). Mosque personnel, such as imams, would thus become employees of the Diyanet and the state would take control of the education of religious professionals. In this respect, one of the distinctive features of Turkey's project of secular modernity is the way the state became actively involved in articulating what was and what was not to be regarded as "true" Islam, as opposed to simply withdrawing from religious institutions.[5]

An important implication of this formulation of secularism is that the conception of Islam that became sponsored by the Diyanet did not precede secular reform, or even the Diyanet itself. Instead, the configuration of Islam that emerged in this period was itself constituted through reforms undertaken in the name of secularism.[6] The 1925 law abolishing religious orders captures well the delicate sorting of acceptable from unacceptable forms of religiosity required of the state:

Law 677. Article 1: All of the *tekke*s and *zaviye*s (dervish lodges) within the Republic of Turkey, whether established as a *vakıf* (pious foundation) or under the personal property right of its sheikh, or by whatever other manner, are fully closed. The rights of property and possession of their owners remain the same. Those presently employed at mosques according to established procedure are to be retained. All of the *tarikat*s (religious orders) using titles such as sheikh, dervish, disciple, *dede, seyit, çelebi, baba, emir, nakib, halife,* fortune-teller, sorcerer, *üfürükçü,* those who write charms to help people attain their wishes; all functions rendered according to these titles and designations; and the wearing of dervish costume, are prohibited. The tombs of the sultans and the tombs of the *tarikat*s are closed, and the profession of tomb-keeping is abolished. Those who reopen *tekke*s, *zaviye*s, or tombs that have been closed, or those who introduce new ones; or those who offer space for the performance of *tarikat* ceremonies, purposefully or even temporarily; and those persons who bear the above titles, or render functions or wear costumes particular to them, will be punished with a prison term of not less than three months and a fine of not less than fifty Turkish liras.

Although leaders of the nationalist movement had initially embraced many of these forms of religious authority as a means to cultivate a new national unity, the passing of this law in 1925 marked a break from a policy of engagement. Amid competing ideas among earlier secularist reformers about the role of Islam in the ordering and binding of society, we encounter here the codification of a model of secularism that sought to place religion under tight state control and, in the process, do away with those forms of religious life that threatened such political visions of religious control.

Rather than incorporating saints, shrines, and religious orders into state-sponsored forms of religiosity, the ensuing efforts to sort acceptable from unacceptable forms of religiosity were driven by a specific desire to eliminate the institutional infrastructure of religious orders while preserving the religious authority invested in the preexisting networks of mosques. The attempted suppression of religious formations alternative to state-sponsored orthodoxy would thus serve two agendas: to subvert bases of political opposition found among the country's network of religious orders and to eliminate the sorts of "superstition" deemed contrary to the national and technological promises of reason, freedom, and science that were to chart the nation's future. Here, numerous religious figures regarded for their ability to bring relief to the sick and dying, such as the *cinci hoca* or *üfürükçü*, would become entangled within the state's redoubled efforts to exert its control over and re-imagine the nation's religious life.

Before continuing, it is important to note that reformers such as Mustafa Kemal (or "Atatürk," as he became known) did not view Islam as inherently at odds with their project of secular modern nation making. Indeed, many secularist leaders during this period imagined a reformed Islam that could both offer meaning to people's lives and complement their project of personal and societal liberation. Accordingly, rather than being opposed to all forms of Islamic practice (as they are often portrayed), these reformers were intensely opposed to religious leaders who were seen as promoting forms of religious interpretation that obstructed a "true" understanding of Islam, in which individual "enlightenment" and "freedom" could be realized.

As I will discuss below, Turkey's project of secular modern reform and societal regeneration intertwined in significant ways with the development of a national medical infrastructure during this period. In particular, as the state came to envision the care of its population's health as one of its central responsibilities, and as the physician gained new power over the health of the citizen, medicine assumed a prominent role in mediating emerging relationships between individual bodies and the body politic. Understanding the institutional expansion of Turkey's medical infrastructure will set the stage for a consideration of how these processes played out on the ground between doctors, patients, and their respective healers.

*   *   *

Not much more than a year after landing in Samsun, as he stood before the newly formed National Assembly in the recently constructed parliament building—a building taking its place amid the widening boulevards and rapidly reconfiguring streets of a new Ankara—Atatürk turned to the challenges that lay ahead: "Being that our greatest goal is to completely bring to life our nation's public order, one of our government's general duties is to take great care of its nation's health and be, in proportion to our possibilities, a healer for its social suffering" (Aydın 1997: 23). Within days, Atatürk would declare his plans for a National Ministry of Health, one of the first such ministries in the world, to be led by Dr. Refik Saydam.

Atatürk's interest in medical reform was not discontinuous with late Ottoman policy. While a multitude of professional and nonprofessionalized therapeutic modalities existed in the region long before the republic—with some being incorporated into what became known as "modern" medicine, and others losing their influence (such as Greco-Islamic medicine[7])—a series of nineteenth-century political reforms in the Ottoman state placed new emphasis on the field of medicine as a domain of state practice.[8] As with other modernization reforms during the late Ottoman period, however, they were introduced through a broader set of reforms that aimed to modernize the military in order to remain competitive with European powers. The military nature of this history of medical reform is reflected in the founding of the first state Faculty of Medicine (Tıphane-i Amire) in 1827, dedicated to training Ottoman military physicians. Tıphane-i Amire was explicitly modeled as a European hospital and emphasized employing European (particularly French and Austrian) medical instructors. The 1827 legal opinion, or *fatwa*, obtained by the sultan's chief physician in support of the medical school argued: "For an army that receives training in a European manner, doctors that receive an education in a European manner are necessary" (Eren and Tanrıtanır 1998: 6).[9]

Despite a recognition of medicine's political potential, the Ottoman state's medical infrastructure was poorly developed during this period, with many of the trained healthcare professionals in the region working outside state control (especially in missionary hospitals). Moreover, as with most Ottoman modernization campaigns, reforms in health policy reached a very limited and privileged set of beneficiaries.[10] While medical training during the late Ottoman period may have been envisioned as an important component of training political and military leadership, it was not embraced as a site of social and political reform to the extent it would be under the republic.

With the founding of the republic, the transformed significance of medicine as a political technology of social reform would become immediately apparent in the state's dramatically increased investment in medical training and services.[11] Based on even conservative estimates, the number of physicians and health personnel employed by the state would increase tenfold within the first twenty years of the republic.[12] As the number of physicians expanded, so too did the geography of healthcare. Dr. Saydam, as the nation's first minister of health and with an eye toward the under-served regions of the country, set about establishing a network of 5–10 bed dispensaries (Muayene ve Tedavi Evleri, Examination and Treatment Houses) to serve as the backbone of provincial and rural healthcare. By 1936, there would be 180 such clinics scattered across the countryside. And by 1950, with more than 300 clinics built on this model, biomedical practice had gone from a nearly exclusively urban phenomenon to a service available in many provincial and village settings.[13]

Along with this commitment to the medical care of individual bodies, the state simultaneously turned its attention to the health of the nation as a whole. During this period, as we will see in the following sections, political rhetoric began to express itself more and more through a vocabulary of health and disease, where the "nation's health" and the "ills of the social body" came to be of great concern in an array of political settings (see Atatürk 1981). The Public Hygiene Law of 1930, conceived as a founding statement within the new field of public health, captures this shifting position of medicine vis-à-vis the state: "It is one of the services of the public state to improve the health conditions of the country, to struggle against all the illnesses or other harmful elements that harm the nation's health, to assure the healthy arrival of future generations and to manifest medical social assistance for the population" (Atatürk 1981). This meant, as Turkish medical historian Erdem Aydın insightfully yet uncritically observes: "The 'right to health' existed for each citizen of the Republic of Turkey" and that, with this, "modern state-individual relations had been announced in the field of health" (1997: 23).

Alongside this rhetoric of collective national health, the state would also become increasingly concerned about collecting reliable data about the health of the "national body." Renewed emphasis, for instance, was placed on measuring the health status of individuals and the population, calculating birth and death rates, generating epidemiological data on the prevalence and distribution of disease, and producing a quantifiable vision of medical services (recording frequency of visits to clinics, treatments administered, supplies utilized, etc.). In a way not seen under Ottoman rule, both biological life and a nation's collective health became corresponding problems of political power (Foucault 1978, 1991).[14]

A closer look at the operations of the planned network of state-run health clinics may prove useful at this point. In this regard, the ten-bed model clinic established in 1930 to serve as the standard for the system as a whole—the Etimesgut İçtimai Hıfzıssıhha Numune Dispanseri (Etimesgut Social Hygiene Model Dispensary)—is particularly illustrative of the trends in medical reform during this period, especially in the way that it brought together a concern for the health of individual bodies and the care of a collective social body. Like other clinics of the period, Etimesgut offered basic inpatient and outpatient medical services. The clinic additionally sent midwives to nearby villages to assist in childbirths and, reflecting the clinic's emphasis on public health education, instruct villagers on such topics as birthing, body and child care, home hygiene, and village environmental health. Alongside such therapeutic and pedagogical work, the clinic set itself apart with its efforts to collect detailed data concerning the health of its patients and the services the staff performed.

In this respect, the clinic would become an important site for the development and introduction of new technologies of medical surveillance. Among these, the "index card system" introduced by Dr. Cemalettin Or (after a year of training in village health and hygiene at Johns Hopkins University in 1935) would become particularly influential (Uğurlu 1994). Following the logic of the recently inaugurated national census, Dr. Or envisioned the use of index cards to individually chart medical case histories as an efficient way to track patients and maintain statistics on the clinic's visitors. Dr. Or imagined that a national network of such clinics, feeding data into a centralized Ministry of Health, could offer detailed snapshots of the nation's health at any given moment. Such a network of medical surveillance would also extend the state's "hands and eyes as far as the village" (*Ülkü* 1933: 253–54).

The Etimesgut clinic served many agendas. In addition to caring for local residents and maintaining detailed health data, it also regularly provided tours to prominent visiting politicians and foreign dignitaries (Sıhhıye Mecmuası 1937; Uğurlu 1994). Writing in the clinic's guest book in 1943, for instance, Brigadier General Leon Fox of the U.S. Army attested: "After travelling all over the Middle East it is a real pleasure to come on to such a real health oasis in the middle of Turkey" (Uğurlu 1994). Atatürk, on a visit in 1937, was impressed by the clinic's orderly, methodical, and speedy services, as well as the daily, weekly, monthly, and yearly statistics and color charts it maintained (Sıhhıye Mecmuası 1937). As he wrote in the guest book: "I toured the Etimesgut Health Center and was very pleased with the information and explanations the valuable director C. Or gave. I saw with satisfaction that modern workings give good results" (Uğurlu 1994). In this regard, Etimesgut—as a symbol of medical efficiency— became an important site where the nation could stage its own modernity, for both domestic and foreign consumption.[15]

The nation's medical infrastructure would expand considerably in the ensuing decades. Between 1925 and 1995, for example, the number of doctors practicing in the country would grow from 2,231 to 65,832 (with 34,405 under the management of the Ministry of Health) and by 2000 there would be 5,700 *sağlık ocakları* (health centers) and 11,747 *sağlık evleri* (health outposts) scattered throughout the country.[16] Few, however, would regard today's healthcare system as a product of deliberate planning. Its development, for instance, would undergo several reformulations over the years—most prominently in the implementation of a nationalized and socialized medical system model during the 1960s,[17] and more recently with the significant trends toward privatization in the health sector. Yet the healthcare system today is nonetheless the direct heir to these early forms of medical-political innovation and experimentation. While a more exhaustive account of its history would of course require a richer consideration of the system's complexity, as well as the competing political ideals motivating reform, my aim here has been simply to draw attention, first, to the overall expansion of the nation's medical infrastructure in the years since its founding and, second, to the increasing reliance on medicine as a site for political and social reform. As such, in this account's broad outline, it is difficult to interpret the growth of the Turkish medical system as anything but a dramatic increase in the availability of healthcare throughout the country, as well as a multiplication of the opportunities for the state to affirm its benevolence in communities and lives—certainly to an extent unimaginable under the Ottoman state.

If one regards the emphasis placed on medical reform in Ottoman efforts of military modernization as an early, albeit tentative, incorporation of modern disciplinary techniques into the state,[18] the Ottoman state's successor fully embraced such techniques of control and wagered its future on more deeply embedding itself in the lives of a newly forming citizenry, here through the fields of medicine and public health. Indeed, these intersecting rationalities of government—what Foucault distinguished as an anatomo-politics of the human body and a biopolitics of population (1978)—would appear time and again in the organization of the healthcare system as well as the medical and public health literature of the time, as we will see in the following sections. Our discussion thus far, however, has captured but one dimension of a far broader expansion of medicine into the everyday lives of Turkish citizens. Namely, the extension of medical services was preceded by and accompanied an extensive campaign aiming to disseminate medical and public health information throughout the country. In tracing this discursive dissemination, we will encounter the distinct ways in which bodies and populations became administrative problems for an emerging nation, as well as sites where newly imagined relationships between biological life and national health could be productively stitched together.

The Scientific Mentality and Its National Health

Despite rumors foretelling the miraculous possibilities of science and technology in the early years of the republic, most people had yet to "come across any health personnel in the village," let alone "see the face of a doctor" (*Ülkü* 1933). At least until the spread of local health clinics in the 1960s, everyday interactions between doctors and villagers were limited. While clinics and hospitals had been established in the provinces, access to them remained inconsistent. A neighbor of mine who had migrated from her village to Ankara in the early 1970s, a woman named Nebahat, describes well the state of rural healthcare during her childhood:

> When we became ill, we went to the provinces and the districts [i.e., the cities or towns that were the administrative centers of provinces (*il*) or districts (*ilce*)]. This is how it was in my father's time. Doctors were really, really, reeeally far away. From our village it was very far. Walking, I'd be on the road four to five hours. When my brothers became sick, my father would take them on his back, walking and walking for four to five hours, over mountains and through forests. He'd reach a road and then catch a ride, and by car they'd take them to a hospital in the town.

Beyond being an extraordinary (but not uncommon) account of the challenges villagers overcame in receiving healthcare, this story captures a noteworthy desire to be treated by physicians. Even before the arrival of health centers and health outposts in villages, the idea of biomedicine and its benefits had entered into social worlds with such force that a father would go to incredible lengths to have his son treated by a doctor. His desire, however, as I will suggest in this section, cannot be taken for granted. Where the previous discussion broadly charted a series of institutional, structural, and technological transformations that created the conditions for the emergence of Nebahat's father's (medical) desire—conditions that owe as much to political and military reform as they do to developments in health policy—I now turn to the particular configurations of health, nation, and citizenship that one finds embedded in Turkey's discursive campaign of medical modernization.

While it was not until the 1960s, with the socialization of the medical system, that the physical presence of the health clinic became an aspect of daily life, the promises of medicine began clearing the way long before. Whereas one can identify several institutions well positioned to undertake this work (such as a national education system), it would require a number of years to develop the infrastructure and training to make them operational. In the meantime, and in addition to the military's efforts to cultivate a new national identity through mandatory service requirements, a prominent means of nationalist re-education during this period was the system of small Halkevleri (People's Houses) and later Halkodaları (People's Rooms) that were established throughout the country. With their origins in fourteen People's Houses established by the Republican People's Party (RPP) in 1931 as cultural centers for all citizens, by the mid-1940s there were thousands of People's Houses and People's Rooms, with the number of People's Rooms reaching 4,371 by the end of 1949 (Öztürkmen 1994).[19]

The activities of People's Houses were explicitly designed to support newly introduced state reforms, with the objective of creating a shared political consciousness through the nationalization of society. Speaking at the opening of a People's House in 1932, Adnan Menderes, who would later become Turkey's first democratically elected prime minister, explained the purpose of the People's Houses in these terms: "One cannot describe a mere mass of human beings as a nation, nor is a nation a collection of people who have established a government . . . the step we have taken today in opening the People's Houses is the beginning of an institutionalization and specialization that will construct and strengthen our social and national body; it is the institutionalization of our cultural element" (quoted in Öztürkmen 1994: 162–63).[20] As historian and folklorist Arzu Öztürkmen summarizes the impact of the People's Houses: "What is now called the 'Turkish national culture' follows, in large measure, the generic structure laid out by the People's Houses in the thirties and forties" (164–65).

The series of journals published by the People's Houses would play a central role in extending state reform to the countryside. Distributed freely throughout the country and regularly read aloud to audiences, these journals were prominent venues for consolidating a common national culture and facilitating the new regime's reforms. As the inaugural issue of one such journal, *Ülkü* (Ideal), explained:

ÜLKÜ goes into publication with the aim of nourishing a new generation's excitement as they leave the dark ages behind and move
towards an honorable and enlightened future, to stir up the revolutionary elements in the social body's blood, to accelerate its progress
towards the future . . . *ÜLKÜ* aims to establish a unity of mind,
unity of heart (*gönül*), and unity of actions for those who have
joined this great journey . . . *ÜLKÜ* aims to serve the national language, the national history, and the national arts and culture . . .
ÜLKÜ aims, through its writing, to spread the zeal of the People's
Houses that are endeavoring to serve all these goals. (Recep 1933: 1)

An important means for achieving these aims, as I will describe below, was
to be found in the ways that the work of the People's Houses and their
publications were conceived as projects of medical and scientific education.

By following the appearance of articles concerned with medicine and
science over the full run of the People's House's popular publication *Ülkü*
between 1933 and 1950[21]—articles that range from detailed scientific texts,
to short fiction concerning physicians, to straightforward proposals for
changes in lifestyle—this section will track the emergence and dissemination of a particular politico-medical thematic that aimed to cultivate the
sorts of dispositions and capacities the new nation would require of its
citizens. Beyond reflecting a desire to create a shared historical consciousness, as Öztürkmen observed (1994), we will also see that the People's
Houses publications embodied a struggle to mold a new political subject in
the image of a clean, healthy, rational, and scientific-minded citizen.

The Scientific Mentality

Writing in a 1933 issue of *Ülkü*, Salih Murat laments that "One of the
great deficiencies in the wondrous developments in science is that there is
not a connection between scientific discoveries and most of our daily
work. For this reason, it is necessary to explain what scientists have
unearthed and what results they have arrived at after so much hard work
and difficulty" (1933: 325). Thus we come on one of the principal missions
of *Ülkü*, the presentation of scientific ideas in a simple and readable format so as to cultivate the citizen's "scientific mentality." For contributors
to *Ülkü*, the cultivation of such a mentality would both push a new nation
toward an "enlightened future" and serve as a means to undermine older

arrangements of religious authority, along with the regimes of truth through which they were legitimated.

The human body held a privileged position in this work. In a series of essays concerned specifically with the structures of the body, for instance, we find authors introducing readers to such varied subjects as human physiology, anthropometrical research, and neurophysiology. Dr. Zeki Nâsır, writing on heart disease in 1934, for example, takes his contribution to *Ülkü* as an opportunity to educate his audience about recent scientific developments in the study of human physiology and the body's interiority, with a detailed explanation of the role of the heart, lungs, kidneys, and blood in the functioning of the human circulatory system. Dr. Şevket Aziz Kansu, in turn, writing in the sporadically appearing section "Anthropology," introduces readers to the field of anthropometry and its relevance for thinking about the "Turkish race" (1939). Amidst expansive tables of bodily measurements (e.g., height, weight, arm span, sitting height, width of left arm, circumference of head, nose length, and so forth), Kansu offers the reader a vision of the quantified Turk and, consistent with the then popular racialist logic of national identity, maps the Turkish race onto a racialized world geography.[22] Kansu would elsewhere return to the importance of human physiology and anatomy in an effort to educate his readers about the evolution of the human brain and the origins of human consciousness. Writing among detailed diagrams of the human brain and its internal structures, Kansu would inform his readers that "It is known that the chief characteristic that distinguishes humans' animal nature from themselves is the expansiveness of their mental faculty" (1936: 111).

These examples each represent distinct moments within a wider politico-anatomical project of re-imagining the significance and truth of the human body. In an effort to provide readers with a basic scientific education, these authors and scientists imagined their work as both filling a void (of ignorance) and cultivating new ways of imagining the body's interiority, mapping and comparing the body's exteriority, and envisioning the relationship between bodily structure and human consciousness. This attention to human anatomy would, in turn, contribute to the larger struggle for societal enlightenment, of freeing a corporate body from superstition and liberating its interiority.[23]

Alongside such anatomical interests, other essays in *Ülkü* aimed to explore the history of science more broadly (Hüsnü 1933; Murat 1933; Aziz 1934). In an effort to explain the "wondrous developments of science"

(*Ülkü* 1933: 325), these accounts introduced readers to a history of great scientific discovery (of atoms, electrons, radiation, X-rays, and laws of thermodynamics), a history animated by great European and American scientists (such as Copernicus, Kepler, Newton, Edison, and Einstein). While it is noteworthy that these historical accounts were fashioned into an evolutionary narrative of progressive scientific discovery (a story that invariably culminates in a European scientific present), I am particularly interested in the ways that these popular historians of science imagined the inseparability of scientific and political development. As Niyazi Hüsnü explained, in his essay "Science and Revolution,"

> The scientific mentality was the biggest enemy of the Sultanate regime, which was convinced that it had received all of its powers from supernatural and divine origins. As it [the scientific mentality] marked in human history the beginning of the search for natural and sensible explanations for the natural events that surround us, its clearest evidence in our history is the toppling of the monarchy and its divine law, and the awakening of the national and public consciousness. For us, in the era of the sultanate and caliphate, there could not have been anything as fake and impossible as SCIENCE. . . . Although in the past the Western civilization that more freely entered into our lives perhaps cultivated people who knew many languages, who spoke well, and dressed beautifully, it had cultivated very few scientific minds until a national and liberated consciousness was awakened in our country. (Hüsnü 1933: 117)

Hüsnü, through an idiom of scientific progress, presents a familiar nationalist theme. Turkey's national regeneration was to depend on the replacement of the old (Ottoman) civilization with a new, scientifically grounded (European) civilization, while maintaining a hold on the unique qualities of Turkish culture. Although European "culture" was present in the Ottoman Empire—in terms of speech and dress—European "civilization" had not arrived, at least until a "national and liberated consciousness had been awakened" (117).

In *Ülkü*'s promotion of scientific literacy, as the above begins to illustrate, themes of nationalism, modernity, and secularism operated as the (often unspoken) organizing principles of its scientific discourse. Even seemingly arcane technical topics such as poisonous gases (Rifat 1934) and the chemical properties of water (Ömer 1933) served to stage a nationalist imaginary, where the state's scientific vision could discern and protect citizens against invisible dangers. This, in turn, reflected a wider reliance on a discourse of science to justify the secular political order and the social revolution it sponsored. "Social life dominated by irrational, useless, and harmful beliefs is doomed to paralysis," explained Atatürk in 1922, "We must begin by purging minds and society of their very springs. . . . Our guide in political, social, and educational life will be science" (Berkes 1964: 465).

While the discursive use of science to promote civilizational change may not have been new to the republic, it nonetheless became, as with medicine, more fully embraced as a technical means of reform for both the state and its citizens. Through the sorts of basic scientific (re)education offered by *Ülkü*—which sought to draw a "connection between scientific discoveries and most of our daily work" (*Ülkü* 1933: 325)—newly conceived citizens were to gain reason, rationality, and order in their understanding of both themselves and the natural, social, and political worlds they inhabited. In the process, older forms of (religious) knowledge, truth, and authority were to be rendered obsolete, and thus incomprehensible. "The esoteric religious man," as Salih Murat described in his 1933 contribution to *Ülkü*, "is not able to understand, let alone does he want to understand, the language of the scholar" (325).

National Health

As opposed to the at times strained attempts to connect science to everyday life, articles considering medicine and public health offered more explicit recommendations to citizens for the alteration of their lives' "daily work." Toward this end, publications such as *Ülkü* not only extolled the promises of modern medicine—laying the groundwork for the clinics to come—but also sought to cultivate a series of new relationships that would be required in the state's project of secular modern reform. Reflecting the journal's goal of constructing a unified national consciousness, we find in *Ülkü*'s consideration of medical topics a shifting conceptualization of how state-individual relations were to be imagined, one in which individual citizens were to assume responsibility for national development as the state assumed responsibility for the health and security of its citizens.

In the first case, as members of a new national community, the health of individual citizens was no longer to be regarded in isolation. Individual health was to be conceived in the frame of the nation's health. As the frequent contributor Zeki Nâsır wrote: "An individual's health means a family's health. A family's health constitutes a village, town, or city's health. All of these establish a country's, or more accurately, a nation's health standard" (1933a: 73). Through such concentric identifications (self, family, community, nation)[24] and the nesting of a nationalist thematic within the discourse of medicine, a healthy body becomes necessary for a healthy nation and, conversely, a sick individual becomes a burden on the family and the nation (Nâsır 1933a; Gönenç 1936). In this context, the implications of such essays as "The Road to Raising Highly Intelligent Children" (Evrenol 1936) gains added significance: a child's development becomes tantamount to a nation's development and, more broadly, individual health is charged with an aura of national responsibility.

A similar set of convictions can be found in the "village monograph" project promoted by *Ülkü*. This project, which urged physicians—among others—to spend their holidays in villages conducting research, led to the publication of a series of concrete suggestions for the improvement of the health status of rural communities (Nâsır 1933b).[25] The suggestions that emerged from this project, grounded in a vocabulary of public health and hygiene, would call for a radical reorganization of village space (in the form of village layout, household architecture, and furnishings; see Figure 2), temporality (with the standardization of meal times), and relations to one's own body (with prescriptions for bodily care, personal hygiene, and proper nutrition). In addition to enlightening the rural peasant about the discoveries of modern medicine, these lay research endeavors sought to build a social solidarity between the nation's urban and rural populations through enrolling *Ülkü*'s readers into a collective effort of improving the health of the nation through improving the health of its villages.

Despite the emphasis on individual bodies as sites of national health, individual action would not be sufficient for national development. "In the civilized world today," as Nâsır urged, "all of the people's and the state's work is done with cooperation" (1933a: 74). Gönenç reiterates this point: "For all of us to have more orderly and better health . . . our working in cooperation is necessary" (1936: 49). As such, the health of the national body, and hence national development, was to be understood as achievable through the personal and collective care of individual bodies.[26] In other words, these examples signal a medically mediated vision of the body's role within the nation's health, such that the individual body is constitutive of

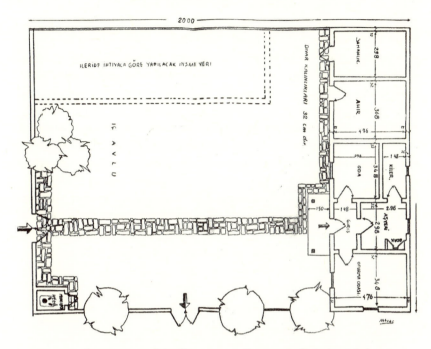

Figure 2. "Hygienic Model Village Houses." From *Halk Sağlığı Bılgıleri*, a free booklet produced to help medical personnel and teachers educate the general public about matters of health and hygiene (Sıhhat ve İçtimai Muavenet Vekâleti 1957).

the national body and the proper care of individual bodies will be vital to the health of the society.

In the second case, the discourse of medicine found in *Ülkü* simultaneously constructed and was constructed by a particular vision of the state and its proper role in the lives of its citizens. Here, individual citizens were not only expected to take care of themselves, and thus contribute to the nation's collective development, but the state was to perform its duty as the defender and guardian of its citizens' health. As a contributor to *Ülkü* explained, "One of the Republic of Turkey's brightest endeavors and triumphs is the state's taking healthcare and social assistance as among one of its foundational political ideals" (*Ülkü* 1933: 255). Building on the revolutionary vocabulary of the War of Independence, citizens were called on to unite as a nation under the protection of the state in order to defend themselves against the invasion of disease.[27]

In order to fulfill its duty as protector and guardian of the nation's health, contributors to *Ülkü* observed, the state would require new forms of legal intervention and technologies of watchfulness. Zeki Nâsır, writing in a 1933 issue of *Ülkü*, for instance, introduces his audience to recent developments in the relationship between health reform and law enforcement. After castigating those who marry too young and thus endanger the future intelligence of their children, Nâsır writes, "How can we expect a strong and healthy generation from mothers and fathers who married extremely young and whose bodies have yet to fully develop? As you see, the government, in the last years, has corrected this improper conduct with a law" (1933a: 74). In concert with such medical interventions into the law, the state would also need to develop its capacity to both perceive and address threats to the nation's health. Here, new technologies of medical awareness would be required to extend and deepen the state's reach. A contributor to *Ülkü* proudly informed his audience:

> Today, if a pestilence breaks out in whatever village of Anatolia, if there is a mother who is not able to give birth, if there is an indigent house with many children, Ankara's ear will immediately hear. . . . One of the obvious attributes of the Republic healthcare system is the extending of its hands and eyes as far as the village. (*Ülkü* 1933: 253–54)

In addition to echoing the vision of total medical awareness that Dr. Or was simultaneously struggling to realize in his experiments with technologies of medical data gathering at Etimesgut, we also encounter here a discourse of national medical surveillance that again articulates a politico-medical imaginary in which individual health and national health are reciprocally bound, with the former contributing to the latter and the latter watching over the former.

*   *   *

"The basic language of Western medicine, with its claims to universalism and modernity," writes Warwick Anderson, "has always used, as it still does, the vocabulary of empire" (1998: 529). For the early reformers of the republic, the reverse proved equally viable: the language of civilization and secular modernity could rely on a medical vocabulary for the articulation of a new political imaginary. While medicine is certainly neither a singular entity nor the exclusive site for such a project, and while Turkey's project of medical modernization was by no means inevitable, medicine nonetheless provided a rich vocabulary for those bent on consolidating a nation and reinventing a state. On the one hand, fabulous promises of an abundant life could be made in the name of medicine and modernity. With the expansion and modernization of the medical system, contributors to *Ülkü* predicted, more people would be born, fewer people would die, disease would fade away, and people would lead altogether longer lives (Gönenç 1936; Ömer 1933; *Ülkü* 1933). And all this abundance would set free an explosive productivity, bringing affluence and prosperity to all.

On the other hand, medicine also proved to be an effective site for enacting the top-down modernization project of the state, where normative claims about self, community, and nation could be introduced under the guise of empirical data and scientific findings. Beyond the well-documented epistemological assumptions embedded within biomedicine (Scheper-Hughes and Lock 1987; Gordon 1988; Good 1994; Mishler 1981), its expansion during this period also came to epitomize new relations between the state and its citizens. In other words, rather than simply reflecting emerging political ideals, medical reform instantiated nationalist ideology by constituting domains of social practice and scientific expertise that articulated corresponding notions of society and citizenship. Health (both individual and national) and development (both individual and national) were conceived as inseparable. And in this conjoining, the terrain of affliction and illness would be carved out anew, with the doctor and public health official being granted expanded power over bodies and communities. As such, medicine turned out to be not only a vital field for a state to enact its role as caregiver and protector of its citizens, but also a site for the introduction of new technologies of government administration and surveillance. Health personnel worked both to care for suffering individuals and to monitor the collective health of a population.

The development of Turkey's healthcare system, as I have argued, thus participated in a larger political endeavor to rationally engineer a new social order and, in the process, consolidate the state's subjects as a nationalized body. In the cultivation of a "scientific mentality" and a "health conscious" population, reformers sought, in the words of Nikolas Rose, to "instill techniques whereby selves would simultaneously practice upon themselves as free individuals and bind them into a civilized polity by means of that freedom and the modes in which it was enacted" (1999: 78). Through these processes, newly imagined citizens would be set free from what Atatürk had described as their "age-old rotten mentalities" and "irrational" submission to unjust communal oppression (Atatürk 1924). In a broad sense then, our discussion has thus far introduced us to the importance of medical care for the political management of collective life, the extensive integration of medicine into the function and organs of state, and the attempted regularization of medicine within people's everyday lives.

In the Shadows of Medicine and Modernity

Given the paucity of reliable sources, it is difficult to gauge how such projects were received at the time of their introduction, let alone how they changed over time. Personal recollections, however, are suggestive. The following account, from a woman who had left her village in the 1960s to move to Ankara with her husband, gives a sense of the transformations brought about by the healthcare system's expansion:

> In the village, when there was no health outpost, and you became ill, you died. In the old days, when you got sick in the village, there was no such thing as a doctor. I can't recall a time when I went to a doctor. But now there is a doctor and a health outpost in the village. My parents for instance—the last one lived to be over 90 years old, and wasn't able to see any longer—had never ever gone to any kind of doctor. Never. Then my brother came along. They would take him to the doctor immediately, even before the tears in his eyes had dried. And the doctors would say there was nothing to be done. This getting sick and going to the doctor, we never felt the need. There wasn't such illness. But now, there are a lot of doctors, and every day there is illness. I didn't know what it was to get sick when I came here. I didn't ever get sick.

Although the chapters to come will consider in great depth the legacy of these medical-political projects of nation making, my neighbor's recollections raise a number of important questions. Her comments are actually quite complicated and there are several intersecting registers of signification at work in them. They seem to indicate, for instance, a recategorization of experience that coincided with the appearance of physicians in her village—the incorporation, for instance, of nonmedicalized experiences (e.g., an expected aspect of aging) into a medical discourse. This would explain the apparent irony of her account, where the presence of physicians seemingly produced more illness. At the same time, it is difficult to separate her reflections from the present tense of the story telling, and the (urban) context of their telling.

To what extent does this story reflect a nostalgia for an idealized rural past, expressed through medical idioms? And to what degree was this absence of illness in the past but an instance of her making a virtue of a necessity—a resignation to the fact that there were few options available to the sick?[28] Each of these questions hinges, however, on the possibility of retrospectively distinguishing nonrecognition of illness from absence of illness. While we arrive here at an irresolvable impasse—for reasons beyond the limits of historical documentation—each question nonetheless confirms the far-reaching and intimate impact of a state's project of nation-making as it was staged in the field of medicine. That is, my neighbor's recollections are inseparable from the decades of discursive and material labor, concentrated in the fields of medicine and public health, that sought to cultivate particular ways of conceiving one's body, relating to others, imagining one's national past, and seeing as well as being seen by the state.

At this point, however, I want to draw attention to what is missing from the recollections and histories assembled in the preceding discussion. Did people, as my neighbor suggested, really do nothing before the state's healthcare system reached the provinces? And when physicians and nurses began arriving, were they necessarily welcomed with open arms? Official accounts would have one conclude that there was nothing before the doctor's appearance, that physicians entered a void of medical knowledge and care. While medicine's official account of its own history industriously covers over any sort of meaningful account of healing practices that preceded doctors (a responsibility that would be relegated to the folklorist, anthropologist, and ethnologist), glimpses of alternative histories nonetheless occasionally surface, even from within medicine's own archive.

Editorials in medical journals of the 1930s, for instance, begin to suggest something other than the unobstructed advance of physicians over ignorance. Writing in the renowned medical journal *Tıb Dünyası*, Dr. Fahreddin Kerim Gökay, in a discussion of Turkey's mental hygiene and psychiatric services, both enacts the preceding discussion (concerning the intersection of secularism and medical reform) and suggests that doctors did not arrive unchallenged:

By accepting secularism, which put a legal prohibition on the rights supporting the organizations that spread the practices of the *üfür-ükçü* and similar false beliefs, the veneration of individuals' freedom of consciousness was recognized as one of the greatest principles. (Gökay 1939a: 4185)

In a later issue of *Tıb Dünyası*, warning of the dangers of too quickly adopting new hospital policy, Dr. Gökay is more explicit:

Harm is possible in such an environment. We risk scaring away and causing to lose enthusiasm . . . a public that has escaped from *üfürük-çüs* and quack doctors and has begun to trust the state's compassionate institutions! (Gökay 1939b: 4287)

A contributor to *Ülkü*, writing in 1933, expresses a similar sentiment:

Altogether ignorant and foul would-be midwives have been giving birth to our mother's children, and of course killing most of them. . . . Under the name of surgery, inexperienced operators are treating wounded, sprained, and broken people, and they are leaving most of them handicapped. Thanks to [the state's role as healthcare provider], the practice of the *üfürükçü* in Turkey flows into the history of false doctoring. The calamities that ignorant midwives, would-be surgeons, dentist barbers, and circumcisers found in their coffee-house-corner offices have been producing for years have passed before us. (*Ülkü* 1933: 255)

The confrontations must have been intense. Even the preeminent scholar of Bektaşism, John Kingsley Birge, who would not normally be distracted by such "folk remedies," felt the campaigns against the *üfürükçü* sufficiently noteworthy to warrant a footnote: "*Milliyet* newspaper for Nov. 19, 1934 reports an arrest of a man for practicing *üfürükçülük*" (1937: 84).

If we follow the path that these passing statements clear before us, we trail into the shadows of the state's history of medicine. Once there, one encounters a multitude of healers employing a variety of therapeutic techniques (such as the *üfürükçü* or *cinci hoca*, the *kurşuncu*, bonesetters, midwives, herbalists, and innumerable holy persons and religious sites), all of which were surely used in a variety of combinations in accord with needs, expectations, and availability. Together, they point toward a history of social and religious formations that do not lend themselves so easily to the sorts of narratives promoted in Turkish medical history—a history, moreover, where the truths of biomedicine may not have been as self-evident, let alone uncontested, as claimed.

Exile

I am by no means suggesting that the hostility directed toward such figures as the *cinci hoca* began with the establishment of the republic. One can identify a long history of animosity to similar therapeutic and religious practices. Ottoman history is replete with disdain for the likes of the *cinci hoca*.[29] Even before the Ottoman Empire appeared in the region, Hippocrates (460–370 B.C.E.) and later Galen (129–200 C.E.) actively condemned "soothsayers," "magicians," and "exorcists" on familiar grounds—for not basing their medical knowledge on observable phenomena and failing to develop systematic therapeutic procedures (Dols 1992). While a scientific critique of such practices was therefore not novel, I am arguing that this critique took on new significance with the emergence of the modern state of Turkey. That is, individuals who offered assistance to the ailing began to enter new regimes of expertise and truth as Turkey sought to realize its project of secular modern development.[30] In particular, as the state increasingly relied on the fields of medicine and public health in the articulation of biopolitical rationalities of governance, which brought together individual and national bodies in an emergent project of political rebirth, healers working outside authorized medical discourses found themselves in conflict with a state's efforts to manage and regulate the health of the nation. At this point, the significance of Dr. Refik Saydam's presence—as a physician—at the moment of Turkey's political birth should be apparent.

While scholars have identified important interconnections between medicine, nationalism, and modernity—especially in contexts of colonialism[31]—this chapter has sought to open a conversation about, first, the particular significance of secularism within histories of medical reform and, second, the importance of the religious healer for understanding the development of both medicine and secularism. In our case, in the name of secularism, a set of social practices and modes of religio-political authority represented by practitioners of "non-scientific" therapies—such as the *cinci hoca* and other forms of religious healing—were structured in opposition to the figure of the modern, secular, rational citizen. Just as a new, modern Republic of Turkey would come into existence by freeing itself from the backward, unenlightened, and corrupt elements of its Ottoman past, so too would the new citizen become enlightened as old habits of thought and sentiment were cast off. The state campaign against practitioners of religious healing thereby emerged as a prominent stage on which secularist reformers enacted their "will to civilization" and desire for societal rebirth, a stage set by an alliance between science and secularism that the fields of medicine and public health would make possible.

Indeed, secularism—as an assemblage of ideas, practices, institutions, and coinciding formations of sensibility, sociability, and governance—was contingently fashioned through the exclusion of such forms of religious authority from the national order as reformers worked to sort and consolidate a version of Islam amenable to state control. We encountered this first in the forcible closure of religious orders, and then in the expansion of a modern, state-sponsored healthcare system. In the latter instance, the development of Turkey's healthcare system emerged as a critical site within the state's project of subject and world making. In tracing the prominent if not fragmentary discursive and material genealogies that assembled here, this chapter has been particularly concerned with the role of medical expertise and scientific literacy in reorganizing existing practices of bodily care, regimes of visibility, fields of social relatedness, and distribution of bodies and sensibilities within a re-imagined community of the nation. In these emergent configurations of truth, expertise, and the sensible, the treatment of injury and the health of the community would come together as a site for new forms of political struggle, a site where technologies of medicine and governance intertwined with a state's desire to regulate and govern collective life. And here, the state-sanctioned imams and physicians would become the speakers and producers of truth—differentiated into religious and clinical forms of authority—as opposed to *evliya*s, *derviş*es, *üfürükçü*s, *baba*s, or other representatives of discredited forms of religious knowledge and practice.

An obvious consequence of these processes was that figures like the *cinci hoca* were no longer available as exemplars of a national past to be celebrated in the name of Turkey's cultural uniqueness, as was the case with "traditional medicine" or "indigenous medicine" in a number of postcolonial settings (Langford 2002; Swartz and MacGregor 2002). Unlike the accepted, nationalized "traditions" of the folk musician or carpet weaver, the practice of religious healing shifted into the shadows of a maligned past. Although the less threatening domain of "folk remedies" would find a new home in the Ministry of Culture rather than the Ministry of Health—as this chapter's opening epigraph noted—the practices of the *cinci hoca* or *üfürükçü* would not be welcomed in either. In the emerging order of the new nation, the *cinci hoca* belonged neither to "civilization" nor to "culture." And once religious healers became associated with an unredeemable past that modernity was to supplant, it was possible to view their continued presence as a revolt of the past against the future. Today, such healers, having failed to "flow into the history of false doctoring," must work in and on the legacy of being positioned as antithetical to the creation of a modern nation and detrimental to the individual freedom of consciousness secularism was to inaugurate.

Although the principles of secular governance institutionalized during the early years of the republic would of course be revised and realized toward different ends as time passed—such as with a military coup in 1960 that would lead to a constitution codifying the military's role as guardian of Turkey's secular democracy, economic reforms in the 1980s that would set the stage for the increasing influence of market forces in the ordering of publics and social lives, and the electoral successes of Islamist political mobilization and the gaining traction of a liberal discourse of (religious) rights in the 1990s—secularism, as a political discourse, continues to organize dispersed fields of political, economic, social, and religious action. In this respect, it continues to be regarded as the foundational and integrative principle of the nation, as well as its encompassing philosophy of life. While we must acknowledge that the ability of the state's project of medical modernization to fully achieve its aspirations was limited, I am nonetheless arguing here that we cannot understand contemporary stories of healing and being healed without appreciating the unanticipated effects of this project's incomplete realization, a history of at times inconsistent visions of reason, rationality, and expertise as they simultaneously formed a nation and gave birth to the conditions of contemporary (therapeutic) experience.

Chapter 2

Healing Difference at the Limits
of Community

When I stopped by to visit Erol, I found him, as I had many times before, sitting in front of his house, book in hand, taking in the afternoon sun. With no work available that day—Erol had been intermittently employed as a day laborer since being laid off from his former job several years earlier—he was passing the hours reading *What Is Alevism?* a book that was quite popular while I was living in Hürriyet. After talking for a few minutes, he invited me in for tea. His wife joined us and, amid the television evening news, we began talking about my research interests in religious healing. Responding in a way that had by then become familiar, Erol insisted, "There is none of that here! None!" He spoke passionately about the uselessness of such practices and the ignorance of those who seek them out. "You'll find most of them over there [gesturing out the window, across the small valley of *gecekondu* homes], because they are more backward than us. We are more advanced, we have science, we have sense (*bilinç*). Sunnis, on the other hand, don't stress science, they don't educate their children." He went on to blame "their mosques"—in terms of both the money "wasted" in their construction and the mentality they fostered. "So there aren't healers like this with the Alevi. And in the future it will be the same with the Sunni, when they catch up with us. For now though, they still have no sense (*bilinçsiz*)."[1]

Although the intensity of this moment would pass, it was hard to ignore the larger ideological project to which Erol was giving voice, a project whose basic architecture had been laid down a generation earlier in the name of a revolutionary modernity and its war against ignorance and superstition. It was also hard to ignore that Erol's comments—articulated through inter-twining vocabularies of scientific progress, secular development, and religious backwardness—took spatial form as they distinguished his own neighborhood from those of, as he put it, "reactionary" (gerici) and "conservative" (tutucu) Sunnis. As I would come to recognize, to speak about religious healing in the neighborhoods where I conducted research was to position oneself within a complex arrangement of intersecting discourses.[2] Just as Erol located himself (and his neighborhood, and the nation) on the horizon of an ideal secular modernity ("we are more advanced, we have science"), he also expressed, reproduced, and mapped local geographies of religious and political difference. Moreover, this was a distribution of difference that also served to demarcate the limits of the sensible, which was at once the limits of both reason and community.

Over the course of my research, I would frequently visit one of these "other" neighborhoods that Erol disparaged with such enthusiasm—where residents were to be universally conservative, passionate supporters of the cinci hoca, and, consequently, lacking in "sense." The neighborhood to which Erol gestured was, in fact, where I had originally planned to base my research, but had been unable to find housing. As I continued to visit friends and acquaintances in this second neighborhood, which I refer to as Aktepe, I would encounter yet more talk—and arguments—about religious forms of healing. Rather than finding a cinci hoca on every corner—as promised by Erol and as I had, given my frustrations, admittedly hoped—I discovered that the vast majority of residents openly rejected, with comparable passion, the forms of religious practice represented by the cinci hoca. They did so, however, on grounds that differed from the residents of Hürriyet. It is this difference, and the ways difference was mobilized to sustain the grounds of community life, that are the subjects of this chapter.

In the twenty-minute walk that separated the two neighborhoods, I would find myself traversing the major religious and political divisions of Turkish society, divisions that similarly cut through the region and the larger Muslim world. Whereas the vast majority of Hürriyet's residents regarded themselves as Alevi—a Shi'i religious minority that comprise 15–20 percent of Turkey's population and are known for their commitment to Kemalist models of secular democratic reform—the majority of residents in Aktepe were Sunni Muslims who regarded themselves as observant, pious Muslims and supporters, broadly speaking, of the pro-Islamist political party that came to power during my research. In this respect, despite the innumerable similarities between the two neighborhoods, Hürriyet and Aktepe nonetheless mapped across some of Turkey's most intensely contested lines of social, political, and religious difference (Sunni/Alevi, Islamist/Secularist, Left/Right).

While the preceding chapter introduced the importance of the figure of the religious healer for political reformers struggling to demarcate the limits of an ideal secular national community, this chapter turns to the ways this discourse of national unity transforms into a language of communal difference as it enters into the weave of social life in the two neighborhoods where I conducted research. Here, I am particularly interested in examining everyday conversations about religious healing as discursive sites for the production and reproduction of difference, wherein divergent visions of social order, community life, and the limits and effects of secular state power are at once articulated and become articulable in the course of talking about religious healing. Attending to these everyday discourses of religious healing is of additional importance because of the vital role they play in mediating relationships between healers and their patients. If we are to understand the capacity of healers to rework the constraints and affordances of human action and subjectivity, the ordering of social relationships, the limits of sensibility and bodily experience, and the imagining of possible futures, we must examine how their representations circulate through the communities and relationships in which they live and practice. Before addressing this entanglement of healing, secularism, and community, however, I want to sketch briefly the economic and political processes that gave rise to the material conditions in which Erol's comments find their home, and out of which we first encounter the concept of the *gecekondu* as a distinctive discursive space within Turkey's urban imaginary.

Disorderly Development

Like other neighborhoods in the area, Hürriyet was a sprawling *gecekondu* neighborhood of single-story homes originally built on land seized from the state by rural migrants. What drew me to Hürriyet was neither foresight nor calculation but what brought most people to Hürriyet—social connections. A friend's wife's uncle's friend was willing to rent me—a young male traveling and living alone—his family's recently vacated apartment. The apartment sat on a modest thoroughfare lined with a handful of multi-story buildings that cut through Hürriyet and formed its commercial center. A common array of businesses and workspaces clustered here—a half dozen small grocery stores and produce stands, a pastry shop, a school supply and stationery store, a post office, a hair salon, a basic clothing store, several inexpensive restaurants, and the occasional real estate office. The apartment I rented was located above one such real estate office.

Both Hürriyet and Aktepe are located in Mamak Municipality.[3] With more than 90 percent of its residents living in illegal or unauthorized housing (Milli Gazetesi 1999a,b), Mamak is considered one of the poorest municipalities of the city. Both neighborhoods were originally settled by residents of villages in the central Anatolian provinces of Çorum and Yozgat. As in other *gecekondu* communities, residents continued to maintain close connections with their natal villages, even across generations of residence in Ankara—regularly talking with relatives, returning during harvest season, maintaining family properties, visiting for holidays, attending funerals, and so forth. Social and familial ties simultaneously stretched throughout the city where co-villagers and relatives had settled, as well as across national borders into Turkish diasporas throughout the world.

The kinds of work available in Hürriyet and Aktepe mirrored those of other such neighborhoods located at the margins of Turkey's economy. For men able to find employment, it was commonly manual labor and, to a lesser but growing extent, work in the service sectors. In both cases, employment was typically irregular and came with few long-term guarantees. The vast majority of jobs, moreover, required lengthy commutes to other areas of Ankara or surrounding towns. While it was not uncommon for women to be employed outside the home in Hürriyet, most worked as homemakers, occasionally selling knit and crocheted items to supplement the household income.[4]

Hürriyet and Aktepe, like other *gecekondu* neighborhoods, came into existence with the massive expropriation of state land that accompanied the industrialization and urbanization of Turkey's economy following World War II.[5] As the term *gecekondu* suggests—literally, "built or settled at night or overnight"—migration to cities was accompanied by an explosion of quickly built homes, sometimes over the course of a single night, without the property owner's permission. Over time, as *gecekondu* settlements became regularized, their residents more organized, and politicians increasingly desirous of their support, urban infrastructures expanded into these neighborhoods—streets were paved, utilities extended, public transportation routes established, and health clinics opened. With these

Figure 3. Hürriyet.

transformations also came property deeds for many residents, however precarious and qualified (such that you could own the home but not the land beneath it). Although neighborhoods like Hürriyet and Aktepe were regarded as peripheral byproducts of economic development, they quickly came to constitute the majority of available housing in Turkey's major cities. Today, in keeping with their founding, such neighborhoods continue to offer affordable housing to maintain a dependable supply of exploitable labor for the regional economy.[6] While the living conditions in *gecekondu* neighborhoods may bear few resemblances to the abject scarcity associated with unregulated housing at urban peripheries,[7] these neighborhoods are nevertheless sites of concentrated poverty that millions of Turkey's unemployed and working poor call home.

In contrast to the material scarcity that characterizes *gecekondu* neighborhoods, discourses about *gecekondu*s are distinguished by their excess. That is, a vast administrative, legal, architectural, academic, media, and literary outpouring has accompanied the emergence of *gecekondu* neighborhoods. From authoritative reports on "Gecekondu Policy in Turkey" (Heper 1978) to satirical *gecekondu* novels (İzgü 1970), from definitive academic studies of *The Gecekondu* (Karpat 1976) to booklets for the public that answer *One Hundred Questions About Urbanization, Housing, and the Gecekondu in Turkey* (Keleş 1983), there is no shortage of words spoken in the name of these neighborhoods—especially by those living outside them. In each, the *gecekondu* neighborhood is defined by its seeming contradictions. Echoing a globalized vocabulary of migration and urban poverty, such neighborhoods are imagined as communities of both virtue and deprivation, honor and volatile excess. Celebrated for their mutual support, the closeness of kin ties, and their ability to maintain the virtues of rural life (honesty, industry, trustworthiness), they are also characterized as spaces of unremitting poverty that breed hopelessness, political and religious radicalism, social conservatism, and uncontrolled criminality. In this regard, given the prevalence of the Turkish suffix "-*siz*" (meaning "without") in these discourses, both *gecekondu* neighborhoods and their residents appear to be defined by what they lack— *işsiz* (unemployed), *düzensiz* (without order), *kültürsüz* (without culture), *mimarsız* (without architect), *imarsız* (without development), and *bilinçsiz* (without sense). Out of these opposing visions of *gecekondu* life emerges a sense that neighborhoods such as Hürriyet and Aktepe are simultaneously sites of nostalgia for Turkey's agrarian past, symptoms of its economic present, and harbingers of a threatening future.[8]

These characterizations were not unfamiliar to the residents of Hürriyet and Aktepe, who frequently described themselves, their neighbors, and their neighborhoods in these precise terms. Everyday discourse about life in the neighborhood—from complaints about dusty streets, irregular bus service, and obtrusive neighbors to commentaries on the pace of community life, the warmth of neighborly relations, and the quality of the air—implicitly organized itself in juxtaposition to an idealized vision of city life, in the process shoring up an otherwise ambiguous boundary between "city" and "*gecekondu.*" A similar dynamic was apparent when residents spoke of the persistently high rates of unemployment in the neighborhood. While quick to describe their lives as significantly "easier" than those of their parents (by virtue, typically, of possessing such consumer goods as washing machines, televisions, automobiles, mobile phones, DVD players, and computers), they still recognized that their economic status in relation to others remained, at best, unchanged. This economic reality was regularly explained in terms of personal failure and urban underdevelopment—of constraints imposed by ignorance or lack of education, which in turn were the result of having grown up in a *gecekondu* neighborhood. This sensibility was reflected in the common depiction of oneself as a "child of the *gecekondu*" to explain one's inability to be socially mobile, a phrase I understood as referring to being born both within the material conditions of urban poverty and through the language spoken in the name of the *gecekondu.*

Even among the already exaggerated depictions of *gecekondu* life, the municipality of Mamak holds a special place.[9] Mamak is regarded not only as an impoverished district of the city but also as an intensely conservative one. In the public imagination, it is an area where women are compelled to wear the most extreme forms of concealing clothing, public space is dominated by (bearded) men, and women are only allowed out of their homes with male escorts. Unlike the city center and its surrounding neighborhoods, Mamak is envisioned as an urban space organized by religion—where mosques are abundant, the day is structured around the five daily prayers, alcohol is forbidden, and one risks being attacked if seen breaking fast during Ramadan. For those particularly fearful about the future of Turkey's secular democracy, Mamak is imagined anxiously as a base for radical Islamists plotting to overthrow the state to make way for a theocratic political and legal order. These traits associated with Mamak, and *gecekondu* settings more generally, will prove vital to our understanding of the forms

of therapeutic authority that religious healers working in Aktepe and Hürriyet are able to cultivate.

Distributions of Life and Death

In describing the differences between the neighborhoods, many residents
in Hürriyet dwelled on the late 1970s as a formative period. These were
the years when political violence threatened to tear apart the fabric of the
nation—when leftists became increasingly organized, their rivals increasingly angry, and both increasingly confrontational. In Hürriyet, these were
years when gun battles erupted between opposing political factions, with
some of the more intense ones taking place just down the main thoroughfare from my apartment. I was also told that these were political clashes—
between leftists and the ultranationalist right—not religious clashes
between Alevis and Sunnis (although, as was quickly added, most Alevis are
leftist and most "fascists," as my neighbors put it, are Sunni). This was a
period before Alevis had begun to assert themselves publicly as Alevis and
before residents of neighborhoods like Aktepe had begun to see themselves
as participants in a worldwide Islamic Revival.

The military and its tanks eventually arrived in Hürriyet, assuming control of the local school as a command post for regular patrols of the neighborhood. "There were police and military all over the place," one neighbor
recalled. "They'd walk around with a list of names and they'd stop you,
and if you were on the list, you'd be taken away. One night, the police
broke into our house and took our son away—his name was on the list.
We didn't hear from him for months." Despite the police presence, gun
battles continued late into 1980, following the declaration of martial law in
the wake of Turkey's third military coup. For those in Hürriyet, the end of
the 1970s marked the beginning of the fragmentation of the left. For those
in Aktepe, the 1980s ushered in the era of Turgut Özal, whose political
leadership would combine conservative social values with rapid neoliberal
economic reform.

The antagonisms that had resulted in open street battles in the late 1970s
had largely been absorbed, by the time I arrived, into a series of state-
mediated political processes. Life and death, and their differing distributions between the two neighborhoods, no longer relied so heavily on the
possession and use of weapons. Rather, matters of survival amid urban
poverty came increasingly to turn on political influence, where control of

the municipal government brought clean(er) water, new health clinics, food distribution programs, and freshly paved roads. Indeed, I moved into Hürriyet just as the municipal government was changing hands from the Hürriyet-supported Republic People's Party to the Aktepe-supported Virtue Party. Within days of the election, I found myself accompanying an Alevi neighbor to a relative's partly constructed home to hurriedly complete the project before newly elected municipal officials could demolish it. Not long after this, Hürriyet's neighborhood health clinic was unceremoniously closed. And just as plans to extend a natural gas line into Hürriyet were canceled, Aktepe residents celebrated the sudden extension of one into their own neighborhood.

While I did not encounter much in the way of armed conflict while I lived there, the border between Hürriyet and Aktepe remained a site of intense exchange. Alongside its materiality within the built environment, this was a border that cut through everyday discourse in both neighborhoods, especially when it came to the topic of religious healing. As my research questions moved between the two neighborhoods, I would come to appreciate the extent to which everyday conversations about religious healing played a constitutive role in shaping how people thought about their neighbors and neighborhoods, how they imagined themselves and their neighborhoods as part of a larger political community, and how they articulated and sought a sense of shared belonging in conditions marked by economic and political marginalization. In time, that is, these conversations would come into view as discursive sites for the production of both community and difference; as they offered a setting for narrating one's inclusion within an imagined ideal of secular modern development, they simultaneously mapped the fields of religious, class, and gender difference that comprised *gecekondu* life.

"We Don't Do That Kind of Crap Here": Enlightenment and Secularist Anxieties in Hürriyet

"Have you ever been to one of these healers?" I asked Nurdan and Hasan, the twenty-three-year-old daughter and twenty-year-old son of a prominent local contractor. We were sitting on the terrace of their newly constructed apartment, which was opulent by local standards—two stories, four bedrooms, two luxuriously decorated salons, and this, the immense veranda on the building's roof. The terrace offered one of those rare views

Figure 4. Hürriyet.

of the neighborhood from above, with *gecekondu* homes spreading carpet-like into the late summer sunset of the Anatolian steppe. It was an uncommon way of relating to Hürriyet, a perspective made possible by their father's accumulation of wealth beginning decades earlier in Germany as a laborer and continuing now in construction and land speculation. I regularly visited Nurdan, Hasan, and their family—talking with Nurdan and her mother while her father was out on business, playing basketball with Hasan and his friends, attending weddings and family gatherings, and passing afternoon hours at their father's office as subcontractors, laborers, and those looking to purchase new apartments passed through. My time with Hasan and Nurdan's family revealed, among other things, the everyday, informal, and unspoken forces at play in the segregation of Ankara's urban landscape. I regularly looked on as families new to Ankara were either welcomed to the neighborhood or politely referred to other areas. I watched as their father and visitors elaborated expansive genealogies in an effort to find common ground and determine what sorts of housing would be appropriate. In that Hasan and Nurdan's father both built and sold apartments, thereby controlling a substantial proportion of the housing market, their family played an influential role in regulating the neighborhood's composition.

Nurdan's response to my question highlighted additional ways in which community boundaries were drawn and redrawn in the course of everyday life. "They are ignorant and stupid, why would I go to them? For that,

you'll have to go over to that neighborhood," as she pointed out across the
expanse of rooftops toward Aktepe. "They all do that *hacı hoca* stuff—the
religiously conservative (*dinci*, *tutucu*) and reactionary (*gerici*). We go to
doctors." Nurdan's family even eschewed the free state clinic around the
corner, opting for the private *poliklinik* down the road. This would prove
to be one of my early introductions to the class geography of healthcare in
the city, and the ways it intersected with a politics of religious difference.
"We don't believe in such healers because we are enlightened, we believe in
science," she said, turning her body and pointing out across the small valley
of *gecekondu* homes toward Aktepe. "You'll have to go where the covered
women are."

Another example. One afternoon while visiting Ali (a retired laborer
whose sons ran a neighborhood store), his wife Sabır, and Feride (a woman
whom Ali and Sabır had brought over to speak with me because of her
expertise in treating people with the "evil eye"), Sabır asked if I was writing
about *muska*, the ritual amulet commonly associated with the *cinci hoca*. I
answered in the affirmative.

> Feride: Tssk. There are no *muska* with US!
> Chris: Who then knows about *muska*?
> Feride: *Hoca*s know about that. Liars know. We do not know.

Feride was repeating what Ali's son had said to me several months earlier,
when he told me about his father going to an *ocaklı* (a descendant of a holy
person who is recognized as having specialized healing powers) because of
discomfort following heart surgery. He took great care in clarifying that
an *ocaklı* was not a *hoca*. "*Hoca*s are not for us. *Hoca*s are for religious
conservatives." While I would come to learn that the relationship between
religious healing and religious conservatism was far from straightforward,
the simple mention of the *cinci hoca* in Hürriyet, especially in these sorts
of group encounters, inspired sweeping condemnations and contentious
ideological debates that served to both mark and inscribe the limits of sense,
which was also the limits of community life.

Alevism as a Public Way of Life

By "we," Nurdan, Hasan, Feride, and Ali of course meant "we Alevi." Yet
according to popular conceptions of Alevism, as well as the scholarly literature on Alevism available at the time of my research, one would not have

expected such an open claim to Alevi identity. Alevis were renowned, after all, for their secretiveness and longstanding commitment to that great Shiʻi tradition of *takiye* (*taqiyya*), or dissimulation—a skill Alevis had refined over centuries of persecution. When it came to the topic of religious healing, however, conversations in Hürriyet inevitably became extended expositions on the nature of Alevi identity and the importance of Alevi traditions. The question I kept returning to was this: How did Alevism come to be formulated in these terms and, specifically, what is it about religious healing that incites such intense and explicit claims to identity?

While Nurdan, Hasan, Feride, and Ali were confident in describing what Alevism was *not*, the popularity of Erol's book—*What Is Alevism?*—suggests less certainty when it comes to defining Alevism in positive terms. Indeed, by "Alevi," Nurdan and the others meant many things. Alevism, nominally a religious designation, encompasses a complex set of interdependent political, religious, linguistic, and ethnic associations.[10] In its restrictive theological sense, Alevism (Alevilik) is commonly conceived as an instance of Shiʻi Islam. Like other Shiʻis, especially those referred to as "Twelvers," Alevi trace the succession of leadership in the early Islamic community directly from Muhammed through his cousin and son-in-law Ali and the Twelve Imams. When asked to characterize the meaning of Alevism today, however, rather than invoking theological differences, neighbors recurrently appealed to a simple moral command: "Eline, diline, beline sahip ol!" (literally, "be the owner of your hand, tongue, and loins"; do not steal, lie, or commit adultery). While it is not uncommon to encounter more elaborated reflections on Alevi philosophy—the significance of an esoteric, intuitive knowledge of God (Marifet) which has as its ultimate goal a union with God (Hakikat, ultimate truth), the striving to cultivate feelings of unity (*birlik*) and love (*muhabbet*) within the community, or one's spiritual evolution through the Dört Kapı (the Four Doors or Gateways to spiritual truth)—asking what characterized Alevism typically evoked broadly construed principles of tolerance, equality, and justice.[11] In this last regard, Alevism represents a rarely acknowledged example of a publicly engaged religiosity in the Muslim world that is not viewed as a threat to liberal secular sensibilities.

Unlike Sunni Aktepe, where there is no overarching structure of community authority beyond the locally elected government official, or *muhtar*, Alevi communities such as Hürriyet are comprised of a number of overlapping social groupings organized around family lineages and headed by a *dede*. In the past, especially before the intensification of urban migration, *dede*s were recognized as both religious and community leaders; they were invested with the moral and spiritual authority to arbitrate conflict, lead communal ritual (e.g., the *cem*), and exile individuals from communal life (*düşkünlük*). With urbanization—as the closed nature of Alevi communities gave way to heterogeneous communities spread across large cities, conflicts between individuals became intercommunal, and the threat of exile became less tenable—the *dede*'s authority would wane substantially. These developments also coincided with a widespread embrace of leftist, liberatory politics among Alevis in the 1970s, which, given their anti-authoritarian and anti-traditionalist emphases, further eroded the authority of the *dede*. By the time I moved to Hürriyet, the role of figures such as the *dede* had become seriously circumscribed, and they carried limited weight in shaping community relations.

Despite the declining importance of the *dede*, as well as other Alevi traditions of communal organization, Alevism appeared to be more important than ever. Residents of Hürriyet regularly spoke of the unprecedented flourishing of "Alevi culture" (*Alevi kültürü*) over the preceding two decades. Alevi religious foundations and cultural centers were expanding, festivals were celebrating Alevi history, young people were embracing Alevi musical traditions, and politicians were actively courting the Alevi vote. Alevism, which had been for centuries a secretive and predominantly rural-based religious tradition, had begun to enter onto a public stage in ways that formerly seemed unimaginable. In this broad transformation, the social institutions and communal structures that had previously defined a sense of common identity among Alevi were giving way to an ascendant celebration of Alevi "culture" as a self-consciously articulated body of ideals, concepts, and images used to assert a sense of shared history and collective belonging—despite the heterogeneity of experience and commitment included under the label "Alevi."

This public celebration of Alevi culture coincided with the increasing involvement of diverse Alevi groups within a wider politics of identity that had begun to gain traction in Turkey during the 1990s (Şahin 2005; Dressler 2008; Tambar 2010). During this period, Alevi ideals of tolerance, equality, and humanist inclusion came to assume a prominent role in Alevi demands for political participation and recognition. While residents of Hürriyet were widely supportive of this public recognition of Alevi heritage and the coinciding demands for the inclusion of Alevi interests in government policy, public debate, and school curricula, many nonetheless read this political shift with great ambivalence. For some, a politics based on Alevi identity represented a betrayal of older Alevi political traditions and was taken as further evidence of the fragmentation of a formerly united leftist political movement. Looking out for specifically Alevi interests, for these critics, was to abandon larger demands for equality and justice for all.

The concurrence we find here of Alevi ideals of the ethical person and Kemalist models of secular citizenship points, in turn, toward a longer history. Not only were Alevis generally enthusiastic supporters of Atatürk and the secularist reform he introduced—as a religious minority that had experienced centuries of persecution under the Ottoman state, they had much to gain by secularization policy[12]—but Alevis were also seen by many secularist reformers as uniquely predisposed to the principles of democratic and secular reform. For some of these early reformers, Alevis were beacons of a new republican model of secular-liberal citizenship.

Today, for those embracing an expressly Alevi politics of identity, the demand for political recognition is at once a call for reinstating such Kemalist principles of political order.[13] These demands, moreover, are emerging in response to a sense that Islamist-influenced political mobilization is threatening the secular foundation of the state, a topic we will return to below. For now, given the distinctly Alevi history of secular reform and the close association of figures such as the *cinci hoca* with Islamist political mobilization, we can begin to understand why the topic of religious healing might incite intense and explicit claims to Alevi identity. We begin to understand, that is, how Alevi commentaries on religious healing emerge out of intertwined legacies of political, economic, and religious transformation.

Development, Difference, Panic

For Aydın, a retired owner of a small grocery store, and someone who had flirted with the idea of following in the footsteps of his village *cinci hoca* while he was a child, far more than individual ignorance was at stake in the continued presence of religious healers. According to Aydın, the nation would be pointing forward, progressing, and modernizing if it were not for the religious healer. As Aydın put it,

> These *hoca*s are always harmful for Turkey. And for the sick they are also harmful. They keep their illnesses from passing and then

they are left with nothing in their hands. No report. No film. No X-rays. *Hoca*s will treat them just to make money—in order to tear away a few cents from a poor patient. The *hoca* says five cents, the patient says three cents, and then the *hoca* starts talking about spirits coming, that the spirits are readying their knives . . . and then the patient believes the *hoca*. Three, five, six months pass, maybe a year passes, and the illness is no better. And when the illness gets worse, not even a doctor can defeat it. *Hoca*s are harmful like that. If there weren't *hoca*s, he'd have gone to a doctor. The doctor would conduct tests, take X-rays, do an analysis, treat him, and he could be cured. But now he can't be treated. And the sick person can't find work anywhere, can't look after himself, can't take care of his family. He's left unproductive, living as a parasite. Only death is a savior.

When I asked why he thought people continued to seek the *cinci hoca*'s assistance, he explained:

Sick people are more ignorant. Here in Turkey, there are a lot of ignorant people. People who have not advanced and who still believe in these *hoca*s. It's as if they don't rely on anything scientific. They don't trust anything scientific. You, for instance, have respect for your mind. From their minds, something is lacking. They are deceived from true nature. They are deceived. *Hoca*s control the people like that. And they leave people still further back. The people do not develop.

Some sixty years after physicians like Fahreddin Gökay, writing in *Tıb Dünyası*, condemned "the practice of *üfürükçüs* and false beliefs like this" for impeding "individuals' freedom of consciousness" (1939a), urban immigrants such as Aydın invoke a nearly identical language to disparage religious healers and their patients. For Aydın—as for Nurdan, Hasan, Ali, Sabır, and Erol—those who believe in *hoca*s are "unenlightened." They are ignorant, uneducated, backward-looking, and blinded from true (scientific) knowledge. Moreover, they bring harm not only to the suffering individual, but to the nation as a whole. In this regard, it is not difficult to hear in Aydın echoes of the contributors to *Ülkü*, as they implored their audiences to conduct themselves like good, rational citizens and rely on modern medicine, as opposed to "superstition," in caring for themselves and others. For

Aydın, as with the contributors to *Ülkü*, to reject the *cinci hoca* and recognize the truth of medicine was to free one's consciousness and to, consequently, become an enlightened and economically productive citizen.

In Aydın's reflections on the dangers of the *cinci hoca*, we also encounter the privileged place that the theme of religious healing holds in positioning specifically Alevi speakers within the horizons of an ideal secular modernity. "We are more advanced, we have science, we have sense (*bilinç*). . . . They are more backward . . . they still have no sense (*bilinçsiz*)." Simply put, "we [Alevi] don't do that kind of crap." Such conversations, in this respect, unfold within discursive fields deeply indebted to an earlier generation's work of political and scientific mobilization. And, given the important role of Alevis in the state's articulation of its project of secular modernity, it is no coincidence that these remnants of past political work exert such a force in Hürriyet today. In their current setting, these conversations not only rehearse an ideological history of nation making, but they also trace contemporary limits of community—which are conceived as the limits of the reasonable and sensible.

When I asked Aydın about the differences between his staunchly secularist, Kemalist neighborhood and nearby Aktepe, he explained,

Do you know the difference? Look, like I said earlier, this is the enlightened area. "To be enlightened," do you know this? It refers to one who goes toward the future. One who absorbs the future. One who thus assimilates the new. For example, if an infidel makes good tea, it is good tea. If a Muslim makes good tea, it is good tea. If they make it good in Japan, it is good. But those who like only what they themselves know, they think that what is made by Muslims is good, and by others is not. Does this make sense? Whoever makes it well, that is good. Right? The other area, well, the *hoca*s are reactionary. And because people get everything from the *hoca*, they do not develop at all. The new is not fitting for them.

In his gesture of humanist inclusion (Why does it matter who makes the tea, as long as it is good?), which was at once a commentary on labor and production (one should not judge the product of labor by the producer's intentions), themes of rationality, science, and development again ravel together and find a particular object in Aydın's Sunni neighbors. For, by "Muslim," he means his Sunni neighbors, and specifically the forms of

Sunni religious conservatism he sees gaining support in neighborhoods like Aktepe. As with Nurdan, Hasan, Erol, Ali, and Feride, the reiteration of a secular modernist discourse that rejects such forms of religious authority operates to express, just as it constitutes, local forms of religious difference. Not only do "we not do that kind of crap," but, always soon after, with a turn of the body and a gesture toward Aktepe—reminding us again of the spatial and bodily entanglements of these discourses of difference—"you'll have to go to the neighborhood with covered women."

As is commonplace in debates about secularism, Islam, and liberal democracy, conversations about religious healing in Hürriyet reliably turned to the topic of gendered religious practice. Beyond providing Alevi speakers the opportunity to assert their distinctively modern and secular identity,[14] these discussions of gender and sexuality in relation to religious healing played a central role in the mapping of religious and therapeutic difference in the surrounding *gecekondu* neighborhoods. Residents of Hürriyet, for instance, repeatedly emphasized that Alevi religious rituals were not segregated by gender, unlike their "conservative" Sunni neighbors. More prominently, as they recurrently pointed out, virtually no women in the neighborhood wore headscarves. Unlike their Sunni neighbors, among whom they imagined covering as ever-present, women in Hürriyet were open (*açık*) and free (*serbest*). For most of the Alevi with whom I spoke, men and women alike, the headscarf epitomized the unjust subordination of women's autonomy to male religious authority within conservative Sunni neighborhoods.

When my Alevi neighbors gestured toward "the neighborhood with covered women" in talking about religious healing, this is what was being expressed—a distinction between the freedom and autonomy of modern women in Hürriyet (symbolized by the absence of the headscarf) and the oppression and subjugation of conservative women in Aktepe (symbolized by the presence of the headscarf). Moreover, for residents of Hürriyet, Sunni women's claims that wearing headscarves was a free choice, even an act of resistance (as many in Aktepe did see such a practice, and as I explained to my Alevi neighbors), were taken as further proof of the dangerous powers of such forms of religious authority. That is, according to my neighbors in Hürriyet, the type of Islamic conservatism found in Aktepe was so powerful that it could make women believe that subjugating oneself to unjust forms of patriarchal religious authority was an act of liberation.

In our considerations of everyday talk about religious healing as a discursive site for the production of difference, it is important also to acknowledge the forms of internal difference these conversations expressed. Alongside positioning Alevi speakers within the discursive limits of an ideal secular modernity, conversations about religious healing in Hürriyet likewise articulated lines of class difference within Alevi community life—a discourse of difference wherein associations between religious healing, traditionality, and the discursive space of the *gecekondu* were particularly insistent. Over the course of living in Hürriyet, this intersection of religious healing and class difference would become particularly apparent to me in a series of complex friendships I developed with two brothers (Bektaş, a greengrocer in the neighborhood, and his brother Fikret) and their families. The following exchanges between Gül, Fikret's wife, and myself illustrate these intersections.

During one of my several visits with Gül and Fikret, while I was complaining about the slow progress of my research, Gül made reference to seeing a *kurşuncu* when their oldest son was a baby. Before I could ask her more, she quickly changed the subject. It was clear that she did not want our conversation to return to the *kurşuncu*. I also could not help noticing her subtle attempts to discern Fikret's reaction. A few days later, as my field notes recount,

> I dropped by Gül's place today because she said that she would tell me more about the *kurşuncu* she had mentioned the other night. I got there at about 11 a.m., knowing that Fikret would have left for work by then. She had just gotten up, and was making breakfast. So we sat down and had breakfast, watching her two sons play. After eating, I brought up the matter of the *kurşuncu* (to which she responded, "Is that why you came?") and asked her if Fikret had not known about her going to the *kurşuncu*. Although he must know now because she said it in front of us all the other night. She said that he had not known until then. And when she said it, she noticed that he turned to her with a startled look. So he knows now. I asked why she hadn't told him before. She said that she hadn't told him because she knew that he didn't agree with it and that he thought such things were wrong. She knew as well that he would get angry. I asked how he couldn't have known, since she had pinned

the lead to the baby.[15] She said she pinned it underneath the baby's vest. "It was pinned there for awhile, but I eventually took it off."

Fikret and Gül were discontented with where they were—in terms of the *gecekondu* neighborhood where they lived as well as what this communicated about their position in Turkey's class structure. They prided themselves on cultivating everything "modern"—from their style of dress to the educational aspirations they had for their children, from their tastes in film and music to the ways they related with each other and their children. Whereas Fikret's brother's family—whose house shared the same enclosed garden—ate their meals sitting on the floor around a large tray, Fikret and Gül sat in chairs at the dining room table. Whereas his brother drank rakı, Fikret preferred whiskey. When his brother took time off to travel with his family to the shrine of Hacı Bektaş, Fikret and Gül were taking week-long vacations on the beaches of the Aegean Sea.

Gül's comments extend our discussion of the relationship between religious healing and visions of secular modern inclusion by demonstrating the ways that notions of traditionality associated with religious healing figure in class politics and their localization in *gecekondu* neighborhoods such as Hürriyet. According to Fikret, what was "wrong" about going to such healers was their traditionality and hence their association with "backward" and non- or anti-modern elements of society. Going to healers like this, as Fikret had insinuated many times before, (re)located them into the *gecekondu*, an area (and its associated ways of life) from which they were desperately trying to extricate themselves. (They were already sending, at great cost, their son to school in Çankaya—a wealthy neighborhood well across the city.) The repudiation of religious healing is thus approached by Fikret as a potential resource in his desire for class mobility—much in the same way that Nurdan's family opted for the private *poliklinik* over the free state health clinic.[16]

*   *   *

These intersecting discourses of religious healing speak toward multiple ends simultaneously. As discussed above, to talk about religious healing is to position oneself as a speaker within the horizons of an imagined ideal of secular modern development. Here, in the everyday dismissal of religious forms of healing, we come upon echoes of larger and older campaigns against "superstition" that sought to enforce particular visions of collective national life, where individual development was to relate metonymically to the development of the nation. Considering how early secular reformers valorized rural farmers as the foundation of the new nation, and given the innumerable campaigns and initiatives introduced in the countryside in an effort to consolidate a social basis of political rule, one should not be particularly surprised by the continuity between early republican secularist attacks on "superstition" and everyday critiques of religious forms of healing among contemporary urban immigrants in Hürriyet.

Unlike the earlier generation, however, where campaigns against "superstition" were part of a larger political discourse of national progress and revolutionary hope, the preceding discussion suggests that an additional set of sensibilities are today gathering around critiques of "ignorant" and "irrational" social practices. On the one hand, in addition to confirming one's enlightened modernity, the topic of religious healing serves to constitute local forms of religious, class, and community difference. In this, discourses about religious healing join with other structuring forces—access to housing, employment, local political patronage—to normalize community boundaries and shape urban segregation. On the other hand, this talk of religious healing is also a language of anxiety, one that expresses a sense that the present political order is under siege and at risk of being lost. Before moving on, I want to briefly address the sense of secularist panic we find working its way through these conversations.

While many residents of Hürriyet may have been broadly concerned about the possible end of secularism and its replacement with some vague sense of "religious law" (depicted as an inverted ideal democracy), the figure of the religious healer gave these concerns concrete form. The religious healer—especially the *cinci hoca*—commanded a dangerously seductive form of religious persuasion, a power that could overwhelm rational judgment and awaken deep-seated passions. This same form of religious persuasion and its accompanying model of communal authority were conceived as animating forces behind the gaining influence of Islamist-inspired political parties in Turkey. Approached in these terms, religious healers and Islamist activists were regarded as involved in a common project of deceiving the uneducated and poor into acting against their own rational self-interest. In the latter case, this entailed convincing susceptible citizens to vote against their own political self-interest, which would then allow Islamists to seize control of the government under the guise of popular consent. In this scenario, the religious healer exemplifies and embodies a form of religious power that not only undermines central secularist principles, but also threatens to render the citizen complicitous in the ends of secular rule.

In noting these secularist anxieties, it is important to keep in mind the larger context of our conversations. Research for this book took shape over a period during which a succession of pro-Islamist political parties achieved significant electoral success. Although these parties would be banned by the Constitutional Court in due course, it was undeniable that such religiously imbued political parties were gaining wide popular support. This was also a period during which support for the dominant Kemalist political party and secularist political establishment was rapidly declining. Although animosity toward religious forms of healing may have a long history, and there is no straightforward relationship between the presence of religious healers and Islamist political activism, these political developments help us appreciate the particular urgency of panic found among Alevis in Hürriyet when talking about the religious healer.

The intensity with which this sense of panic (for the future of secularism) coursed through everyday conversations about religious healing is also a reminder of the specific aesthetic entanglements of healing and secularism. That is, these discourses of societal decline, as they give voice to a sense of fear and anxiety, are simultaneously marking the limits of sense, or *bilinç*—a threshold of the sensible across which (political) reason does not travel. Moreover, in that this threshold assumes its material form in the boundary between Hürriyet and Aktepe, we find here an aesthetics of secularism, healing, and community allying in a common project of partitioning the sensible and distributing—across the surrounding landscape of *gecekondu* neighborhoods—the possibilities for participating in a common world. As we turn our attention to Aktepe, we will encounter a discourse of religious healing that differs sharply from these assumptions, yet attracts a complementary set of concerns and anxieties. These concerns and anxieties will nonetheless configure in distinctive ways and, in so doing, articulate divergent limits of sense and sensibility as they express alternate configurations of political power, secular order, and community life.

Piety, Superstition, and Victimhood in Aktepe

Alevism is not a religious tradition to which one can convert. A person is born into an Alevi family. On numerous occasions in Sunni Aktepe, however, when it became clear that I was not Muslim, the possibility of my conversion would transform into a palpable, if not always spoken, force shaping conversations. One afternoon, for instance, an older gentleman with whom I was talking about my interest in religious approaches to healing and recovery decided that there was a person with great knowledge on the subject that I had to meet—the local mosque's imam. Beyond assisting me with my research, he envisioned our chance encounter as an opportunity for me to learn about Islam from someone with authoritative knowledge. With evening prayers approaching, he brought me to the mosque, where I waited along a wall in the back to be introduced to the imam. As prayers proceeded and I reflected on the approaching conversation with the imam—whom I had only met casually up to this point—I was suddenly overcome by an intense fear. What if someone from Hürriyet were to see me come out of this mosque?

The disgust with which my neighbors in Hürriyet described this area, and its mosques, came insistently to mind—stories of dangerous passions and irrational rage (against secularism, against the West, against the modern) being fomented in mosques, tales of violent disregard for the non-Muslim foreigner (*gavur*, or "infidel"), and bloody accounts of the murder of Hüseyin at the hands of Sunnis in their struggle for control over the early Islamic community.[17] I had an exaggerated sense that, if I were seen by friends from Hürriyet, a range of relationships would be betrayed. Already, and repeatedly, I had been less than forthcoming about my trips to this part of the municipality. Friends in Hürriyet had openly expressed their disapproval. "What can you learn from such reactionary and ignorant people?" The likelihood of encountering a neighbor from Hürriyet outside a mosque in Aktepe was, of course, exceedingly low. Despite the short walk that would take you from one neighborhood to the other, I had yet to meet anyone in either neighborhood who knew a resident of the other. To traverse the two neighborhoods, in spite of their proximity, was to pass between two dramatically different local moral worlds (Kleinman 1991).[18]

The imam proved to be gracious and extremely helpful. I would end up speaking with him on numerous occasions. The anxiety that swept over me that evening while waiting in the back of the mosque, however, would always remain close. In addition to being a powerful reminder of the ways my experience of Aktepe was so thoroughly mediated by my living in Hürriyet, it also signified the transgression of a largely imperceptible boundary, one that had settled deep within my body. Indeed, little outwardly distinguished Aktepe from Hürriyet. Residents came from the same provinces of central Anatolia, lived in or had ties to similar villages, had built similar houses, worked at similar jobs, and similarly struggled to gain legal ownership of their land. Expectedly, one found widespread conformity in terms of speech, food tastes, styles of sociability, and even traditions of healing between the two neighborhoods.

Aktepe and Hürriyet were also bound by mutual disdain. As we have already encountered, residents of Hürriyet regarded Aktepe with contempt. They viewed Aktepe as uniformly reactionary (*gerici*, *irtica*), conservative (*tutucu*), intolerant, and a breeding ground for radical Islamist movements threatening the secular state. Aktepe was envisioned as a neighborhood where individuality was suppressed in the name of a consuming, dogmatic, legalistic religiosity; where women were systematically subjugated to an unbending Islamic orthodoxy; where not only democracy but modernity as a whole was rejected; and where, consequently, *cinci hocas* were to be found in abundance. Residents of Aktepe, in turn, viewed Hürriyet as the home of radical leftists threatening the moral fabric of society. As residents of Aktepe saw it, because neighborhoods such as Hürriyet promoted a form of social and political life devoid of an ethics grounded in Islam, their residents had fallen prey to some of the most corrupting dimensions of Turkey's project of secular modernity, especially those associated with Westernization: women had lost their modesty, male authority was no longer privileged, and the young no longer respected their elders. When Aktepe residents were being generous, the Alevis of Hürriyet were described as Muslims who had lost their way. In this respect, Alevis were regarded not so much as a separate religious sect as a class of deficient Sunnis. As friends in Aktepe occasionally explained, "Alevis are so far from religion that they must first become Christians before they can become Muslims." In such a theological hierarchy, Alevism was depicted as representing a "shamanic" or "animistic" precursor to the true Islam represented by Sunnism.[19] As this begins to suggest, if residents of Hürriyet argued that Sunnis needed to move forward and progress in order to become modern, residents of Aktepe argued that Alevis needed to move forward and progress in order to become true Muslims.

This mutual disregard was not, of course, uniformly present. As should be expected, opinions about Alevism in Aktepe and Sunnism in Hürriyet varied considerably from speaker to speaker and setting to setting. Despite this variability, I would nonetheless find that conversations about religious healing in Aktepe inevitably engaged similar themes of secularism, religious authority, and the limits of state power. Yet these themes would configure in distinct ways to articulate contrasting visions of the limits and possibilities of an ethical community life.

*   *   *

Unlike in Hürriyet, where religious healing was closely associated with the *cinci hoca*, conversations about religious forms of healing in Aktepe commonly included a discussion of the general therapeutic potential of proper religious practice. The following example from my field notes illustrates this point, as it also introduces some of the distinctive dynamics of public discourse about religious healing in Aktepe.

> On the way to the bus stop this evening, I dropped by Ahmet's shop [a small grocery store, or *bakkal*, that he ran with the assistance of his wife and, to a lesser extent, his aging father]. As Ahmet and I talked, customers came and went. And as time passed, I noticed that more people were coming than going. By nightfall, there were some six people gathered in the cramped space of Ahmet's shop, talking about various topics—the weather, the latest inflation adjustment, the most recent scandal, the price of bread. The man Ahmet had pointed out to me before—the one who had recently returned from Egypt after receiving religious training—eventually entered the shop. Ahmet, eager for us to talk, commanded me—from behind the counter, across the shop floor crowded with others—to talk with him about my research. Realizing the now publicness of my interests in religious healing, I instinctively cringed and prepared myself for an assault. My neighbors in Hürriyet had similarly and repeatedly announced my research to others, so as to poke fun at me, the American, for being interested in something so patently absurd. Against my initial expectation, the new visitor politely and with all seriousness explained that he knew little about the topic. Another visitor then reacted with disdain, insisting that such practices were useless. Others then turned on him, extolling the healthful benefits of prayer, fasting, and reading the Qur'an—especially those verses known for their curative powers (*şifa ayetleri*). The conversation then shifted to a well-worn discussion of the various ways that Islam

was no longer respected and the state was obstructing their right to religious freedom.

A noteworthy feature of this exchange is how it resembled, in its broad outline, conversations in Hürriyet. As in Hürriyet, these conversations were never merely about religious healing, or even the therapeutic value of religious practice. Instead, they invariably seemed to operate as vehicles for wider social commentaries. In this case, as in Hürriyet, the topic of religious healing incited a public debate that expressed a collective sensibility of a community under siege by larger societal forces, just as it highlighted lines of difference internal to community life. At the same time, this exchange begins to suggest the ways everyday conversations about religious healing in Aktepe gave voice to a distinctive set of assumptions, sensibilities, and anxieties concerning the meaning and effects of secular political rule.

In Aktepe, the topic of religious healing was closely associated with matters of faith and proper religious practice. As many of the men gathered at Ahmet's shop insisted, regularly performing prayer and reciting passages from the Qur'an could have positive therapeutic effects if carried out with sincere and heartfelt intent (*niyet*). Yet, as they also insisted, realizing such an ideal of regular and heartfelt religious practice has grown increasingly difficult to achieve within contemporary political and economic conditions. For those gathered at Ahmet's shop then, if I wanted to understand the possibility of religious healing today, I had to understand this relationship between sincere religious practice and contemporary societal conditions.

Osman, a thirty-year-old shoe repairman and lifetime resident of Aktepe, would later elaborate on this point. Osman was seeking the help of the local imam for recurrent headaches and a feeling of debilitating listlessness, which were making his fourteen-hour workdays all the more unbearable.

> Nowadays, the youth are being steered completely backward. They are trying to distance themselves from Islam. I don't think there really are any youth who are going [to healers]. This newly maturing generation, what can I say about them? Unbelievers? Indifferent? It is the more mature people who go to healers. By "mature," I mean maybe over 30. I suspect that this is the majority of those who go. But, nowadays, there is no one among the youth who does perfectly the five daily prayers (*namaz*). If you go to the mosque at prayer

time, for example, you'll see that most of the people there are retired
people. 90% of them are retired. This is also because, as I said earlier, it is impossible to do prayers in some places. At work for
instance. In work places, they are even banning prayer. This, now,
is because of the government. In the past there was no such prohibition. But two or three years ago, they introduced this ban. Moreover, they closed the *imam hatip* schools [for training religious
personnel]. And they are still closing them. That is to say, they're
trying to strike Islam with a battleaxe. So help me God. . . . We, I
believe that in the end, sooner or later, the world will come to an
end. We believe that the time of the next world is going to come.

In making sense of Osman's comments, it is useful to recall Aydın's account
of the corrupting influence of the *cinci hoca* in the nation's political and
secular development.

For Aydın, the continued presence of religious healing was symptomatic
of "backwardness" and "ignorance," which were attributed to the forms
of religious conservatism associated with neighborhoods like Aktepe. For
Osman, however, it was not ignorance that explained the persistence of
religious healing. In fact, it was the lack of real faith that was leading to the
demise of (acceptable) forms of religious healing—a sense of loss he narrated, like others, through themes of generational difference. As a seventy-
six-year-old resident of Aktepe explained this situation, "Although there
are many more mosques today than there were in the past, if you go inside
there are only four or five people. There are mosques, but there is no religious community (*Cami var, cemaat yok*)."

Unlike in Hürriyet, the declining significance of religious healing was
not necessarily read as a sign of modernity. Rather, it was taken as evidence
of a pervasive insufficiency of faith that was a product of Turkey's secular
modern development and a materialism associated with a consumer-
oriented market economy. In particular, residents like Osman placed specific blame on what they saw as the state's undemocratic, authoritarian
suppression of religious freedom, as well as its unwillingness to regulate the
spread of cultural forms associated with the West. In this formulation, the
state—in both its excessive and insufficient action—undermined the forms
of religious practice and ethical commitment that Osman understood as
central to religious healing. Whereas Aydın viewed the prevalence of religious healing as a part of the threat of Islamism, Osman viewed the waning

recognition of the healthful benefits of religious practice as yet another sign of a threat to Islam from an unjust state.

Osman's account, as well as other conversations about religious healing in Aktepe, must be placed in the context of the broader Islamic Revival, of which they are in part an expression. While Alevi political and religious life was firmly rooted in a national, Kemalist political imaginary, the Sunni Muslims with whom I spoke in Aktepe, while certainly expressing a strong commitment to the nation as a political community, also imagined themselves as taking part in an Islamically constituted global community of believers, or *umma*. Although I will have more to say about this in Chapter 4, for now it is important to note that a model of ideal religiosity based in the concept of the pious religious subject was largely normative to community life in Aktepe. In addition to emphasizing religious practices commonly associated with orthodox Islamic practice—profession of faith in the singularity of God, praying five times daily, distribution of alms, fasting during Ramadan, and completing if possible the pilgrimage to Mecca—residents of Aktepe placed special importance on realizing in one's everyday activities and interpersonal conduct a pious and ethically grounded life. For instance, increasing numbers of residents of Aktepe, men and women alike, had become actively engaged in traditions of religious legal interpretation previously limited to religious scholars and jurists in an effort to realize such an ethical life—a development that reflects wider trends in the Muslim world (see Eickelman and Piscatori 1996; Mahmood 2005; Hirschkind 2006; Deeb 2006; Meeker 1991; Hefner 1998; Roy 2004). Coinciding with these changes, residents of Aktepe were also becoming active in various forms of Islamist-inspired political mobilization and regularly supported pro-Islamist political parties in local and national elections. While the reasons for such political commitments were numerous, there was a shared sense that such religiously imbued political parties would work to facilitate one's ability to fulfill pious obligations within current political structures, not in opposition to or in spite of them.

In addition to expressing concerns about the ethically compromised nature of contemporary society, conversations about religious healing in Aktepe also articulated a sense that present conditions were ripe for the proliferation of corrupted forms of Islamic authority and practice. Residents of Aktepe, for instance, repeatedly noted that the tight regulation of religious expression in public institutions, as well as the limited ability to appeal to religion in the political system, meant that Islam remained overly distant from centers of political power. Meanwhile, the continued margin-alization of the *imam hatip* schools in the educational system left the coun-try, and Aktepe in particular, with an insufficient number of properly trained religious scholars. Moreover, the promotion of economic policy that emphasized a consumer-based free market economy undermined the ability of parents to inculcate in their children the forms of moral conduct they regard as necessary to leading a pious life. In short, the decline of "true" Islam and the upsurge of "false" Islam were seen as interdependent aspects of a single destructive process.

While the therapeutic value of religious practice may have been widely accepted in Aktepe, claiming the ability to intercede with God in order to produce miracles or to influence the world of *cins* in order to create worldly effects was not. Rather, such claims—which are the claims of many reli-gious healers—opened a person to accusations of heresy, especially within the forms of Islamic law regularly invoked in Aktepe. Here we arrive at the limits of a broad consensus regarding the therapeutic role people were will-ing to ascribe to religious practice. At this limit, we also encounter a form of discourse that both resonates unexpectedly with the critiques of religious healing in Hürriyet and displaces the grounds of these critiques in impor-tant ways.

As with Hürriyet, forms of impermissible religious practice were regu-larly dismissed as products of "ignorance" and "superstition." As with Hür-riyet, they were also regarded as backward "traditions" that must be abandoned in the name of rational progress. In Aktepe, however, the terms of the religious healer's critique carried connotations that were absent in Hürriyet. For instance, those who claim the ability to exert control over *cins*, such as the *cinci hoca*, were accused of relying on forms of religious knowledge that were distorted approximations of a "true knowledge" grounded in Islam, here understood as a rational order of religious knowl-edge, practice, and ethics. Similarly, accusing religious healers and their patients of being "superstitious" suggested that they were engaging in forms of practice that were both unscientific ("irrational" and not based on empirically observable phenomena) and founded on "false belief" (as an unauthorized or impermissible form of religious knowledge). In both cases, abandoning such practices was a prerequisite for progress, conceived in this instance as one's ethical development.[20]

These accusations, in their basic outline, are not new. There is a rich history of debate among Islamic scholars about the permissibility of a wide range of therapeutic practices, debates that run through centuries of medieval Islamic scholarship and similarly turn on questions of the empirical validity of such claims. Given this history, one could regard critiques of religious healing in Aktepe as but a continuation of these debates. What strikes me as distinctively contemporary about their current formulation, however, is the specific role assigned to individual believers in discerning permissible from impermissible forms of religious practice and, alongside this, the ways individual responsibility for failures of discernment are construed.

In a setting where doctrinal debates that had previously been the purview of scholars and jurists were regularly informing everyday moral reasoning, the act of distinguishing permissible from impermissible religious knowledge and practice gains both new significance and a new locus. Rather than simply heeding the opinions of legal scholars—as was imagined to be the case in the past—ordinary Muslims were expected to ground their conduct within authorized doctrinal sources or identifiable forms of Islamic reasoning. Similar to Hürriyet in fact, people's continued dependence on illicit forms of religious and therapeutic authority was explained as the persistence of personal "ignorance." In this instance, however, the inability to distinguish "true knowledge" from its heretical distortion was a failure of discernment that reflected an insufficiently cultivated piety.[21] While accusations of ignorance in Aktepe and Hürriyet may share a vocabulary of "truth," "rationality," and "progress," they nonetheless take part in distinctive discourses of reason. Yet, and this is the important point, the ultimate responsibility for this pious failure was rarely placed exclusively on the back of the individual.

Rather, responsibility was commonly ascribed to structural forces. What made the corruption of Islam possible—what undermined people's recognition of the healthful benefits of prayer, fueled the spread of *cinci hocas*, and distorted people's ability to discern "true" Islam—were the conditions of social life fostered under the state's regime of secular governance. In contrast to Hürriyet, the presence of fraudulent healers, as well as their ability to deceive patients, was taken in Aktepe as evidence of an ethically diminished state. Although the state was not necessarily seen as the sole or immediate cause of societal corruption (that could be located elsewhere —in the media, in foreign films and music, in the United States and Europe, in consumer advertising), the state was viewed as unwilling to regulate or incapable of controlling the effects of these corrupting forces.

Moreover, the state was seen as systematically obstructing the ability of non-state institutions and community structures to take on such a regulatory role. In other words, in Aktepe, the presence of religious forms of healing, however permissible, was read not as a sign of personal failure—of ignorant people failing to embrace reason and freedom—but as the failure of a state to allow the flourishing of a publicly authorized religious sensibility that would at once stem such corrupting forces and cultivate in citizens the forms of religious appraisal necessary to discern "true" Islam from its distorted approximation.

Accordingly, the problem of ignorance and the persistence of corrupt healers was not to be solved by tighter state regulation or by a more active campaign of scientific literacy—as had been the preoccupation of early secular reformers, and was recurrently suggested in Hürriyet. Rather, the "problem" was going to be most effectively addressed by the state withdrawing from community life to allow for a communal ethics grounded in Islam to fulfill its proper duty. Importantly, and in contrast to the expectations of Hürriyet's residents, this was a demand for limiting government, rather that its reorganization. We do not encounter here a desire to overturn either secularism, as a political principle, or the state. In fact, many residents of Aktepe saw in secular-liberal principles of individual rights the precise sorts of freedoms (especially of religious expression) that might offer a solution to the ethical challenges of the present.

Within such discursive configurations of secularism, ethics, and community, accusations of "superstition" served not so much to differentiate the "enlightened" from the "ignorant," but as the basis for claims of having one's religious liberties obstructed by the policies of an illiberal state. Indeed, despite the demographic majority enjoyed by Sunnis (who make up some 75–80 percent of Turkey's population), residents of Aktepe envisioned themselves as representing a religious minority being suppressed, if not persecuted, by an unjust state. Omar's assertion that "the government is trying to strike Islam with a battleaxe" captures this sensibility precisely. In contrast to the secularist anxieties about an impending Islamist threat that animated conversations about religious healing in Hürriyet, these conversations in Aktepe expressed a counterposing sense that a moral community was under siege by an ethically compromised or misguided state.

In other words, while debates that erupted around religious healing in both neighborhoods conveyed a shared sense of religious marginalization and persecution at the hands of powerful political and religious forces, they nonetheless expressed divergent arrangements of marginalization and belonging—whether it be a secularist minority being oppressed by a religious majority, or a religious minority being oppressed by an authoritarian state. I would, in time, come to regard these visions of fear and siege as mutually conditioning commentaries on the proximity of political rule: if the state was imagined as overly close in one neighborhood (as it interfered in a religiously grounded ethics of community), it was imagined as overly distant in another (in its failure to regulate "anti-modern" religious sensibilities and fulfill its welfare state promises).

At the same time that the discursive work being accomplished by conversations about religious healing in the two neighborhoods converged to express a common sense of marginalization and victimhood, it also gave voice to distinctive visions of the limits of community life, which was at once a distinct commentary on a community's sense of national belonging. Unlike in Hürriyet, conversations about religious healing in Aktepe did not work to draw sectarian boundaries between Sunnism and Alevism. Instead, they emphasized the need to delineate the boundaries of a "true" Islam. When sectarian difference was invoked, it was to elaborate political differences—Alevis were, in these instances, leftists overly invested in Kemalist models of authoritarian secularism.[22] Religiously, again, Alevis were regarded simply as "bad Muslims." Accordingly, where collective identity in Hürriyet may have been defined by the question "What does it mean to be an Alevi?" it was defined in Aktepe by the question "What does it mean to be a good Muslim?" Or, as the local imam in Aktepe explained, "When Alevis come to the mosque, we look at them with Sunni eyes."[23] For many Alevi, such comments confirm the extent to which Sunni forms of Islamic religiosity maintain an unspoken hegemony in the national political imaginary.

As we have discussed in this section, everyday conversations about religious healing and the therapeutic potential of religious practice in Aktepe, as compared to Hürriyet, invoked distinct commentaries on the relationship between religious authority, secular political rule, and the limits of state power within community life. Foremost, discourses of religious healing in Aktepe expressed a common sense that the role of religion in the ordering of social and national life was becoming perilously diminished. This concern was confirmed along two fronts. Not only were people failing to recognize the healthful benefits of proper religious practice, but they were less able to discern "true" religious knowledge from its heretical distortion. Unlike in Hürriyet, where the religious healer's voice was inherently dangerous, the presence of such corrupted religious practices in Aktepe suggested that either those who spoke with correct religious knowledge were not heeded or listeners had lost the capacity to discern what warranted their attention.[24] If everyday conversation about religious healing in Hürriyet marked the limits of reason and sense, which were also the boundaries of a local moral world, its principal accomplishment in Aktepe was to trace a series of moral limits internal to community life. Rather than marking the limits of a spatially circumscribed community, that is, commentaries on religious healing and the therapeutic value of religious practice served to identify a series of shifting thresholds at which the limits and effects of state power within a common moral life were both articulated and critiqued. These were thresholds, in turn, whose political stakes turned on cultivated practices—and failures—of discernment, appraisal, and moral reasoning.

Difference and Repair

Victor Turner famously argued that ritual healing among the Ndembu of central Africa succeeded by bringing into the open that which was "rotten in the corporate body" (1967: 392). Through the performance of collective ritual, individuals and acts that strayed from the social order could be compelled to return, "sealing up the breaches in social relationships" and reconfirming the vitality of community. For Turner, the social force of rituals was not to be found simply in the abstract, disembodied meanings of symbols or the explicitly formulated ritual objectives, but rather in the performative processes that enlivened symbols and engaged participants. In this chapter, I have found myself posing an analogous question of religious healing, a question that in this case folds back upon itself. What if the rotten element in the corporate body is ritual healing itself? Can "healing" be healed, so to speak, as a means to reconfirm the vitality of particular visions of community life?

In an effort to address these questions, I have attended to everyday conversations about religious healing as discursive sites through which visions of community life are sustained and the limits of community are continually drawn and redrawn. Where Turner emphasized the unity of the corporate body and the reproduction of normative meanings through ritual, I have instead taken these conversations as a means to push beyond commonplace assumptions about the unity and homogeneity of *gecekondu* neighborhoods. In addition to highlighting the heterogeneity of social lives that find their homes in such neighborhoods, this attention to seemingly quotidian conversations about religious healing and the therapeutic potential of religious practice has also brought into view the otherwise unremarkable—and un-remarked upon—ways that prevalent lines of social differentiation are produced and reproduced in the course of everyday social lives (in this case, Sunni/Alevi, Secularist/Islamist, Left/Right). In so doing, I have considered the ways that discourses about religious healing articulate and map multiple forms of difference in the process of reconfirming the vitality of distinct visions of community life and political order. As such, my central concern in this chapter has been not only with the forms of religious, political, and community difference that the subject of religious healing names, but also with the ways that difference becomes speakable in the process of talking about religious healing.

Although the residents of Hürriyet and Aktepe may have spoken about one another in terms that seem to deny the possibility of commonality—in much the same way that "Secularists" and "Islamists" are opposed in typical accounts of Turkey's political culture—approaching the question of communal difference through the language of religious healing has captured the play of less absolute and more contingent processes of differentiation. In so doing, this has also allowed us to avoid the common mistake of hearing in expressly religious critiques of state practice a categorical rejection of secularism, as is commonly the case in interpretations of political dissent in neighborhoods like Aktepe, or even the municipality of Mamak as a whole. Instead, by attending to the ways residents of both neighborhoods debated and argued about the validity of the religious healer's claims, we encountered a series of interrelated and mutually informing struggles to formulate viable arrangements of religious authority, the limits of state power, and an ethic as well as aesthetics of community life.

Although we must remind ourselves of the historical specificity of these commentaries—this was a period, again, during which Islamist political mobilization was gaining significant electoral power, and the dominant Kemalist political party was losing support—it should also be clear that such sensibilities arise out of a significantly deeper history of secular modern nation making. These are sensibilities that have long since settled into the "sensible texture of the community," as Rancière would suggest (2009: 8), and the common sense of bodies—where accusations of ignorance and immorality incite visceral disgust, the turning of bodies, and the panic of an inexperienced anthropologist. Taking a cue from these discursive, spatial, and visceral entanglements, rather than accepting the neighborhood boundaries offered by the city planner and map maker, I have instead attended to the ways everyday discourses about religious healing offer unique insights into the processes through which a common sensibility of community is both articulated and reinscribed in the folds of everyday social life. Here it became possible to understand divergent conversations about religious healing as taking part in a common project of charting the limits of reason and sense, which in turn marked the limits of community. Here, as well, we again encountered the fear and anxiety that the voice of the religious healer is able to elicit—a voice that was to be not only distrusted, but regarded as containing an obscured force that threatened rational judgement, individual autonomy, and, with them, the entirety of Turkey's project of secular modernity.

Given our discussion up to this point, it may be difficult for the reader to imagine why anyone would ever seek out such healers, to say nothing about why someone would ever desire to learn such therapeutic practices. Considering the intense hostility that the figure of the religious healer attracts from police, reporters, and neighbors alike, it would appear that the subject position left to the religious healer is thoroughly uninhabitable. How could such forms of speech and practice gather an audience? How could they engender desire? And who would ever seek their assistance? With these questions in mind, we now return our conversation to Zöhre Ana, the *evliya* whose followers we met briefly at Anıt-Kabir, as they confronted the caretakers of Atatürk's tomb.

Chapter 3

Hagiographies of the Living: Saintly Speech and Other Wonders of Secular Life

In these times, language and nation form the historical body of all religious passion.

—Jacques Derrida, "Faith and Knowledge"

Along the far edges of the city, separating the sprawling neighborhoods of Aktepe and Hürriyet from a similarly sprawling military base, runs a highway that leads eastward out of Ankara toward the Black Sea port of Samsun. Lest we forget, Samsun was the site of the nation's conception, where Mustafa Kemal (Atatürk) landed on May 19, 1919, and, casting his eyes across a newly imagined homeland, began his campaign of organizing the countryside for a war of national liberation. Traveling in the opposite direction along the Samsun Highway—as its name changes from May 19 Boulevard (commemorating Atatürk's landing), to Turgut Özal Boulevard (after the former prime minister and president regarded widely as the architect of the economy's neoliberal transformation) and, before heading back out of the city, to Mevlana Boulevard (in honor of the great Anatolian Sufi philosopher and poet Jalal al-Din Rumi)—one soon approaches Anıt-Kabir, where Atatürk's body is entombed.

Between these points of political birth and death, just off the highway, on the margins of one of Ankara's many *gecekondu* neighborhoods, can be found the compound of a living saint of significant local repute whose prophecies and visions have brought about miraculous cures, predicted death, and foretold new life. Accounts of her deeds, along with her name— Zöhre Ana—circulate ceaselessly in the surrounding neighborhoods. Her words and reputation draw visitors from across the nation, hundreds at a time, in search of blessings, recovery, and renewed hope. Yet word of Zöhre Ana's powers, and the power of Zöhre Ana's words, do not circulate without resistance. Just as her saintly voice attracts audiences of admirers—as it takes shape along this passage between political birth and death—it has been ordered silent by police, commanded to speak before courts, recorded secretly by government agents, and rebroadcast without permission by the media. Indeed, given the environment she works within, Zöhre Ana realizes a form of saintly speech that is difficult to sustain—one that is fundamentally unstable and, as we will see, destabilizing.

This chapter turns to a topic that has remained at the horizon of the discussion, a topic that has organized medical reform and neighborhood gossip alike: those modalities of exilic religious life able to find a home in conditions born of Turkey's ongoing project of secular modern development. In tracing the efforts of a living *evliya*, Zöhre Ana, to cultivate therapeutic and religious authority within a thoroughly inhospitable setting, this chapter returns to the series of intersecting questions posed at the outset. On what grounds might the religious healer gather an audience today? How might the illicit or criminalized speech of the religious healer interact with other types of permitted religious, political, and medical speech? And what might this tell us about the possibilities of speaking and being heard under contemporary conditions?

These questions—which are ultimately questions about the possibilities and limits of speaking, truth, and healing—also return us to the book's overarching concern with secularism's politics of aesthetics. As introduced earlier, the approach to aesthetics being formulated here attends not only to the sensory effects of perceptible phenomena (an audience's response to music, a reader's response to a text, a viewer's response to an image, and so forth) but also to those discursive and material processes which render certain phenomena perceptible, speakable, or possible, as they render others imperceptible, unspeakable, or seemingly impossible (Rancière 2004, 2009). Aesthetics, approached in these terms, thereby presupposes a series of distinctive social and bodily relations, such that a critical component of an aesthetic regime's "distribution of the sensible" (2004) is the organization of bodily capacities and sensible intensities in space and time. Accordingly, the relationship between what can be said and who can be heard, between the visible and what can be imagined as possible, is at once a relationship of inclusion and political recognition. Who, in a given aesthetic regime, is recognized as having a voice, and thus able to participate in a common political life?

In elaborating on the political and therapeutic implications of such an aesthetics, I am particularly interested in exploring the way that secularism —understood as an assemblage of ideas, policies, institutional practices, and coincident formations of sensibility, sociality, and governance—presumes a particular theory of language and operates with a series of assumptions about the possibilities of speaking and listening within a specific set of conditions. Given these concerns, Talal Asad's reflections on the secular liberal ideal of free speech are useful in setting the parameters of our inquiry (2003; see also Asad et al. 2009). For Asad, the public sphere of free speech does not simply emerge with the confinement of religion to private spaces and personal sentiment. The "public sphere," in this formulation, is not an empty space for carrying out debate. Rather, it is an ongoing production of dispositions, sensibilities, and possibilities for speaking and listening that is inseparable from liberal models of political rule. "The enjoyment of free speech presupposes not merely the physical ability to speak but *to be heard*," Asad writes, "a condition without which speaking to some effect is not possible. If one's speech has no effect whatever it can hardly be said to be in the public sphere, no matter how loudly one shouts" (2003: 184).

For Asad, this speech without effect means not only that there are limits to what can be said or heard in this public sphere (some limits being formal or legal, and others conventional), but also that secularism should be recognized as a set of processes that work, while assuredly not always in concert, to cultivate embodied dispositions, capacities for speaking and being heard, and what Rancière would refer to as "common sense"—a shared modality of sense upon which community turns and the limitations of the sensible are inscribed. In short, as Asad concisely puts it, "there is no public sphere of free speech in an instant" (2003: 184). That is, the secular public sphere—as with the secular citizen capable of speaking with effect—is not merely what is left behind after religion has evacuated public spaces and political institutions, but a positive domain that depends on, as it is constituted through, the active production of affective and bodily dispositions, ways of relating with others, and modes of conceiving and inhabiting the world.[1]

While I share Asad's interest in those typically unacknowledged assumptions about the relationship between language and space that inhere within secular models of political governance, I want to approach this problem from a position that may appear counterintuitive. Rather than engaging actors and spaces that directly challenge secularism, or self-described "Secularists" who endorse such models of secular political rule and public sociability (see Navaro-Yashin 2002; Özyürek 2006; Turam 2008), I approach secularism through examining a form of speaking that was systematically excluded from the public sphere of free speech and rational debate in Turkey's history of secular reform—the divinely inspired speech of the saint.

As a means of interrogating secularism as an aesthetic project of subject, history, and world making, this chapter therefore takes seriously a saintly figure who would appear, by most accounts, to be marginal if not irrelevant to prominent struggles between "Islamists" and "Secularists" over political power—struggles that have become imagined as the primary if not exclusive site for working out new models of secular democratic rule in the Muslim world. Approaching the entanglements of language, space, and secular forms of sociability and governance through such exilic forms of religious life, however, will require a sensitivity to the dynamics of speaking and listening that is decidedly more open and multiplicitous than what Asad's, or Rancière's, formulations might suggest. In fact, I regard the language of the saint—with its ambiguities of authorship, its uncertain temporalities and localizations, the multiple forms of participation it allows for, and its unclear responsibilities (who, ultimately, is responsible for what is being said?)[2]—as uniquely positioned not only to disrupt secularism's presuppositions regarding the distribution of (linguistic) possibility, but also to complicate assumptions regarding speaking and listening one finds among prominent critiques of secularism, critiques that turn on a model of language that tends to delimit speech within a conceptual horizon of political action and subjectivity.

In the course of attending closely to this form of saintly language—and the distinct ways it is bound to a particular setting and understood to take material and spatial form—we will come to understand the speech of the saint as a site of both struggle and return. That is, we will encounter here the legacy of a history of secular reform that marked in advance the speech of the saint as a site of future struggle. In turn, we will also consider the ways that the speech of the saint, as a disqualified and illicit form of speech, comes to represent an important site of return—where the unresolved violence of secularism's origins is staged and the interweaving of therapeutic power and political rule grows particularly dense. It is at this intersection of historical struggle and future return where the generative intimacy of secular rule will come into sharp relief, as its idioms and forms are offered as signs of popular wonder—just as they offer up the possibility of healing wounds and repairing damaged relationships.

Hagiographies of the Living

By the time I met Zöhre Ana, an ever-growing number of former followers regarded her as socially dead. For them, she had long since squandered whatever spiritual powers she had gained at the moment of her initial visions. In their eyes, she was a contemptible and dangerous fraud—a morally inexcusable exploiter of those in desperate need of help. Among her current followers—for whom she is, alternatively, an *evliya*, a possessor of *keramet* (the capacity to perform miracles), a *pir* (or spiritual guide), the *ermiş* one (having been spiritually enlightened), or simply Ana (lit. "mother," a term also used to describe a female spiritual leader)—other forms of death were spoken. Her previous self, as well as her birth name (Süheyla Gülen), had long ago passed on in order to make way for Zöhre Ana the *evliya*. As an *evliya*, she was no longer to be bothered with earthly concerns. And as an object of intense devotion, she no longer belonged to herself. While she was most assuredly alive in the biological sense, to approach Zöhre Ana as a person in the biographical sense proved most challenging.

How does one write about those who are dead but not yet entombed? How is the ethnographer, aware that his audience anticipates a rendering of subjects in their personal and emotional fullness, to write about a person who never seems to be "off stage" and whose sainthood is premised, in many regards, on the departure of this "person" from the stage? It is in the name of this ambiguous relationship between death, person, and biography that I gesture at the outset toward the hagiographic—the religious and literary tradition of writing about the lives and miracles of saints. With its gift for weaving together the miraculous and the commonplace, the tradition of hagiography captures well the challenge of writing about a figure such as Zöhre Ana, whose truth resides as much in biographical "fact" as in accumulated rumor—whose "truth" actually resides somewhere in the subordination of the former to the latter.

In keeping with the conventions of the hagiographic, we begin our account at Zöhre Ana's origins. Zöhre Ana's saintly birth follows a trajectory recognizable within many Islamic traditions and broadly resembles the structure of stories attached to *evliya*s and holy persons whose tombs are spread across Anatolia, and well beyond. As she chronicles these events,

> I married when I was sixteen. In 1982, on exactly the day of November 10, the first sign began. It was Thursday. It was around 4:00–5:00, my son had come from school. I was going to make him work on his homework. Just as I was lighting the lamp, I began to hear voices. I had been hearing them for days, but had not been able to tell anyone. It was as if there was someone inside. But I couldn't see them. I began to search. While I was lighting the lamp, everything became enveloped by a green cloud. I didn't understand that there was a divine radiance (*nur*) inside the house. I could see the light, yet I could also see the house. Thinking that the coal stove was burning intensely, I ran up and touched it. It wasn't. It didn't burn me. I suddenly understood. I said a prayer and knelt. There was a radiant cloud and it showered the wall with a rainbow of colors. The stove sat there, and my children were looking on with amazement. I gathered myself, and I gave them their food.

With this, not two years after Turkey's third major military coup and with a nation still under military rule, on the day commemorating the death of Mustafa Kemal Atatürk (November 10, 1938), an Alevi woman in a meager *gecekondu* home witnessed a divine light and received her calling as an *evliya*. Her calling thus marked, though not yet fully realized, she gathered herself and continued on with her domestic duties.

Her family was initially skeptical. "As soon as I would lie down, Gülbaba³ would come and he would say: 'You will be heard worldwide, you will spread across the globe. We will open a *dergâh* here for those who love you, for those who respect you, for those who have fallen on hard times. And you will bring cures to those who visit it.' And then he would disappear. I would later explain it to close family members—my mother, my father, and my brother. At first, they didn't believe." As time passed, it became evident that she was no longer the same person. The number of visions multiplied. Her touch brought about miraculous cures. Neighbors and relatives began to give birth to children after doctors had declared it

impossible. Jobs were secured, exams passed, and lotteries won. Rumors of
the existence of a woman able to effect cures began to circulate through the
surrounding neighborhoods. As word spread and networks of obligation
expanded, she came to be recognized as possessing *keramet*, the God-given
capacity to perform miracles.[4] She hence became for many an *evliya*, or
"saint," and assumed the name Zöhre Ana.[5]

As is common to accounts of sainthood in the region, Zöhre Ana's
calling and initial visions came involuntarily. They were neither intention-
ally sought after nor prepared for by study and devotion. "In my family
and surroundings there was definitely no *dede*s or *ebe*s (midwives),"
explained Zöhre Ana, "nor was there this practice of *hoca*-ing. I never saw
or learned these things. Whatever I learned from school, that is what I
knew." The model of saintly authority that Zöhre Ana came to embody
reflected the Alevi religious and political milieu in which she was raised.
The Twelve Imams and Hacı Bektaş Veli (a thirteenth-century saint who is
highly regarded among Alevi) assumed prominent positions in her practices, as did other figures of primarily Turkish Alevi significance, such as Pir
Sultan Abdal and Kaygusuz Abdal. Followers described her healing touch as
"the paw of Ali," in reference to the cousin and son-in-law of Muhammed,
who is commonly depicted as the "Lion of God." And the principal communal ritual of the Alevi, the *cem*, became a centerpiece of her early practices. Despite her Alevi lineage, however, large groups of Sunnis also began
appearing at her doorstep as word of her miraculous powers spread
through the surrounding neighborhoods.

Zöhre Ana's popularity and powers expanded in tandem. By summer
1997, when I first met her, she had hundreds of people visiting her daily,
scores of assistants regulating ritual conduct, and an instituted inner circle
that helped administer her charitable foundation—the Zöhre Ana-Ali (va)
Sosyal Hizmetler Vakfi (Zöhre Ana-Ali Social Services Foundation).[6] Visitors were no longer simply relatives and neighbors, and they no longer
visited Zöhre Ana in the *gecekondu* home in which she received her first
visions. By this point, she had taken over an abandoned coal storage facility and transformed it into what many of her followers referred to as her
dergâh, a term typically used to denote the lodge of a religious order. As
her reputation spread, it became increasingly difficult to attribute a specific profile to her visitors. While still mostly Alevi, guests and visitors
came to represent a spectrum of religious, political, educational, and occupational experiences and commitments. Just prior to my extended period

of fieldwork, an audience of some 1,000 people gathered to celebrate the opening of a newly constructed *dergâh* and foundation headquarters.

Zöhre Ana's notoriety with local authorities also grew with her popularity. Stories of repeated arrests, followed by miraculous escapes, were prominent elements of the lore that flourished around her. Soon after the new building's opening, for instance, a popular investigative news program—*Objektif Program*—aired an episode that captured a number of her assistants on hidden cameras receiving what appeared to be inappropriately large donations. As had happened on previous occasions, Zöhre Ana was arrested and charged with fraud, exploiting the ill, and operating an illegal religious organization. Later, in 2002, a national wiretapping scandal would reveal that police had been illegally recording phone conversations at her foundation, along with dozens of other prominent political parties, trade unions, media organizations, and universities.

Although Zöhre Ana's public appearances would become greatly restricted during these periods, one such event provided me the rare opportunity to meet with her privately. During a visit to her *dergâh* in 1999, only a few weeks after her release from jail following the scandal on *Objektif Program*, I was unexpectedly ushered in to speak with her. As my field notes recount:

> I was taken to the top floor of the crescent-shaped wing of the new building. I had not expected to see her today, let alone meet with her in private. Since our last meeting, she had become an increasingly distant figure. I came out of the narrow stairwell to an open room that was lined with windows overlooking the courtyard and rose gardens. Zöhre Ana stood hunched over the windowsill across the room, gazing absently out the window. She seemed sullen and dejected. It was in such stark contrast to her public, ritual demeanor. She struck me as a beleaguered celebrity off camera.
>
> She greeted me in an offhand and unceremonious manner, inviting me into her meeting room. We passed bent over through a small, arched door into the adjacent room and sat on the deep, high couches. Massive quantities of food soon appeared. We all knelt around the low table and began to eat. I asked about the media scandal and she grew visibly enraged. No longer speaking softly, she loudly explained how she had treated them as guests, that "they had eaten breakfast right here, and look what they did." They [the reporters]

had come four times she said. She continued this particular invective for some time, pausing only for a belch or to refresh the gum she had already chewed into submission. Eventually getting so close that I could feel her breath on my face (and smell the spearmint scent of her gum), she grumbled angrily: "They are dishonorable. They are shit."

Many months would pass before I was offered another private audience with Zöhre Ana. As the scandal intensified suspicion, and increasing numbers of police cars passed slowly before the *dergâh*, Zöhre Ana withdrew into her public persona. The networks of gossip that formed around her would also turn against me briefly, drawing connections between my unanticipated appearance and her arrest.

Despite the regular surveillance, repeated arrests, and coincident fluctuations in her public appearances, Zöhre Ana's practice experienced a dramatic expansion between 1982 and 2005, when I last visited her. Fed by divine inspiration, the suggestions of her inner circle, and the demands of visitors, the scope of her ritual expertise grew remarkably during this period, coming to encompass and ritually mark all major transitions in the life course. Over the same period, her practice would move from the *gecekondu* home where she received her original calling, to the refurbished coal storage facility, and then into a newly constructed three-story building and surrounding compound. Meanwhile, her reputation began traveling along transnational circuits of Turkish labor migration. Although visitors continued to be drawn primarily from Ankara and nearby towns and villages, Zöhre Ana's practice—in the span of a decade—developed into a globally dispersed network of admirers and followers. Even as Zöhre Ana took part in a long tradition of saintly devotion in Turkey—a tradition whose scope and historical precedent can be easily observed in the innumerable tombs of saints and holy persons that one finds in nearly any neighborhood, town, or village—she nevertheless distinguished herself by both the scale and the public nature of her saintliness.

The Breath of the Saint

At the center of Zöhre Ana's religious and therapeutic authority, as both the basis and evidence of her miraculous powers, is her capacity to communicate and intercede with deceased *evliya*. If we return to our opening questions—regarding the forms of disqualified religious speech and truth that are able to gather an audience within secularist regimes of aesthetic possibility—we begin to arrive at a response in Zöhre Ana's saintly utterances and the innovations that they announce. While subsumed in the *Umman* (literally, "ocean"), a condition in which Zöhre Ana takes on the stylized persona of visiting saints, deceased *evliya* are once again able to communicate with the living. Through these visiting *evliya*, events and voices that were formerly unknown (or simply forgotten, a distinction that can be difficult to determine) are brought back to life, and the past is again able to comment on the present. In what follows, I am interested in considering such forms of saintly speech—which take shape at the intersection of saintly authority and secular regimes of speaking and truth—as sites of return wherein unspoken histories of political-theological exchange and the forms of violence that marked secularism's origins are brought to bear on the present. To begin such an inquiry, however, we must first consider some of the defining features of this genre of saintly speech.

At times described with a sense of fear and awe, and other times as precipitating a feeling of inner peace, few visitors to Zöhre Ana remained untouched by her speaking. Within the larger corpus of Zöhre Ana's saintly language, special importance was attributed to her *nefesler*. While the term *nefes* (singular of *nefesler*) carries the literal connotation of "breath," it also refers to lyrical poems attributed to Alevi and Bektaşi poets. In the present instance, the term *nefes* refers to the divinely inspired poetic speech that issues from Zöhre Ana while within the *Umman*. Set off from her everyday speech by both their performativity (as she embodies the visiting saint) and their poetic form, Zöhre Ana's *nefesler* offer commentaries on the present as they give voice to a long genealogy of saintly authority. Her transcribed *nefesler* fill two volumes—*Cemden Gelen Nefesler* (1991) and *Mehtaptaki Erenler* (1996)—and a third volume was in preparation at the time of my last visit.

To offer a sense of the conventions of the *nefes*, the following transcribed *nefes*, along with her continued commentary while still in the *Umman*, is in many regards characteristic of the genre:

Begin thus, from the word
In the *cemevi*, from the beloved soul
One of its attributes being Ali
He who dwells in the sea of *nefes*

Oh enlightened ones! Oh enlightened ones!
Those who come to the *cemevi*
Show me the way my old friend
Those who granted me this authority

I looked to the right, Imam Hasan
I looked to the left, the *cem* becomes still
Out comes Hüseyin
He becomes excited, it is God who excites

He who trusts in his authority
From the spirit (*dem*[7]) of Güvence Abdal
Every dervish looks to Bektaş
He who brings a grape in hand

You are the pitcher in the hand—let me see
Let me plead for a glass
I am thankful, I owe a debt of gratitude
Don't be caught off guard, Come!

.   .   .

Even you brave heroes, Come!
Bury the corpses
Your name has descended from God the Exalted
You are of the spirit of Güvence Abdal

I lay to rest these martyrs of mine with Hüseyin's permission. For
those who have come and gone, for those who have died while
within the cem, for those martyrs who died at Kerbela but will
remain forever with us. Let my heart and head be with God (Hüda)
my Sultan, with the spirit of Güvence Abdal. Without hesitation my
Sultan, such a sanction was granted that even I may desire justice.
Because in my time, there was only one sanction, in war.

Zöhre Ana's *nefesler* offer little in the way of moral guidance or explicit
models of ethical conduct for listeners. Nor do they represent a form of
speech that aims to persuade by drawing listeners into elaborately woven
narratives. Indeed, visitors to Zöhre Ana frequently remarked on the difficulty of comprehending the meanings of individual *nefesler*. Instead, listeners emphasized the corporeality of the *nefes*'s enunciation (of Zöhre Ana

subsumed in the *Umman*, taken over by deceased *evliyas*, their words emanating from her twisting body) and the enumerative quality of her saintly speech (in the repetition of recognizable holy people, places, and deeds).[8]

While the names of religious figures commonly recognized as saints throughout the Muslim world appear in her *nefesler*, a large class of visiting saints, as mentioned earlier, comprise a distinctly Shi'i and Alevi cosmology (e.g., Ali, Hasan, Hüseyin, the Twelve Imams) and have particular Turkish relevance (e.g., Hacı Bektaş Veli, Pir Sultan Abdal, Kaygusuz Abdal, Yunus Emre). As with the enumeration of saintly names, Zöhre Ana's *nefesler* also evoke an expansive religious landscape, one that includes such recognizable sites as Mecca, Kerbela (the setting of Hüseyin's martyrdom), Khorasan (a region of central Asia renowned for the dervishes it sent into the world, such as Hacı Bektaş Veli), Konya (the location of the tomb of Jalal al-Din Rumi, the founder of the Mevlevi order of dervishes), and innumerable less well-known locations of tombs dispersed across Turkey's countryside. Taken together, listeners attempting to fix meaning to Zöhre Ana's *nefesler* regarded these enumerative and performative qualities as comprehensible signs gesturing toward a fuller meaning that seemed to reside just beyond one's ability to make sense of them.

A distinctive feature of this genre of ritual language, a feature that contributes to their opacity for listeners, is the ambiguity that surrounds the authorship of Zöhre Ana's *nefesler*. Although *nefesler* issue from her body (and one could well question the extent to which this speaking body, at these moments, *belongs* to Zöhre Ana), the identity of the speaking subject regularly shifts over the course of individual *nefesler*. A *nefes* that begins with the visiting saint speaking in the first person to Zöhre Ana may well end with Zöhre Ana, as the primary speaker, addressing the visiting saint. As such, any single *nefes* may contain multiple points of subjective coherence, or, more precisely, Zöhre Ana's *nefesler* regularly enclose multiple coherences of subjectivity. A significant effect of this ambiguity is the sense that a multitude of saintly figures can gather, simultaneously, within Zöhre Ana's *nefesler*.

Much the same could be said about the spatiality of her *nefesler*. Just as the vacillating identity of the speaking subject allows Zöhre Ana to join a chorus of established saintly voices, the continually transforming landscapes and settings of the *nefesler* facilitate the sense that these voices can share a common space.[9] In the reclaiming and gathering of lost voices that characterize her *nefesler*, Zöhre Ana becomes a constitutive participant in the sacred topography that she gives voice to.[10] In addition to signaling the (miraculous) ability of her *nefesler* to bring together figures and landscapes from the sweep of history into a single (linguistic) setting, such a genealogy of names, spaces, and events also designates Zöhre Ana as the manifestation of an ancient voice, a capacity to speak that has passed along an unbroken chain of holy figures who share a common spirit, or *ruh*. These shifting capacities of speaking and inhabiting space that characterize her *nefesler*, as well as the aura of "past-ness" that enframes them, will prove important for our consideration of Zöhre Ana's saintly language as a site of return.

As much as these features of her *nefesler*—the entwining of voice, name, and place through enumeration—position her squarely within an established tradition of sainthood, the saintly form of speech that emerges through the *Umman* is also an important source of innovation. In this respect, Zöhre Ana's *nefesler* represent a form of speech that is at once iterative and unstable, for it is from the *Umman* and in Zöhre Ana's *nefesler* that unknown or forgotten elements of the past are revealed anew in the present. While submerged in the *Umman*, not only does one encounter familiar names and places, but unknown *evliya* also make their first appearance, new truths are announced, novel rituals come into existence, and a wide range of developments are introduced—from the expansion of foundation services to guidance on the design and construction of buildings.

The play between the iterative and innovative is encapsulated well by the two central saintly figures that surround Zöhre Ana. On the one hand, Ali assumes a central position among the many *evliya* that visit Zöhre Ana in the *Umman*. Given his importance within Alevism, his prominence here is not unexpected. On the other hand, it is through Zöhre Ana's *nefesler* that we first learn that Mustafa Kemal Atatürk, Turkey's arch-secularist and modernist founder, had similarly inherited Ali's *ruh* and was, consequently, an *evliya* (Figures 5 and 6). As she explained to a disbelieving reporter when he first saw images of Ali and Atatürk side by side at the *dergâh*: "Yes, Atatürk, in his first life, went by the name Hacı. One of his brothers was named Bektaş, and the other's name was Veli. The three of these, in a later age, came to the world at the same time as Hünkar Hacı Bektaş Veli. Hacı, in his most recent appearance, was Mustafa Kemal, Atatürk that is . . . Atatürk, of course, was an *evliya*." And as an *evliya*, he is again able to speak to his public, through Zöhre Ana.

Unlike the common public invocations of Atatürk's voice—the reading of his speeches before crowds, their distillation into slogans to promote competing political visions, or simply the theatrical and cinematic stagings

Figure 5. Ali, Zöhre Ana, Atatürk. Used with permission of the Açık Kapı
Derneği.

of his life—Zöhre Ana's saintly speech establishes Atatürk as once more the
agent of his own voice. With Zöhre Ana's body and voice subsumed in his
presence, Atatürk proclaims:

> I left my glory to Turkishness
> For those ignorant of religion I was unenlightened
> Now I dispatch a message with you
> Make me known Zöhre Ana

> Mustafa Kemal is coming
> He is extending his glory from Ankara
> He who knows who is dying
> I did not die Zöhre Ana
> . . .
> The entire world knows of the Turkish military
> I established sovereignty, a national homeland
> The truth of God is proclaimed in many languages
> I brought peace and accord to the world

Figure 6. Zöhre Ana, 2011. Used with permission of the Açık Kapı Derneği.

Mustafa Kemal's eyes are like the sea
All people were born of Adam and Eve
Turn back the English, French, and Greeks
Whoever is in need of help while at Kocatepe[11]

.   .   .

They added to my name Atatürk
I gave my declaration, Ali is my Pir
My guide Zöhre Ana is my representative
The Latin alphabet spills from my tongue[12]

.   .   .

Speak, my Zöhre, speak! Speak without pause
Write from the radiance of the dervish's pen
Sometimes boasting, sometimes blushing
Mustafa Kemal's essence belongs to God

Hoca,[13] you cannot fathom the essence of the Alevi
Come establish your Islamic party, it will be for nothing
Even I cannot discern Islam, and you? God forbid!
Mustafa Kemal Paşa is the one who established secularism

In many regards, there is little that distinguishes this from other *nefesler*. As with a typical *nefes*, we find a deceased *evliya* holding forth before his audience, recounting the major events of his life, confirming his position within an ancient saintly genealogy, castigating those who presume to understand God's intentions, and criticizing unwelcome developments in contemporary society. As with other *nefesler*, the narrating subject shifts repeatedly over the course of the *nefes*, becoming at points a composite of Zöhre Ana and the visiting saint. As with other *nefesler*, we encounter a conjoining of name, place, and event that gives the *nefes* both historical specificity (in terms of the life of the visiting saint) and temporal ambiguity (in terms of the living status of the saint's speech within the present).

Although conventional in many regards, this *nefes* is distinctive in how it juxtaposes idioms of saintly revelation and secularist critique. In this instance, to recount the saint's life and miraculous deeds is to recount the story of the nation—the leading of Turkey's nationalist movement against foreign invaders, the defense of Turkey's sovereignty, the establishment of secularism as the organizing principle of both state and society, and the sweeping political reform of society (e.g., introducing the Latin alphabet to replace the Arabic script, as with the wonderful image of "The Latin alphabet spill[ing] from my tongue"). Here, where the historical time of the nation-state—that homogeneous, empty time of successive events (Benjamin 1968; see also Anderson 1991)—braids together with the ancient genealogical time associated with saints, we also encounter the interweaving of proclamations of Atatürk's oneness with God ("Mustafa Kemal's essence belongs to God"), humanist calls for inclusion ("all people were born of Adam and Eve"), and saintly articulations of explicitly secularist critique. The closing quatrain is exemplary in the latter case, where Atatürk reproaches the claims of Islamists not simply as "the one who established secularism," but simultaneously as an *evliya* whose proximity to God allows him to see the incomprehensibility of Islam. Beyond these specific juxtapositions—which I will return to and expand on below—we should also not lose sight of the larger irony that is Atatürk's saintly manifestation. With Zöhre Ana's assistance, Atatürk—a person who regarded appeals to the dead for help as uncivilized and disgraceful—becomes the object of just such an appeal.

Atatürk's presence at Zöhre Ana's *dergâh* is not limited to her *nefesler*. Alongside his recurrent appearance in her ritual language, Atatürk's image repeats itself incessantly within the *dergâh*. His portrait, reproduced as an enormous banner, periodically hangs from the building's roof. A reproduction of his signature, cast in large bronze letters, is fixed permanently on the building's exterior. And myriad less substantial representations of Atatürk, along with Ali and Zöhre Ana, are everywhere to be found—hung on walls, carved into stone, pinned to lapels, raised onto flagpoles, cast in cement, color-copied, silk-screened, and put on sale in the gift shop.

Returns of Language

In that *evliya*s are entrusted with the charge of bringing people back onto the (spiritual) path from which they have strayed, their work is understood as being inescapably anchored in the past. Unlike the *peygamber*, or prophet, whose principal task is to bring word of altogether new paths, the *evliya*'s job is to revise the present through reclaiming lost voices. It is a corrective voice, as Zöhre Ana's followers explained, one particularly attuned to undoing accumulated historical inaccuracies and mistakes. Given Zöhre Ana's efforts to engage—or be engaged by—deceased *evliya* in a project of historical revision, what are we to make of Atatürk's presence in Zöhre Ana's economy of saintly language? What is to be made, in other words, of this convergence of language, death, and visions of state power in Zöhre Ana's divinely inspired poetic speech? Although Atatürk's appearance in Zöhre Ana's *nefesler* can be read as an instance of an expanding fragmentation of his meaning as he and his legacy are recruited to support countless political causes and social ambitions (Özyürek 2004), I want to draw attention to the way that it also marks an important site of return.

In struggling to make sense of this intersection of language, death, and power, I have found myself returning time and again to Michel de Certeau's (2000) commentaries on the outbreak of demonic possession and accusations of sorcery that gripped seventeenth-century France, which led up to the well-chronicled trials at Loudun. For de Certeau, the key to understanding these events resides in the ways that the language of possession was able to express, as it simultaneously took part in reworking, wider societal reconfigurations of political, religious, and medical authority. In the events surrounding the trials, as representatives of each struggled to claim the right to speak the truth of possession (such that a form of speaking that had once been the priest's to discern would become, with political backing, a voice to diagnose; where the enigmatic would be transformed into objects of medical classification), one encounters both the instability of truth in the circulation of language and its capacity to reveal social and historical processes that would otherwise remain, as de Certeau put it, "nocturnal."

> It always comes as a surprise when the nocturnal erupts into broad daylight. What it reveals is an underground existence, an inner resistance that has never been broken. This lurking force infiltrates the lines of tension within the society it threatens. Suddenly it magnifies them; using the means, the circuitry already in place, but reemploying them in the service of an anxiety that comes from afar, unanticipated. (2000: 1)

For de Certeau, such forms of speech both set the stage for the emergence of something new and bring into the open that which usually remains latent or unspoken: "The possession rekindles former conflicts, but transposes them, offering them a different range of expression. While presupposing earlier rifts, it constitutes a different experience, with a new language" (23).

As I read de Certeau, such forms of language, when set in motion, are simultaneously iterative and anticipatory. "These languages," as he put it, "seem to reject both the limits of a present and the real conditions of its future. Like scars that mark for a new illness the spot of an earlier one, they designate in advance the signs and location of a flight (or return?) of time" (1). In other words, these forms of language—of possession for de Certeau, of divinely inspired poetic speech in our case, as I would suggest—not only display an affinity for attracting expressions of the past (former conflicts, unresolved traumas, the nocturnal), but also, in their very expression, establish a site for their future articulation. It is in this regard that I am interested in exilic forms of religious speech as sites of return.

The irony of Atatürk's voice in Zöhre Ana's *nefesler* stages just such a return. Recall, for instance, that Atatürk—as a sign for the expansive economies of secular modernity that condense around his name, and continue to organize political and social fields—regarded the forms of popular Islamic practice represented by Zöhre Ana with deep suspicion and actively sought their elimination. Recall, as well, that a critical dimension of the secular reforms introduced under his leadership consisted of the forcible closure of the networks of religious orders and lodges, many organized around the tombs of holy persons, in an effort to subvert bases of political opposition and to consolidate a version of Islam amenable to state regulation. The forms of religiosity associated with the veneration of saints also emerged here as prominent targets in the state's struggle against the sorts of "superstition" deemed contrary to the national and technological promises of a rationally organized society. Through secular reform, the forms of truth offered by such figures as the *evliya* were to be discredited and replaced by those of state-sanctioned imams (for addressing moral and religious concerns) and physicians (for treating disorders of the body). In an effort to reorder preexisting relationships between speaking and truth that were held together around such figures as the *evliya*, the saintly or prophetic voice was to become an anachronism of a subordinated era, a speaking-out-of-time that was to be distrusted.[14]

With Zöhre Ana, the very idioms and temporalities of secularist critique that supported the suppression of such forms of religious authority return to authorize her status as an *evliya*. Turkey's project of secular reform thereby both represents the conditions of possibility for Zöhre Ana's saintly speech (as a prohibition, an illicit form of outmoded speech) and marks the language of the saint in advance as a site of future return. In this respect, Atatürk's presence in Zöhre Ana's *nefesler* can be understood as participating in a much older aesthetic commerce between secular-nationalist ideologies and Islamic institutions in Turkey, one that in turn indexes a series of ambiguities that characterize the nation's secular origins. In what Ayşe Kadıoğlu regards as the hyperreality of Turkish nationalism (1998), state policy, particularly in the early years of the republic, was laden with Islamic motifs and depended heavily on religious symbols to produce a unifying nationalist sensibility.[15] Given this history, the contemporary manifestation of Atatürk's voice in Zöhre Ana's saintly language could be regarded as but one moment in a long-running mimetic exchange between state power and (exilic forms of) religious authority. As I will address in a more sustained fashion below, we could indeed read Atatürk's presence here as indexing a return of the signs and idioms of secularism to their originary political-theological entanglements.

The regimes and economies of discursive practice authorized in the name of Turkey's project of secular modern development, which explicitly targeted such forms of religious authority in an effort to subordinate religious life to state power, thereby give rise to an aesthetics that folds back on itself. In the political-theological economy of idioms and forms that Zöhre Ana's *nefesler* indicate, we encounter not only the traces of a secularist labor to reform state and society but also a distorted version of the state's own desire for devotion being realized at the economic margins of society. As the book's opening vignette has already demonstrated—where security guards at Atatürk's tomb confronted Zöhre Ana's followers—these returns can prove threatening. As much as the state wants to draw on the unifying potential of worshiping Atatürk *as if* he were a religious figure, to actually worship him *as* a religious figure not only invokes the wrath of security guards, but also threatens to bring into the open that which is supposed to remain concealed.[16]

The significance of this chapter's opening scene—of Zöhre Ana's saintly speech taking form along the passageway between political birth (Samsun) and political death (Anıt-Kabir)—should, at this point, be apparent. Although we will return in later chapters to the work required to ready visitors to listen to Zöhre Ana in particular ways—we cannot, after all, reduce the effects of her speaking to the illocutionary force or performativity of the speech event itself—we have nonetheless begun to engage in this section the sorts of truths that she is recognized as being able to speak. As opposed to the desires of Turkey's early secular reformers—who would have transformed the voice of the *evliya* or holy person into a dead language—it appears here as a site of intense creativity, where new forms of religious life are able to flourish in the interstices of religious and state

Figure 7. Zöhre Ana visiting Anıt-Kabir, the burial site of Atatürk. Used with permission of the Açık Kapı Derneği.

law. In doing so, however, Zöhre Ana's *nefesler* also come to mark a site of return. "It reveals something that existed," as de Certeau describes, "but it also, and especially, permits . . . something that did not exist before" (2000: 23). This point will become more clear as we shift from a discussion of the possibilities of saintly speech to the organization of space and the distributions of abilities in space that this form of language both authorizes and represents.

Museums, Ethnographic and Hagiographic

Is the knife sharper than breath, or is breath sharper than the knife? We've come to a state where no distinction can be made. . . . I, unhappy soul, have seen the breath of a great Hoja [*hoca*] taken in a leather bag from one village . . . to another, and used bit by bit as a remedy for sickness. (Makal 1954: 172)

The term *nefes* carries several connotations. While the preceding discussion focused on the *nefes* as a form of divinely inspired poetic speech, the term also connotes, again, one's breath. Unlike the breath of an ordinary person, however, the breath of the saint is often regarded as possessing curative powers. To feel the breath of the saint is to be touched by the saint. In such an approach to the therapeutic possibilities of language, the force of Zöhre Ana's speech can thus be understood as residing in at least two additional dimensions. Along with its performative-enumerative quality, we encounter here an important spatiality that inheres in Zöhre Ana's saintly language. If feeling Zöhre Ana's breath, or *nefes*, is to be touched by her, then we can understand the effects of her speaking as depending on a relationship not only to language but also within space—insomuch as feeling her breath presupposes a proximity to her. Moreover, this is a relationship to language in its materiality—such that, as with Makal's image of the traveling *hoca*, knife and breath and language can be conceived as mutually transportable substances.

In the performance of Zöhre Ana's *nefesler*, language and space are tightly coupled. Not only does the enumeration of names of holy sites map a geography of saintly manifestation, but her saintly speech simultaneously animates the religious landscape she moves through while submerged in the *Umman*. In this section, I want to examine an additional dimension of this coupling of language and space—the importance of, first, the setting of her saintly enunciations and, second, the way in which the language that emanates from this setting is understood as taking material form within the built environment of her *dergâh*. It is within this materialization of her saintly discourse where the implications of our concern with the returns of language will become most evident.

As one might expect, visitors and followers approach the complex of buildings that make up Zöhre Ana's compound as being of special significance. The buildings and grounds are regarded not merely as a passive context within which ritual takes place but, in many respects, as an extension of her *keramet*. Guests, for instance, commonly marked their entrance with prayer and a ceremonial touching or kissing of the outer gates; being within the *dergâh*'s courtyard elicited and demanded modest conduct; visitors regularly attempted to collect soil from the grounds in the hopes that it contained miraculous powers. While the buildings associated with Zöhre Ana's foundation attracted expressions of general reverence, primary importance was given to the *dergâh*. For casual visitors and committed

Figure 8. Fabricated model of Zöhre Ana's *dergâh*, 1996. Used with permission of the Açık Kapı Derneği.

followers alike, the *dergâh* was the focal point of devotion. The *dergâh* was not only the building in which Zöhre Ana received visitors and where the majority of ritual activities occurred, but its design signified the singularity of Zöhre Ana's saintly presence.

Built according to architectural plans that came to Zöhre Ana in a series of visions while in the *Umman*, the *dergâh* is a three-story building that, when viewed from above, forms a star and crescent (Figures 8 and 9). While resembling the pragmatic and utilitarian modernist vocabulary of much of Turkey's urban architecture—cement buildings composed of repetitions of parallel lines and corresponding angles—it also expresses a series of departures, particularly in its need to accommodate a range of specialized activities. Evidencing the dramatic expansion of her ritual repertoire since her initial calling, the building consists of spaces for communal worship, an area for performing sacrifices, a kitchen and cafeteria, a wedding salon, a gift shop, a tea salon, numerous guest rooms, an area for preparing bodies for burial, and the administrative offices of her foundation.

Although the building was constructed in accord with a pre-established architectural plan, an exuberance of personal devotion and ornamentation fills out its basic infrastructure. Statues of various sorts are scattered about the grounds. Framed pictures, plaques, and innumerable forms of craftwork adorn the walls. Oversized vases and urns border ritual spaces. Expansive, well-maintained rose gardens fill out the *dergâh*'s grounds. Posters and images of Ali, Ana, and Atatürk are ubiquitous. In the gift shop, one can

Figure 9. Zöhre Ana's *dergâh*, 1999. Note the portrait of Atatürk adjacent to the Turkish flag.

buy everything from porcelain plates displaying Zöhre Ana's image to basic pencils, from elaborately decorated ceramic figurines to simple stickers and miniature flags advertising Zöhre Ana-Ali Social Services Foundation. Although the building had been open less than two years when I began regularly visiting in 1999, successive layers of sedimented adornment were already apparent.

In sharp contrast to the design and organization of space in the main building, much of the *dergâh*'s subterranean structure has been enclosed and modeled to resemble the interior of a cave. Constructed with walls of textured cement, this space consists of an area cordoned off for receiving visitors, a fireplace for cooking, a simulated well, a series of small ponds lining the walls, a lion-shaped spigot dispensing sacred water (*zem zem*), and myriad items labeled "antiquities valuable to history" strewn across the floor and hung on the walls (Figure 10). When the area is staffed—as is often the case on spring and summer weekends—visitors will find female followers reenacting a version of domestic village life: women wearing loose-fitting combinations of homemade sweaters, skirts, and headscarves sitting before the open fireplace cooking *gözleme* (a popular stuffed flat-bread) that is to be blessed by Zöhre Ana and sold upstairs in the gift shop.

Figure 10. Interior of cave, 2009. Used with permission of the Açık Kapı
Derneği.

The overwhelming aesthetic of the cave is of a self-consciously construed
traditionality, what one reporter—after a visit to Zöhre Ana's *dergâh*—
referred to as its underground "culture complex" (*kültür kompleksi*) (Sabah
1999).

I want to pause over this "culture complex," and its juxtaposition to the
aboveground sections of the building, for what it communicates about the
possibilities of organizing saintly space within conditions incited by Turkey's
project of secular modern development. As I read this space, the simulated
cave relates to the larger *dergâh* in much the same way that Atatürk's presence in Zöhre Ana's *nefesler* relates to her larger corpus of divinely inspired
poetic speech. The cave, rupturing the linear and symmetric consistency of
the rest of the building, combines architectural discourses that belong alternatively to the vernacular vocabulary of the tomb (*türbe*) or dervish lodge
(*dergâh*, *tekke*) and the state-sponsored ethnographic or folklore museum.
On the one hand, references to popular Islamic and Alevi themes are unmis-
takable. The term *zem zem*, for instance, is used popularly to describe water
attributed with miraculous healing powers and refers specifically to water
derived from a well found in Mecca. The image of the lion, in turn, appears
regularly in the iconography of Alevism and Bektaşism, here in reference to

the lion-headed fountain found at the tomb of Hacı Bektaş Veli. And the meaning of the cave carries multiple, overlapping connotations—as the setting of the Qu'ran's revelation to Muhammed, as the birthplace of innumerable saints, and as the destination for many pilgrimages. On the other hand—with its markers identifying objects as "antiquities valuable to history," the staged production of an idealized village life, the unmistakably manufactured character of its traditionality—Zöhre Ana's cave simultaneously draws on the architectural idiom of the ethnographic museum.

If we conceive of Zöhre Ana's *nefesler* as a site of return, what additional returns might we find at play within the organization and materiality of this saintly space? If we witnessed in Zöhre Ana's *nefesler* the staging of a historical exchange between state power and (exilic) forms of religious authority—such that idioms of secularism could be read as signs of the miraculous—what sorts of return might we discern in her *dergâh*? We can begin to answer these questions by noting that this is not the first time that such forms of religious practice and the ethnographic museum have come together. In this respect, although we may have learned earlier that an important component of Turkey's project of secular nation building was the closure of religious orders, lodges, and tombs during the early years of the republic, we have yet to speak of their contents. "All tombs of the Sultans and all tombs in connection with *tekke*s were . . . declared closed and," as John Kingsley Birge informed his readers in 1937, "a later law was passed requiring that all articles within the *tekke*s—candles, swords, wall pictures, begging bowls, musical instruments, etc.—should be held for the use of the Ethnographical Museum" (1937: 84–85). Indeed, many of the former lodges of religious orders—as well as abandoned churches—would in due course be transformed into museums and filled once again with the objects that had been confiscated from them.

As an expression of the same "will to civilization" introduced in Chapter 1—according to which the "civilizational" was differentiated from the "cultural" in a systematic effort to re-signify the emerging order of the nation—objects confiscated from religious orders and tombs were converted into museum collections and displayed as evidence to support the nation's account of its own past. This was a past, moreover, that was to be experienced as distant and outmoded, one that had been surmounted in the nation's progressive movement forward. As institutions that offered historical and archeological support for a secular political order, ethnographic museums thus worked at the front lines of the state's consolidation and materialization of a nationalist historical imagination (Kezer 2000; Gür 2007), one that conceived the nation's founding as a decisive historical partition on which would hinge the nation's development (from tradition to modernity, ignorance to enlightenment, illness to health, and subjugation to freedom).[17] Of particular importance to our discussion, these ethnographic and folklore museums would play a defining role in efforts to desacralize and repurpose spaces and objects that ran counter to secularist visions of appropriate (or at least nonthreatening) forms of Islamic religiosity.

Much as the historical time of the nation wove into the ancient, genealogical time of the saints in Zöhre Ana's *nefesler*, the *dergâh* both rehearses and problematizes the partitioning of the "traditional" and the "modern" on which the temporality of the secular nation relies. In particular, in the materiality of Zöhre Ana's *dergâh*, a secular-nationalist ethnographic and archeological idiom reappears to authorize forms of speaking and truth disqualified in the state's aesthetic project of secular modern world making. In this economy of architectural forms, Zöhre Ana's *dergâh* thus enacts—and carries forward—a central transaction between religious and state power that was foundational to Turkey's history of secular nation-building.[18] That is, a vital aesthetic form through which the emerging nation validated itself and its own historicity, a form premised on the forcible subordination of particular religious idioms and spaces to secularist regimes of governance, becomes manifest here as evidence of saintly legitimacy.

The commerce between political and religious authority that revealed itself through Zöhre Ana's *nefesler* thus appears again in the materiality of her *dergâh*. Indeed, I would suggest, Zöhre Ana's *dergâh* stands as a concretization, artifact, and record of her saintly voice as it enters into dialogue with the exuberant devotion of her followers. Yet where her saintly speech draws into the open, as it challenges the limits of secularist regimes of truth and speaking, the forms of return we witness in her *dergâh* reveal a related engagement with the organization of space, the ordering of time, and the distribution of abilities in space that characterize secularist aesthetic regimes of possibility. In so doing, Zöhre Ana's *dergâh*, as the material externality of her saintly speech, stages the originary conditions of both political and saintly possibility within Turkey's project of secular modernity. And just as her *dergâh* can be read as confirming the strength of the state's hold on discourses of historical traditionality and accompanying formations of historical consciousness, it simultaneously brings to light the degree to which this hold can become unstable as discourse is set into motion and assumes material form. As much as her *dergâh* represents a site of return, it also signals a space of new possibility.

Sainthood Before the Law

In that Zöhre Ana enacts a project of world making that is at once therapeutic and religious, it is not surprising that she frequently finds herself before the law. After all, as we have already learned, the right to tend to wounds and injury was monopolized by the state early in its project of secular modern nation making. Among her visitors and followers, however, Zöhre Ana is distinguished less by her oppositionality in relation to the law than by her ability to manifest a saintly identity *through* the law. In this final section, I want to examine the ways Zöhre Ana's productive engagement with the law embodies what Achille Mbembe has described as a certain "conviviality" of power.

For Mbembe, relations of power defined in convivial terms cannot be reduced to logics of opposition or resistance, but should be recognized as processes of mutual borrowing—where, in Mbembe's terms, "officialdom" and "popular vulgarity" rely on one another's repertoire of idioms and forms in a common desire for "majesty" and "grandeur" (2001: 110). Relationships of subjection are thus marked not simply by disjunction and opposition but by familiarity and domesticity, in that state power and the "popular world" share a common living space (110). Building on Mbembe's observations, I am interested in the ways that the articulation and materialization of Zöhre Ana's saintly speech—as well as the stories of healing and being healed that I will return to in Chapters 5 and 6—tread across spaces of domesticity and intimacy that are shared with those forces aligned with instating and maintaining the binding status of political rule. Appreciating this shared intimacy will allow us to approach differently the question of returns that ended the last section.

The following petition, submitted by Zöhre Ana to the directorate of the Turkish Parliament (TBMM), the Constitutional Courts, and the Ministry of the Interior in defense of her practice, captures the way her saintly authority gains a voice within the juridical structures of Turkey's secular modernity:

For the last 7–8 years, I have been translating prayers that reach my consciousness through divine revelation to people that, because of my beliefs, have come to visit me. That is to say, I am helping them as I recite prayers. They come on their own to receive the prayers and I do not invite anyone. I am not someone to spread propaganda about myself in any form whatsoever. Additionally, I do not think about material gain at all. I continuously reject such offers from those that come to me. Before everything, I am a Turk and a citizen of this country. I am a person who longs for peace and security to be found within the unity and integrity of this country and this Turkish nation, and that our citizens will truly love one another. Furthermore, I am a person who is opposed to divisiveness, super-stitious thought, and outdated ideas.

I am a person who is bound to the Republic of Turkey; a person who believes in the ideals of social peace, including national solidar-ity and just tolerance; a person who respects human rights; a person bound to the nationalism of Atatürk; a person who believes in the basic principles of a democratic, secular, and social civil state, prin-ciples that were made clear from the beginning and which received a place as a foundational element of the second article of the Consti-tution. Yet, I have had complaints lodged against me at the Police Headquarters and other such places by several people with various goals and hidden intentions. I have been under continual surveil-lance and supervision by the Ankara Police Headquarters. To be spared this negative treatment and to enjoy that which is decreed by the 19th article of the Constitution, that "everyone possesses per-sonal liberty and safety," I would like to invoke the Constitution's 20th article: "Everyone possesses the right to demand that their per-sonal and family life be respected. One's privacy in one's personal and family life is untouchable."

Investigations about myself have been undertaken on numerous occasions by the Ankara Police Headquarters and the Office of the Political Directorate based on malicious accusations that claimed I practiced such things as *üfürükçülük*, that I offered cures in exchange for payment, and that I proclaimed myself a prophet and an *evliya*. At the end of the trials that were opened against me, in Ankara's Sixth, Seventh, and Ninth Criminal Courts, I was acquitted. In one of them, in the Ninth Criminal Court, the trial was rejected. And now I find myself facing accusations of producing propaganda for a religious sect. . . . As mentioned above, I wish to make use of the human rights and freedoms guaranteed under the Constitution. The continuous inspections and trailings by police officers is bringing discomfort to my family and my children. Based on the decisions of the court presented in this petition's appendix, I respectfully petition and request that the necessary legal steps be taken to stop this particular matter.

We must of course remain mindful that this document was produced for a particular legal, bureaucratic audience and, as such, lends itself to the effusive. Beyond illustrating her command of secular liberal discourse, however, I include it here because Zöhre Ana and her followers do indeed take these ideals as central ethical injunctions.

Moreover, this document begins to demonstrate the ways Zöhre Ana gives voice to a saintliness that operates not from outside the law (whether in oppositional, antiquated, or superseded terms) but, rather, from within the law. "Before everything," she is a Turk and a citizen of the Turkish Republic. She is committed to the foundational principles of a democratic and secular state. She demands tolerance, inclusiveness, and respect for human rights. She promotes freedom of religion and religious pluralism, yet opposes forms of divisiveness that could threaten the integrity of national unity (as charismatic religious leaders have been accused in the past; see Mardin 1989). She promotes the fundamental importance of privacy and individual rights, the equality of all before the law, and the necessity for a strong, unified state. Accordingly, she demands that her *dergâh* be an open institution—freely accessible to the public and transparent in its operation. And, of course, she is strongly opposed to regressive forms of religiosity, such as those practiced by the *üfürükçü* or *cinci hoca*, that run contrary to the enlightened modernity that Atatürk established.

For her followers, Zöhre Ana's appeal to secular liberal principles of democratic citizenship was not secondary to her saintliness. Rather, it was precisely her capacity to inhabit the law as a saint that was taken as evidence of her miraculous powers. One of her followers explained:

There is a defense that she wrote against the public prosecutor, have you read it? My, how beautiful! How beautiful! A legal expert, a parliamentarian, even a public prosecutor could not have written it that beautifully. It was from when she was arrested and thrown into jail. Zöhre Ana's defense, so beautiful. From a legal point of view, from a social point of view, from a linguistic point of view, this was a miracle (*mucize*).

The beauty and miraculous implications of Zöhre Ana's contemporariness was a recurrent theme in interviews. "In my mind," as an initially skeptical visitor recounted his first meeting, "I was imagining a particular type of person. She would be veiled, with only her eyes visible, covered from head to toe—wearing, in fact, a face shield and a veil that covered her entire body—sitting in a dark room, affecting others while in her mystical state." Yet, when he arrived, "Zöhre Ana was not covered, she was not veiled. She does not like the headscarf at all. Her head was uncovered, her face was without makeup. In short, she is a modern Turkish woman." Zöhre Ana, this visitor observed, rejects the dominant symbol of feminine religiosity and piety—the veil—and embraces a secular nationalist discourse of ideal womanhood as an idiom of her saintly identity.[19] As he went on to explain, "She was wearing a plain skirt and blouse. Her fingernails were unpainted, but perfectly clean. She was the image of the Republican generation's fully modernized Turkish woman" (Figure 11).[20]

İsmet—a self-described amateur anthropologist and frequent visitor to Zöhre Ana who had himself investigated, out of curiosity, comparable forms of religious practice along the Black Sea coast—depicts a similar sense of wonder at the contradiction between what he expected and what he found when he first visited Zöhre Ana:

Of all the *hacı*, *hoca*, *üfürükçü*s, or *muskacı*s that I had seen, she was quite different. She showed a more modern form. [C: A new form?] She showed a new form. This intrigued me. And I continued going. When I first saw her, she was uncovered, her hair was uncovered, and she had this green sacred cloth. The type of people engaged in this line of work usually have their heads covered, or they're constantly clicking their *tespih* [prayer beads], and blowing. They are people who use the Qur'an, and religion, as an instrument. This, Zöhre Ana, is a very different structure. Zöhre Ana is someone who doesn't fit into the standard form of what it means to be an *evliya*. When I first saw her, I saw that she didn't use the Qur'an, specious reasoning, or Muhammed for instrumental purposes. I saw that she

Figure 11. Zöhre Ana. Used with permission of the Açık Kapı Derneği.

was a person who had embraced modern life, who was contemporary, someone who was not outdated or backward.

In a similar vein, visitors recounted their astonishment when first witnessing Zöhre Ana's mastery of the language and vocabulary of "modern medicine"[21]—her elaboration of physicians' treatment protocols, her familiarity with medical and neurological genres of explanation, and the ease with which she wielded statistical data. Likewise, there was her and her assistants' fondness for invoking the wisdom of such literary figures as Shakespeare, Dostoyevsky, Hugo, and Tolstoy; the rumors of Thomas Edison revealing

himself as an *evliya* through Zöhre Ana; and the numerous proverbs and
aphorisms posted around the compound attributed to the likes of Emerson,
Washington, Goethe, Keats, Cervantes, and Helen Keller. As these examples
begin to suggest, in people's accounts of their initial visits to Zöhre Ana's
dergâh, there was a pervasive sense of being surprised to encounter the
familiar or recognizable—the language of medicine, political and legal principles of secular liberalism, figures of European and North American
cultural distinction—appearing within an unexpected setting. And it is precisely this disjuncture between the familiar and the unexpected, as opposed
to simply the former, that her followers and visitors would regard as making her distinctively "modern."

Rather than regarding these features of Zöhre Ana's practice as parodies
of modernist or secularist desire, I want to suggest that this sense of unanticipated familiarity is better approached through Mbembe's notion of
"conviviality." The form of saintliness articulated by Zöhre Ana was not
defined in opposition to the law or secular modernity—as was expected of
her, and the reason why Zöhre Ana regarded other healers as ignorant
impostors. Instead, she realizes her sainthood in large measure through her
ability to exemplify a range of secularist sensibilities. Contrary to expectations of sainthood (elderly, wearing a veil, and relying on false, instrumental, or overly literal readings of the Qur'an), visitors were surprised to find
a middle-aged woman who wore "modern" clothes (often a business suit)
and cut her hair in a "modern" style; an *Atatürkçü* who staunchly defended
the ideals of secularism and democracy; a religious figure who called for
the gender integration of religious worship and emphasized religious inclusiveness and pluralism; a religious figure who displayed an expert command
of medical and scientific discourse; and a "modern woman" who passionately argued for the equal rights of women and men.[22] In her dress, bodily
comportment, styles of reasoning, literary tastes, legal and medical expertise, and the identity of the deceased *evliya*s who spoke through her, the
"signs and language of officialdom"—as Mbembe would put it—and popular formations of sainthood come to borrow from one another's "majesty"
and "grandeur" (2001: 110). In this regard, Zöhre Ana creates and inhabits
a space where seemingly incompatible forms of reason can share a common
living space. Although this point will require further attention in subsequent chapters, I am suggesting here that this conviviality of saintly and
state authority attests to the generative force of secular rule, where its idioms and forms come to be read as signs of popular wonder.

Acknowledging the logic of conviviality at play in Zöhre Ana's saintly authority is significant because it compels us to think differently about the relationship between state power and what I have described as exilic forms of religious life. While other scholars have identified the critical role played by "popular" religious practices in relation to modernity, colonialism, and globalization, the present analysis diverges in critical ways. Focusing on such topics as witchcraft accusations and occult economies in Africa (Comaroff and Comaroff 1993, 1999, 2002; Geschiere 1997; Meyer and Pels 2003; Moore and Sanders 2001), spirit possession and spirit mediumship in southeast Asia (Ong 1987; Morris 2000), ghosts and ancestral spirits in China (Mueggler 2001), and shamanism in South America (Taussig 1983, 1987) or Mongolia (Buyandelgeriyn 2007), anthropologists have been at the forefront of demonstrating how "popular" religious formations—especially those that address misfortune and affliction—play a vital role in managing, responding to, and making sense of large-scale social and economic transformation concurrent with processes of colonialism, modernity, and global capitalism. Beyond showing how such practices are thoroughly embedded within modernity—rather than being anachronistic vestiges of a premodern "tradition"—these studies have offered a powerful means of conceptualizing forms of religiosity appearing at the margins of political orders as counter-hegemonic responses to and embodied critiques of colonial, state, or capitalist forms of domination, exploitation, and abstraction. While indebted to this line of analysis, my approach to secularism's politics of aesthetics through exilic forms of religious life offers an alternate means of conceptualizing the relationship between religion, political power, and subjectivity that these studies presume. The following chapters will elaborate this relationship further; here I merely want to draw attention to the intimacy of secular rule that Zöhre Ana's saintliness begins to indicate.

Approaches that emphasize the counterhegemonic modernity of "popular" religious practices are built on a common conceptualization of both the distance that separates religious life from political power and the characteristic means by which this distance is bridged. In the settings that these studies portray—where political institutions are either "weak" or communities are geographically isolated from centers of political power—structures of state or colonial authority are rarely experienced as a mundane, institutionally routinized presence in the everyday regulation of community life. Rather, they are more often experienced as a spectral force that reproduces its authority through a combination of seemingly arbitrary enactments of brutality and those fantasies of power that such distance and arbitrariness can breed. While the Turkish state certainly exercises authority through periodic enactments of explosive violence (more frequently in some parts of the country than others), and while the political order is sustained by multiple fantasies for the state (see Navaro-Yashin 2002), the idea of the state has nonetheless settled deeply into the weave of social life in neighborhoods like Hürriyet and Aktepe as a predictable frame through which people order their everyday lives, interpersonal relationships, and future aspirations.[23] Here, it is useful to recall the long history of social and secular reform that invested tremendous resources into fashioning early residents of such neighborhoods—and especially their rural parents—into the mold of an ideal republican citizen. In this context, the state's presence is neither conceived as radically external to lived worlds nor defined exclusively by a dynamic of external pressure. This is not, however, to suggest that this normalization of the idea of the state is free of violence and coercion, only that its powers are recognized as familiar, mundane, and domestic.

At the Limits of Speaking

The preceding chapters introduced a history of thought, practice, and institution building through which the figure of the religious healer was cast out of Turkey's project of secular modern development, becoming then a menacing presence against which boundaries of community life—of both nation and neighborhood—were, and continue to be, forged. This chapter focused attention on one such figure in an effort to examine a set of subjective capacities—a repertoire of miraculous abilities of acting and speaking made possible by one's proximity to God—that were supposed to be impossible to sustain in contemporary distributions of the sensible and possible. In tracking the manifestation and elaboration of these capacities, the chapter asked: What formations of saintly language and space are capable of drawing and holding an audience today, in such a terrain of exile? What arrangements of speaking, listening, and dwelling become possible along the figurative and geographic passage between (Atatürk's) political birth and death?

Exploring Zöhre Ana's efforts to address these questions revealed how the assemblage of discursive practices, arrangements of sensibility, and possibilities of speaking integral to secularism can conjure an aesthetic economy capable of betraying its own origins. Here, idioms and forms of Turkey's project of secular modernity would come to nourish formations of religious life whose subordination was the condition of secularism's possibility. Approaching secularism's politics of aesthetics through Zöhre Ana's saintliness also allowed us to understand how the history of the state's efforts for secular modern world making marked in advance the speech of the saint as a site of future struggle, which simultaneously marked the saint as a site of future return.

I noted in Chapter 2 that the common association of religious healers with an antiquated, historically superseded sense of traditionality made their continued presence appear as a return of the past (if not a revolt against the modern); this chapter introduced a parallel set of returns circulating through the articulation and materialization of Zöhre Ana's saintly language. Significantly, these returns cannot be characterized simply as nostalgic recollections of an idealized past (see Özyürek 2006, 2007), a form of relating past to present that would reproduce the temporality of the secular nation. Although the returns of saintly language may, at times, take part in such a nostalgia for the past, they nonetheless speak toward something decidedly less comforting and assuredly more alive, and hence volatile, than the nostalgic. In Zöhre Ana's *nefesler* and in the built environment where they find a home, one comes upon traces of typically unacknowledged, subjugated historical transactions that reassert the unspoken violence of secularism's origins. Moreover, in the ways the language of dead saints circulate through Zöhre Ana's *nefesler*, and the ways Zöhre Ana's language circulates amid such death, we are reminded again of the commerce between death, healing, and political power that I noted at the book's outset.

We are reminded, that is, of the seemingly inescapable entanglement of therapeutic power and secular forms of political governance. In particular, conceptualizing healing and secularism as overlapping projects of world making with a shared set of aesthetic stakes—a mutual concern with the constraints and affordances of human action and subjectivity, the ordering of constellations of social relatedness, the limits of sensibility and bodily experience, and the building of possibilities for alternate futures and re-imagined pasts—allowed us to understand how Zöhre Ana can articulate a saintly voice that is not defined merely by its opposition to the secular modern. This is not simply a voice of resistance, nor is her speech simply an expression of state power, or its parody. It articulates a relationship to power that cannot be reduced to a discourse of appropriation and instrumentality.

Instead, Zöhre Ana's presence takes shape as a persistent process of formation and return within the conviviality of saintly and state power, where the two can rely on one another's repertoire of idioms and forms in a common desire for "majesty" and "grandeur" (Mbembe 2001). While this cannot fully explain why people are drawn to Zöhre Ana—a matter that we will consider in later chapters—the conviviality of saintly and state forms one finds in her *nefesler*, for instance, nonetheless attests to the generative force of secular rule at the limits of speaking, where the state's ideological repertoire can be read as evidence of popular wonder. And through this popular wonder, we can conceive of Zöhre Ana as offering her audiences a novel language for participating in and—for better or for worse, welcomed or not—finding a home within the state's ongoing project of secular world making, at the same time that it offers the possibility of healing wounds and repairing broken relationships. Before taking up these therapeutic possibilities, and the specific possibilities of listening that Zöhre Ana's saintly voice both requires and calls forth, I want to continue examining this intersection of therapeutic power and secularism's politics of aesthetics by turning our attention toward a second form of religious healing, one that is associated with the figure of the *cinci hoca*.

Chapter 4

The Therapeutics of Piety:
Ethics, Markets, Value

Few are loathed as much as the *cinci hoca*. Inextricable from a history of secular reform that turned with particular passion on the figure of the *cinci hoca*—as a regressive form of religiosity, as the embodiment of irrationality, as an affront to individual autonomy and freedom of consciousness, as a corrupting force within the civilizing mission of secularism, as an anachronistic submission to "tradition" that undermines the health of individuals and the nation—the *cinci hoca* today continues to be derided as untrustworthy in his deceitfulness and dangerous in his cunning. Indeed, accounts of the *cinci hoca*'s many exploits and insatiable lust (for money, power, and young women) circulated with such regularity through both the national media and everyday neighborhood conversation that I would come to regard them as comprising a distinct genre of story, in which the *cinci hoca* figures as the ever-present allegory of social and moral decay (Dole 2006). Given the enmity *cinci hoca*s attract, it should require little effort to imagine the severity of the challenge that confronts those who want to lay claim to the *cinci hoca*'s religious and therapeutic power.

Scholarly accounts of such forms of religious practice offer a similarly discouraging prognosis. In the rapidly expanding literature that charts contemporary formations of religiosity within the Muslim world, the types of religious practice associated with the *cinci hoca* inevitably appear as unelaborated foils of an outmoded traditionality against which pious Muslims assert the modernity or authenticity of their piety (see Hart 2009; Deeb 2006; Mahmood 2005). For those embracing orthodox models of pious religiosity, fellow Muslims who seek the assistance of the likes of the *cinci hoca* are characterized as uncritically (if not ignorantly) reproducing a set of cultural practices that lack doctrinal justification, practices that run contrary to the pious modern ideal of purposeful ethical conduct supported by authorized forms of religious reasoning. Much like the role played by the religious healer in Turkey's history of medicine—a resemblance that is not coincidental—such forms of religiosity are regarded as relics of an undifferentiated "traditional" past, where people did what they did simply because that was how things were done.

When one pauses to consider the multiple and varied formations of religious life that gather and disperse amid the flow of everyday life in neighborhoods like Aktepe and Hürriyet, however, such distinctions between "traditional" religiosities and "modern" forms of piety prove difficult to sustain. One also quickly recognizes that an incredible diversity of practices, sensibilities, and experiences are being subsumed under either side of this distinction. The practices of the *cinci hoca* and *evliya*, to take but two examples that typically fall together under the category of "traditional," reflect notably dissimilar approaches to the limits and capacities of the world and people. Each implicates a host of divergent assumptions about possible relationships between authority and subjective change; power and visibility; the force and materiality of language, text, and speech; and the limits of the sensible and common sense. To rely on the theoretical vocabulary we have set for ourselves, there are a series of distinctively aesthetic assumptions that differentiate the practices of the *cinci hoca* from those of the *evliya*. By taking these sorts of difference seriously, this chapter will introduce an additional means of approaching our larger concern with the entanglement of therapeutic power and secularism's politics of aesthetics.

In particular, I want to consider in this chapter a corollary to the question that has guided our discussion up to this point: If we approach healing as the remaking of worlds—as opposed to simply a return to "normalcy"—how might *different* forms of healing participate in and reformulate competing projects of world making *differently*? Given the mutual investment of healing and secularism in the constraints and affordances of human action and subjectivity, the ordering of social relationships, the limits of sensibility and bodily experience, and the imagining of possible futures, how might different modalities of healing articulate within secularism's politics of aesthetics in distinctive ways? And what lesson might we derive from this capacity for mutual articulation?

Where Chapter 3 examined the *evliya*'s gift for drawing into the open a series of expressly political assumptions and sensibilities embedded within Turkey's project of secular modern world making, this chapter introduces the sorts of economic and ethical entanglements of therapeutic power with secular forms of political governance at play in the work of the *cinci hoca*. In particular, I am interested in exploring the unexpected ways that market forces and pious ethics fold into one another within the therapeutic intimacies of the *cinci hoca*'s ritual practices. How does one develop therapeutically viable arrangements of piety and value capable of managing the ambivalences and the sorts of economic-moral critique that the practices of the *cinci hoca* attract—in which they are disparaged for reducing prayer to the vulgarities of financial transactions and their patients are accused of irrationally squandering their limited resources? In tracing what I refer to as the micro-practices of secularist differentiation that emerge in response to these challenges, I also want to reflect on the specificity and mobility of the pious forms that the *cinci hoca* embraces. How do those models of piety and virtue central to contemporary ideals of modern "orthodox" Muslim religiosity—which are, again, typically defined in opposition to the likes of the *cinci hoca*—form and circulate in the sorts of bodily economies and interpersonal relationships that comprise the *cinci hoca*'s field of specialization?

In large measure, I owe my understanding of these therapeutic entanglements of piety, markets, and value to my relationship with Ibrahim, a practicing *cinci hoca* who will figure prominently in this chapter's analysis. Over a six-month period, Ibrahim and I met regularly to talk about his work as a *cinci hoca* and the new possibilities this work opened for himself, his family, and his patients. During this time, I spent many long afternoons and evenings in his home as he met with patients, prayed, crafted *muska*, and visited with neighbors, family, and the occasional old acquaintance (who had come to meet the young American scientist investigating the powers of the *hoca*). In keeping with Ibrahim's emphasis on the fundamental importance of ritual proficiency and expert religious knowledge in his treatment of patients, I begin my discussion by considering in some detail the defining practices and principles that organize the therapeutic work of the *cinci hoca*. This extended introduction to the work of the *cinci hoca* is of additional importance given the lack of serious attention such practices have received in the scholarly literature.

The Science of Talisman, an Art of Conditions

Ibrahim's time in prison proved to be a pivotal period in his professional life—not so much as a period during which his character would be reformed under the disciplinary impress of the penal institution, but as an opening in his life wherein new career opportunities presented themselves. Ibrahim was in prison for murdering, in a fit of uncontrollable rage, his wife's lover. In recounting the events that brought him to prison, Ibrahim described a period in which he became progressively consumed by a mounting sense of agitation. He found himself unusually nervous, unable to sleep, easily angered, and overall out of sorts in the months leading up to the attack. "I would just explode in anger. I was like a car that had lost its brakes." As he later saw it, these factors prepared the ground for the murder he would commit, as they conspired to make him unable to control his anger once he learned his wife was involved in an extramarital relationship.

Only after entering prison did he realize that additional forces were at play in laying this ground. With continued sleeping problems while in prison—a manic pacing that left other inmates convinced that he was erratic and dangerous—he asked relatives to retrieve the mattress from his home, with the hope that it would help him sleep better. When they moved the mattress, seven *muskas* fell to the ground. His relatives would find more hidden under the couch cushions in the den. With the discovery of *muskas* under the bed and couch, Ibrahim realized the source of his sleeping problems and irritability, as well as the distal cause of his murderous rage and subsequent imprisonment.

These revelations provided Ibrahim with a firsthand lesson in the logic of *büyü*, a term commonly translated as "magic." In this instance, the magic his wife initiated with the assistance of a *cinci hoca* did not seize direct control of him. Rather than compelling one to act against one's own will, the form of magic experienced by Ibrahim exerted its force on the conditions of his conduct. As Ibrahim frequently did in our interviews, he illustrated his point with reference to sexual intercourse:

Let's say a woman's sexual desire is bound (*bağlamak*). She won't be able to be with a man. No man will be able to do anything with her. He'll be inoperative. How is this? Just as wax softens when it gets close to a flame, so happens to a man's manhood when it

approaches certain verses from the Qur'an. It becomes inoperative.
In this case, the man's manhood is bound.

Büyü thus works not through directly controlling individuals but through
indirectly compelling certain sorts of actions or decisions: a woman who
runs away from her husband becomes unable to sleep in a bed other than
the one she shared with her husband; a husband begins to have nightmares
if he sleeps in any bed but his own; an adulterous husband can no longer
get an erection when with his lover. In Ibrahim's case, his wife had found
a *hoca* willing to perform "bad" magic that would provoke his agitation
and thus draw his attention away from her suspicious behavior.

Once he learned of his wife's use of magic, Ibrahim sought out, among
his fellow prisoners, the followers of a shaykh from Konya who would help
him dispel the forces that had fueled his murderous rage. Ibrahim needed
their assistance because the effects of the magic initiated by his wife persisted. He continued to feel agitated, easily angered, and "out of his mind"
(*kafası karışık*). With the assistance of the followers of the shaykh—who
were in prison for failing to pay taxes on their own work as *hocas*—he was
eventually able to break the magic's hold. In the process, he also began to
see the future promise of such work. Not only was he impressed by the
breadth of their religious knowledge, and not only did he see it as fulfilling
his lifelong interest in caring for others and his commitment to justice (of
"giving people what they deserve"), but it also seemed like a viable means
of securing a modest income given his age and limited contacts, marketable
skills, and education. By the time we met, Ibrahim had remarried, become
the father of a young boy (in addition to two adult children from his first
marriage), and was receiving patients full-time.

* * *

For Ibn Khaldun, the fourteenth-century philosopher of history, individuals who wield magical powers could be divided into three categories: (1)
those who exercise an influence upon others and the world of the elements
through psychic powers, without any instruments or practical techniques;
(2) those who use astrology, the temper of the elements, or the secret properties of numbers to create effects on the phenomenal world; and (3), those
who exercise influence through the powers of the imagination, by the use
of phantasms, images, and illusions. Philosophers, says Khaldun, call the

first sorcery, the second talismans, and the third prestidigitation. The difference between the first two forms of magical ability—and this is the important distinction for Khaldun, being that the third form of magic is based on illusion and, thus, "not real"—is that talismanic magic requires the assistance of external procedures and forces to exercise an influence on the phenomenal world. "In sorcery, the sorcerer does not need any aid, while those who work with talismans seek the aid of the spiritualities of stars, the secrets of numbers, the particular qualities of existing things, and the positions of the spheres that exercise an influence upon the world of elements" (1967: 394). The philosophers say, Khaldun continues, "that sorcery is a union of spirit with spirit, while the talisman is a union of spirit with body (substance)" (394). For Khaldun, both are sciences, and all three may cause harm, which means they together belong in the same class of forbidden things.

The ritual skills that Ibrahim began to learn over the final months of his imprisonment fell principally into this second order of magical ability, the talismans. To become a *hoca*, Ibrahim would have to master a large body of ritual formulas and techniques for the fabrication of ritual objects that, when properly used, could realize a desired effect on others and the world. The precise configurations of prayers, practices, and objects were to be determined by, he learned, the combined influences of the patient's problem or intent (*niyet*), the patient's astrological sign (*burç*), his or her defining element (*tabiat*, such as earth, air, water, fire), and a numerical value attributed to Arabic characters used in the spelling of the patient's and/or patient's mother's names (which are, in turn, generated by assigning Arabic equivalents of Turkish characters). These factors, whose possible arrangements were seemingly endless, combined to determine the form and ordering of ritual procedures necessary for the treatment of specific patients and problems.

The *cinci hoca*'s work is premised on an understanding of a world thick with *cin*s (Arabic, *jinn*). Described in the Qur'an as spirits born of a smokeless flame, *cin*s are a broad class of spirits who are regarded as being of an ontological status distinct from the phenomenal world (Crapanzano 1973). Although invisible to most humans, their effects on the world visible to humans are nonetheless multiple, if not unpredictable. In this respect, *cin*s are widely known for their capriciousness—their facility for being in turn kind, clever, mischievous, and malicious. It is the *cin*'s ability to influence the world invisibly that the *cinci hoca* seeks to harness through his repertoire of ritual practices and objects.[1] "They are like the laser beams in your remote control," Ibrahim explained. "It is an energy that you can neither see nor capture, but, when you push the button on your remote control, the channel changes." The vast majority of afflictions treated by *cinci hocas*—such as marital and familial conflict (likely the most common), a range of symptoms associated with children and childhood (e.g., nightmares, daytime fears, seizures, and general misbehavior), sleeping difficulties, infertility, problems at work, and any number of everyday aches and concerns (from headaches to a child's success on a school exam)—can be traced back to the influence of *cins*.

Although known for their skills in summoning and controlling *cins*, *cinci hocas* are able to realize but a finite number of specific effects on the world. As Ibrahim learned from his own experiences, the scope of a *hoca*'s influence on others is constrained by the necessity to work on the conditions of their experience. A critical component of the *cinci hoca*'s work thus involves proficiency in altering the parameters of conduct to induce self-motivated action, so that one comes to desire what the magic (and the person ordering the magic) intends. Toward this end, the *hoca* relies on a limited repertoire of objects and ritual techniques that are able to produce a circumscribed range of results. By properly arranging such objects and rituals, however, the skilled *hoca* can enact a complex calculus of moods, relationships, and circumstances to generate the worldly effects desired by clients and patients.

As this description begins to indicate, the *cinci hoca*'s therapeutic abilities are closely bound to his ritual expertise. Unlike the *evliya*, whose powers are conceived of as being granted if not imposed, the *cinci hoca*'s are acquired. Anyone who is willing to lead an exceptionally pious life, risk the dangers that accompany interacting with *cins*, and commit oneself to an intense regimen of study can become a *cinci hoca*. For Ibrahim, it would take years of continual study to learn what he described as the "art" (*sanat*) of the *hoca*, which was at once a "secret science" (*gizli ilmi*). Over this period of training, he would have to learn such skills as writing in Arabic, the proper method for cleaning oneself before treating patients, the appropriate prayers and verses of the Qur'an to recite, the materials necessary for the production of *tılsım*s (talismans) techniques of Qur'anic recitation, and the ideal times for preparing *muska*. In addition to such technical skills, he had to learn strategies for arranging these techniques and objects so as to create the conditions for a desired result.

Ibrahim's training occurred outside formal religious institutions. While he received occasional guidance from a shaykh in Adıyaman, he was largely self-taught. "This science (*ilim*) is a science known the world over. Anyone who can read can learn this. There are books after all. Whatever you want to do, you can find in these books. Everything is in the books." Ibrahim was referring to two books in particular, both described as *Gizli İlimler Hazinesi* (Repository of the Secret Sciences) and each comprised of multiple volumes available under the titles *Havasu'l-Kur'an ve Kenzü'l-Havas* or simply *Kenzü'l-Havas*. These texts, which contained extensive compilations of ritual instructions, would prove indispensable in Ibrahim's efforts to learn the skills of the *cinci hoca*. "For fifteen years, there wasn't a day when I wasn't reading these books. I was continually reading them, day and night, day and night."

It is worth underscoring the significance of these texts, for they offer us a valuable lesson on the distinctive relationship between language, truth, and healing at play in the *cinci hoca*'s therapeutic practices. A defining feature of the *Gizli İlimler* volumes is their organization into several hundred individual entries, each containing a brief description of a specific problem or intent for which the entry is appropriate, prayers that are useful in addressing such intents, the ideal time of recitation, the required number of recitations, and the text of the prayer (often in Turkish and Arabic). Although the organization of these texts seemed to suggest a relatively straightforward and consistent system of diagnosis and treatment, their actual use involved considerable technical complexity. As was particularly evident in Ibrahim's treatment of different patients with identical afflictions, there were many ways to arrive at a desired outcome, and these many paths toward a common effect could each be pursued through varying combinations of ritual practice. Even though Ibrahim would come to memorize those sections of the books that he used regularly, the books continued to play an important role in his everyday practices, especially in dealing with what he regarded as the more complex cases.[2] On many occasions, for instance, I would watch Ibrahim scour the indices of several volumes as he devised the ideal treatment regimen given the nature of a patient's intent and specificities of the conditions within which this intent was to be realized. In short, for Ibrahim, learning the ritual techniques of the *cinci hoca* required learning the methods for using these texts.

Understood in these terms, and in contrast to the authoritativeness of the *evliya*'s voice (whose force derives from its divine origins), the therapeutic and religious authority of the *cinci hoca* operates principally as a form of ritual expertise grounded in a distinct and exilic textual tradition. Unlike more widely recognized textual traditions of Qur'anic exegesis, the *cinci hoca*'s engagement with the *Gizli İlimler* volumes did not seek to elicit moral guidance or illustrate theological principles. Even though the Qur'an figures prominently in the *cinci hoca*'s practices, Qur'anic passages appear as fixed components within a larger assemblage of ritual prescriptions that make up an individual entry within the *Gizli İlimler* volumes. By gaining proficiency in this textual tradition—learning to navigate the books' complex indices, elaborate ritual formulas, and varied prescriptions for attracting and repelling *cins*—Ibrahim would learn to arrange obstacles, resistances, and incitements across a terrain of everyday social life in an effort to orchestrate conduct toward a desired end.

The therapeutic intersection of text and ritual that we begin to see in the *Kenzü'l-Havas* texts—as technical manuals of ritual expertise—finds its fullest realization in the *muska*, the ritual object with which *cinci hoca*s are most closely associated. A *muska* consists of a piece of paper on which a Qur'anic verse, a ritual prescription, the patient's name, the patient's mother's name, and/or the object of the spell's intent have been written in Arabic. The paper is then folded, frequently into a triangle, and put into a pouch. This pouch can be carried by the individual (as a form of protection) or placed in prescribed locations to create a specific effect—as we saw with the *muska*s found under Ibrahim's mattress and couch cushions. Alternatively, the *muska*'s effects can be realized through burning it or submerging it in water, after which the water is consumed. As the principal material vehicle of the *cinci hoca*'s powers, the *muska* exemplifies a distinctive understanding of the material force of words and their potential influence on the world. For the *cinci hoca*, much as Doumato describes the practices of Qur'anic healers in Saudi Arabia, "the pharmacopoeia of Qur'anic words included not just the uttering of words but also physical extensions of them. Words were conceived as capable of communicating their goodness to patients when written down on paper and buried, worn, or consumed through drinking the ink with which they had been written or the saliva of one who had uttered them" (2000: 138).[3] In other words, where the power of words for the *evliya* inhered in their divine inspiration and enunciation, here they gain their worldly force through the ritual reproduction of text and, frequently, its physical ingestion.

Although *cinci hoca*s are closely identified with the production of *muska* (such that the term *muskacı*, "maker of *muska*," is also used to describe the *cinci hoca*), *muska*s are in fact but one of an array of ritual objects—or *tılsım*s, as Ibrahim described them—produced by *hoca*s. Over the months of visiting Ibrahim's home, I would spend considerable time watching as he methodically wrapped hollowed walnut shells with blue silk thread, prayed over salt, drew elaborate charts with saffron-scented inks, and repeatedly locked and unlocked small padlocks as he prayed. As will prove significant to a later discussion, it is also important to note that the ritual prescriptions used by *cinci hoca*s like Ibrahim dictate the precise day and time when rituals are to be performed, so that a majority of the *cinci hoca*'s work occurs outside the patient's presence.

Although there may be no typical *cinci hoca*, Ibrahim does provide a general introduction to the prominent ritual and therapeutic principles and practices that organize this form of religious healing: the mastery of ritual formulas, prayers, and practical techniques for the production of objects that can, when arranged properly, realize a desired effect on the world. Unlike the *evliya*, again, the *cinci hoca*'s powers turn not on his possession of a divine gift of *keramet*, but on his studied ritual expertise and cultivated religious knowledge. Perhaps for this reason, *cinci hoca*s are rarely regarded as charismatic figures. Although the occasional *cinci hoca* may attract a modest following—even though, in many of these cases, the label *cinci hoca* is being misused to designate the leader of a religious order, or *tarikat*—the more commonly encountered *cinci hoca* is decidedly small-scale: clients typically come from the same neighborhood, they only visit when they are ill or are otherwise in need of assistance, and they rarely seek religious and moral guidance on matters beyond the problem at hand.

Markets, Piety, Value

"How can they justify taking money in exchange for prayer?" This is the question I would hear time and again from critics of the *cinci hoca*, of which there were no shortage. It was the sort of question that led into an extended commentary on the immorality of the *hoca*'s receiving financial compensation for his religious expertise. As this suggests, many had a difficult time imagining the work of the *cinci hoca* as a productive (let alone therapeutic) convergence of piety and commerce. Yet, after spending countless hours listening to Ibrahim, meeting with Zöhre Ana's followers and visitors, and listening to the stories of personal loss and familial suffering so common to these healers, I would find myself posing the opposite question. How could the two be held apart? Why wouldn't one expect the exchange of money—such a ubiquitous and commanding currency of value—to assume a prominent place in these relationships of hope, desire, and need? Given the prevalence and authority of market forms, why shouldn't we expect to find them circulating here?

By exploring the ways *cinci hoca*s like Ibrahim respond to such questions —how *does* one justify taking money for prayer?—I want to examine in this section the novel arrangements of ethics, markets, and value that I see being worked out in the folds of social life within which the *cinci hoca* labors. I am particularly interested in tracing the means through which Ibrahim, working outside formal religious institutions, struggles to combine an ethics of piety with idioms of commercial professionalism in an effort to cultivate an authoritative, therapeutically productive, and morally palatable approach to the ritual expertise of the *cinci hoca*. In contrast to abstract debates about the relationship of "religion," "politics," and "economics" so common to conversations about secularism, this ethnographic consideration of the *cinci hoca*'s everyday financial and ethical negotiations will bring into relief the ways that large-scale configurations of secular order and economic power are established and reproduced in the sorts of interpersonal relationships that constitute social life.

The figure of the *cinci hoca*, we already know, has long been an object of ridicule. Among the many vices for which the *hoca* is renowned, his proclivity for accumulating substantial wealth at the expense of vulnerable clients incites perhaps the greatest animosity. In this respect, there is a distinct economic logic to be found in the popular disdain for the *cinci hoca*'s practices. The commercial component of the *cinci hoca*'s work, for instance, regularly attracts accusations of unbridled greed, financial exploitation, and undeserved wealth. Similarly, clients and patients of *cinci hoca*s are ridiculed for their economic failings—the ease with which they are deceived and their irrational "squandering" of large sums of money on "false" and "unscientific" promises. Together, *hoca* and patient are an affront to the economically rational ideal citizen who is to constitute the nation's democratic, scientific, and economic development.

It is important to note that these critiques assumed a distinct intensity within the transforming economic conditions that coincided with my fieldwork. Over the course of the research for this book, Turkey's economy entered into a period of severe financial crisis, during which the value of the currency dropped dramatically and, by 2002, the unemployment rate had nearly doubled. Especially in the sorts of neighborhoods where I was living and working, the deteriorating economic conditions would become quickly apparent—as the number of unemployed steadily grew, family savings gradually disappeared, and local business owners struggled to maintain their businesses. In such a setting, accusations of fraudulence and economic irrationality leveled against the *cinci hoca* served to condense a pervasive sense of market-driven social decay. For his critics, the *cinci hoca*'s financial exploits exemplified the ways basic social and religious bonds of trust and respect had broken down with society's modernization, especially as seen in the expansion of a consumerist-oriented market economy. Stories of *cinci hoca*s able to accumulate substantial wealth in such difficult economic conditions only confirmed this sense of betrayal. If the *cinci hoca* was not meant to survive Turkey's secular modern development, it surely was not supposed to represent a feasible means of succeeding in the new economic order.

Given these discursive and material conditions, *cinci hoca*s practicing in neighborhoods such as Hürriyet and Aktepe went to great lengths to distinguish their practices from public images of corrupt and exploitative healers. Working in a climate particularly sensitive to financial deceit, *cinci hoca*s confronted the formidable challenge of negotiating an economically viable practice without threatening the trust of potential clients. As I want to consider here, a prominent strategy for achieving this balance—one that anticipated these financial critiques—was to emphasize one's pious ethics through idioms of commercial professionalism.

Ibrahim, for instance, explicitly developed his practice on the model of a small business. Recounting the reasons why he legally incorporated his practice under the name "Medyumluk" (Mediumship), Ibrahim explained:

> I chose the name Mediumship because "medium" is a modern title. When you say "hoca," everyone is afraid. When you say "medium," people are thinking about fortune telling—the reading of coffee grinds, the reading of palms. The public delights in such simple things. Yet when you say "hoca," they become scared and they lodge complaints against you with the authorities. They say you are involved in an illegal enterprise, and they are afraid. But being that I'm working openly, I call myself a "hoca" and I call myself a "medium." I'm not afraid.

Ibrahim's desire to appease the fears of clients by developing a businesslike environment was a recurrent theme in our conversations. By the time he received his first patients, he had purchased a book of receipts from which he issued individual receipts to paying "customers," or *müşteriler*—a term he emphasized repeatedly. To publicize his services in the surrounding area, he designed and had printed business cards, which he distributed to neighbors, relatives, and patients. As time passed, he extended his advertising efforts by targeting commercial areas near his home and distributing cards to local businesses, asking owners to distribute them to their clientele. All the while, Ibrahim maintained meticulous records of his business-related expenditures and revenue. Although the income generated from treating patients remained modest, he would eventually hire an accountant to assist him in tracking his finances and preparing his taxes.

In cultivating a pious, market-friendly presence, Ibrahim was not simply attempting to cast his work in a positive moral light. These efforts were also motivated by a tangible fear of arrest and imprisonment—as his prison acquaintances from Konya had demonstrated, and as frequent news reports about the arrest of fraudulent *cinci hoca*s confirmed. In this regard, Ibrahim envisioned his business practices as part of a larger effort to manage his public image in such a way as to avoid state and media attention. Rather than working clandestinely, as other *cinci hoca*s were known to do, Ibrahim continually emphasized the importance of his openness and transparency. Ibrahim's strategy of managed visibility is captured well in his approach to taxation:

> There are people who come to me from all over Turkey. There are also those who go to other healers, of course. But I work openly. I pay taxes. For those who come to me, for instance, I write them receipts. If I were to receive an amount of money from them, I have an accountant for paying taxes on it. I go to him, he figures out how much I owe, and he records this. He takes my file to the office of taxation and tells them that there is this medium that has done this amount of work, received this amount of money, and has this amount of value-added tax (*katma değer vergisi*). He is then told how much in taxes I owe. He brings me the receipt, I sign it, and I pay the taxes. That's how it's done. I am therefore working openly. Because of this, the police can't just come in here and arrest me. If I were doing this illegally, they could, and I would be afraid.

On a separate occasion, as Ibrahim and I watched an evening news segment that featured a *cinci hoca* being caught on hidden cameras taking large sums of money from patients, he (angrily) elaborated on this point: "If you have a certificate of taxation . . . this, this is fake. Being that he doesn't pay taxes, this is fake. If you submit an application and get a certificate of taxation. . . . How is this possible? Where in the world is this fake? When you open a shop, you pay taxes, right? I'm paying taxes. You are bound to taxes, and I am bound to taxes. If you are doing commerce, are you not bound? I am. Where is this swindler? Where is this?"

Ibrahim understood his conscientious payment of taxes as being both a realization of his pious virtue and inseparable from his legitimacy as a *cinci hoca*. It signified his willingness to practice in the open, which thereby held him accountable to patients in a way that those who practiced "illegally" were not. According to Ibrahim, as with any other legal business, his customers could complain to authorities without fear of retribution. At the same time that Ibrahim's embrace of taxation was intended to communicate a sense of professional legitimacy capable of attracting and reassuring suspicious patients, it was also a strategy to escape the notice of state authorities and a scandal-hungry media. In its basic form, Ibrahim's strategy was to take part in the state so as to escape its punitive gaze.

Ibrahim's approach to taxation reflected a more pervasive economic logic organizing his practice. Along with his tax preparations, for instance, he maintained a detailed accounting of his ritual practices and their material requirements—a ledger of revenue and ritual expenditure through which he sought to make his business more efficient and profitable. Ibrahim would frequently rely on these ritual and economic calculations to justify the price of treatments. As he explained to a client whose wife had run off with another man, "I will make a *muska* for 25 million (lira). Of this 25 million, at least 10 million will go to materials for the *muska*. 10 milligrams of ink like this costs 15 million. And if I buy musk for the ink, I'll buy 5 or 10 milligrams. And if I buy saffron, I'll buy 10 milligrams. And if I buy some herbs, or a lock, that's another 15 million." Ibrahim continued in a similar vein, explaining the additional expenses that factor into the rates he charges, such as rent, utilities, bookkeeping, advertising, garbage collection, mobile phone service, coffee and tea, and so forth. While these accounting practices may seem unremarkable, especially given Ibrahim's meager income, it is important to draw attention again to the context of their explicit formulation. After all, there were many ways that Ibrahim could have justified the value of his ritual expertise to a potential patient.

Although Ibrahim spoke enthusiastically about his uncompromising business ethics and fastidious payment of taxes, I do not want to exaggerate his generosity. While he regarded paying taxes as a fulfillment of his moral obligations as a businessman, citizen, and pious *cinci hoca*, he also went to considerable lengths to avoid paying taxes. In fact, if Ibrahim was as dutiful in paying his taxes as his ideals suggested, he would have been an exceptional business owner in the neighborhood. Like other small business owners, Ibrahim actively worked to minimize his tax obligations by regularly issuing receipts for amounts far lower than what was actually paid. I mention this not to confirm the image of the deceitful *cinci hoca*, but, rather, to highlight how conventional Ibrahim was as an entrepreneur. Although he did not develop formal ties with businesses in the area, he nonetheless drew on the strategies they had refined for financially managing their legibility in relation to the state—paying just enough taxes so the state would not look too closely at one's books.

* * *

It is worth asking at this point why such models of entrepreneurial professionalism might be so appealing to an individual's claims of religious and pious expertise. Despite the tendency to view the prevalence of commercial forms among contemporary religious healers (in Turkey and elsewhere) as yet another example of the corrupting impact of markets and their commodities, I want to suggest that such an economic explanation cannot fully account for the willingness of *cinci hoca*s like Ibrahim to imagine their relationships with patients in the model of a financial transaction. In particular, I argue that the religious healer's embrace of commercial models of entrepreneurial professionalism in Turkey has as much to do with the effects of specific economic transformations—especially the introduction of neoliberal economic reforms in the 1980s, which would make market forces a more tangible presence in everyday social life—as with the withdrawal from the social field of particular forms of religious institutional authority. Pursuing this point briefly will also afford us the opportunity to detail a specific example of the way that Turkey's history of secular political reform—with its efforts to regulate religious expression and consolidate a version of Islam amenable to state control—intertwines with a series of economic transformations coincident with market reform.

Although the figure of the *cinci hoca* has maintained a continual presence within this history—as an oppositional figure against which ideals of the secular modern were asserted—the practices of actual *cinci hoca*s have nonetheless experienced significant change. From the late Ottoman era to the present, for instance, there has been a dramatic shift in the bases on which the *cinci hoca* claims authority. Under Ottoman rule, those practicing the forms of healing represented by the *cinci hoca* commonly emerged from or claimed association with such state-authorized institutions as the *medrese*—the theological schools that to a significant extent represented the institutional backbone of Islamic orthodoxy in the Ottoman Empire. Although such practices as exorcising *cin*s were certainly not part of formal *medrese* education (being long regarded as impermissible), older residents of both Hürriyet and Aktepe recalled stories about *medrese*-trained clerics visiting their natal villages and regularly engaging in practices associated with the *cinci hoca*. Much as Aktepe's neighborhood imam was willing to engage in practices commonly associated with the *cinci hoca* and of questionable theological permissibility in an effort to appease those seeking his help, the *medrese*-trained clerics appear to have been willing to play into local visions of religious power in everyday transactions with village residents. Conversely, just as traveling *medrese* clerics drew on local expectations of religious authority, village *hoca*s were known to make claims of being trained by *medrese*-educated religious scholars.

With the secularization reforms of the early republic, however, as *medrese*s were closed and religious orders banned, claiming authority based on one's association with religious institutions took on significantly different connotations. Rather than representing one's inclusion in state-authorized institutions, as older associations with *medrese*s could have been read, the emerging political conditions resignified the *medrese* into an antiquated and anti-modern institution. *Medrese*s were regarded as promoting forms of thought and truth ill suited for—if not antithetical to—the modern, secular political community that was being called into existence. Rather than marking one's inclusion in state power, associations with *medrese*s could thus be read as a gesture of political opposition.[4]

In this transforming religious and political landscape, the *cinci hoca*'s claims of religious authority based on *medrese* training or *tarikat* membership would no longer carry the force they once had. Together with the expansion of Turkey's education system, the increasing accessibility of texts such as *Kenzü'l-Havas* (in terms of both translation into Turkish and affordability), the growing influence of market forms in shaping social life, and the shift of therapeutic claims of authority onto the figure of the physician, the stage would be set for the emergence of what some refer to as the *ticaret* or commercial *hoca*. The same confluence of events and conditions would also lead to the proliferation of self-taught *cinci hoca*s such as Ibrahim.

Although Ibrahim's experiments with combining market forms and pious ethics are surely indebted to the ongoing effects of a specific set of economic transformations, the above alerts us to the importance of recognizing how the ground for these experiments was cleared by the withdrawal (if not active destruction) of those forms of institutional religious authority that *cinci hoca*s had relied on previously. Given this play of market expansion and religious withdrawal, we can begin to understand the distinct appeal of commercial models of entrepreneurial professionalism for a *cinci hoca*'s claim of religious and pious expertise. That is, instead of reading the *hoca*'s commercialization as but an episode within an encompassing economic history—of the ineluctable advance of market capitalism and its commodity forms—I take these transformations as indicative of the sorts of everyday religious, political, and economic entanglements that together constitute a history of secular reform in Turkey.

*   *   *

In response to customer expectations, fear of arrest and media scandal, and a desire to lessen the suffering of others—in a setting that offers limited religious institutional support for such forms of religious practice, to say nothing of economic opportunity for a retired laborer trying to survive on a meager pension—we find *cinci hoca*s like Ibrahim experimenting with contingent alignments of piety, commercial aesthetics, and business ethics in the intimacies of therapeutic exchanges. Before we consider these exchanges in more detail, I want to emphasize here that Ibrahim's experiments in commerce and ethics were not undertaken without ambivalence. Despite the order and safety he sought through his accounting practices, and the seeming clarity they might bring to his therapeutic ethics, Ibrahim struggled to establish a meaningful, and morally satisfactory, balance between the exchange value of his services and the religious principles that guided his care for others. To be clear, Ibrahim was not concerned simply about the presence of money in his therapeutic relationships. As he would be quick to point out, healers have long received compensation for their ritual expertise. Moreover, if we are to learn anything from the central role of merchants and business owners in Islamist political mobilizations and the way Islamist political parties have for decades been at the forefront of promoting neoliberal market reforms in Turkey, it is that market capitalism and an ethics of religious piety are by no means incompatible.[5] In our case, Ibrahim's ambivalence turned not on the exchange of money per se but on the form this exchange was to assume—of appearing to literally exchange prayer for money.

Ibrahim was particularly concerned that his ethics of religious care—his commitment to ameliorating the suffering of others through appeals for God's assistance—might be overtaken by the financial aspect of his practice. The allure of the latter, according to Ibrahim, was substantial. As he frequently explained, "If I were willing to do bad things, I could make a lot of money. There's a lot of money in this business. A whole lot." At the same time that Ibrahim was sensitive to accusations that *cinci hoca*s were reducing religious matters to the banalities of financial gain, he also felt that he had the right to be remunerated for his expertise—as long as it was a reasonable amount and his labor was used toward "good" ends, unlike the "dark" work done by his former wife's *hoca*. As this begins to indicate, Ibrahim struggled to find some respite from the anxieties and ambivalences that gathered at the intersection of religious ethics and economic rationality, an intersection where his practices were squarely located.

Despite Ibrahim's effort to forge a viable balance between value and ethics, there appeared to be little chance that it would ever be settled. What he deemed morally appropriate, what he regarded as a reasonable expense and a legitimate amount to charge, or what distinguished "bad" magic from "good" magic were all situationally determined. In his everyday interactions with patients, he was continuously revising the coordinates of this relationship between a pious ethics and monetary value as he encountered new situations, and as he and his family struggled to make ends meet. Although I initially regarded Ibrahim's emphasis on paying taxes, his detailed accounting of ritual expenditures, and other attempts to cultivate a professional presence as primarily an effort to anticipate critiques of fraudulence and economic irrationality, I would in time come to appreciate them as moral practices in their own right—as attempts to mitigate the ambivalences surrounding the financial component of his practice, for both him and his clients.

I also came to regard Ibrahim's efforts to inhabit this intersection of pious ethics and economic rationality as capturing the seemingly mundane and rarely acknowledged ways that the assumptions of secularism were being made and remade in the course of everyday life. As micro-practices of secularist world making, which were also micro-practices of secularist differentiation, Ibrahim's delicate yet diligent endeavor to hold "religion" apart from "economy" to satisfy his and his clients' pious expectations were indicative of the sorts of continual productions (of affective and bodily dispositions, ways of relating with others, and modes of conceiving and inhabiting the world) necessary for maintaining the seeming inexorability of those structural differentiations associated with secularism and secularization —where religion is distinct from politics, which is distinct from economy, science, art, and so forth. Approached ethnographically, therefore, secularism comes into view here not as an abstract machine that overrides local moral worlds and overwrites reality. Rather, in Ibrahim's improvisational micro-practices of secularist differentiation, we catch sight of those typically unspoken assumptions, anticipations, moral and visceral sensibilities, and innumerable labors of social life necessary to reproduce a sense that this is, simply, the world's inevitable order. To fully appreciate the complexity of this social, economic, and ethical production, however, we must also consider in some detail the sorts of therapeutic possibilities this production underwrites.

Therapeutic Effects of Piety

To understand the politics of secularism in Turkey, one must understand its politics of piety. Over the past several decades, reflecting wider trends throughout the Muslim world, secularist assumptions about public life in Turkey have been challenged by the growing influence of conceptualizations of religious piety that emphasize the importance of Islamic forms of sociability and public visibility, especially as they relate to the dress and care of one's body, styles of interpersonal relating, and everyday forms of public speech. These forms of visibility and sociability are, in turn, closely aligned with a repertoire of deliberative practices of ethical cultivation—the regular performance of prayer, the reading of the Qur'an with heartfelt intentionality, a continual mindfulness of God during the performance of even the most mundane of activities, a striving to bring authorized forms of doctrinal reasoning to bear on one's everyday conduct and interpersonal relationships—that together aim to encourage a set of bodily, affective, and rational capacities associated with the ideal virtuous subject (see Mahmood 2005; Hirschkind 2006; Asad 1993, 2003; Henkel 2007). As we learned from everyday discourse about religious healing in Aktepe, this model of religious piety is defined in opposition to those forms of ritual practice attributed to the *cinci hoca*. In addition to lacking doctrinal support, the continued presence of the *cinci hoca* and people's continuing reliance on the *cinci hoca*'s ritual services are understood to represent a set of obstinate social habits that result from a blind submission to an unreformed traditional past.

Piety, approached in these terms, is not merely a personal quality one attains or possesses, but the ongoing effects of an intentional process of ethical self-fashioning. As Saba Mahmood has written persuasively about such forms of piety in Egypt, "Among mosque participants, individual efforts toward self-realization are aimed not so much at discovering one's 'true' desires and feelings, or at establishing a personal relationship with God, but at honing one's rational and emotional capacities so as to approximate the exemplary model of the pious self. . . . The women I worked with did not regard trying to emulate authorized models of behavior as an external social imposition that constrained individual freedom. Rather, they treated socially authorized forms of performance as the potentialities—the ground if you will—through which the self is realized" (2005: 31). In this conception of pious virtue, attending to the modesty of one's clothing or the propriety of one's interpersonal conduct is not regarded as just a secondary expression of one's inner belief. Rather—and reflecting a set of specific assumptions about the relationship between bodily capacities, ethics, and subjectivity—such outward forms of pious conduct are conceived as a vital potential means for producing the affective and ethical dispositions necessary for sustaining a virtuous life.

In this section, I want to consider a set of alternate forms of subjective capacity that such regimes of ethical practice can give birth to, especially as they enter into the therapeutic labors of the *cinci hoca*. While Chapter 2 introduced us to the ways that the forms of public sociability and Islamic visibility associated with these ideals of piety served to mark the moral limits of community—in their rejection for the residents of Hürriyet, in their embrace for the residents of Aktepe—I return to the topic of piety here in order to highlight both the specificity and the mobility of pious forms as they move through the interpersonal tissue of community life. I am particularly interested in examining the distinct entanglement of piety and politics that comes into view when we track ideals of pious religiosity as they form and circulate within the *cinci hoca*'s therapeutic practices. In the course of following these movements of piety, we will come upon a fugitive configuration of desire, ethics, and bodily capacity that is both indebted to and betrays the pious origins of the *hoca*'s ethics of care.

*   *   *

Ibrahim worked tirelessly to cultivate a piety that could sustain his therapeutics. In contrast to *evliya* like Zöhre Ana, who received the divine gift of *keramet* with neither warning nor preparation, the therapeutic and religious abilities of the *cinci hoca* are, again, conceived as the product of his ritual proficiency, expert religious knowledge, and a refined piety. In this respect, Ibrahim's capacity to influence worldly conditions with the assistance of *cin*s was made possible by a continuous ethical labor—of diligently performing regular and heartfelt prayer, striving toward virtuous conduct, attending to his body's and home's order and cleanliness, and maintaining an attentiveness to God that would permeate his everyday activities.

As Ibrahim explained to a visiting patient who threatened to go to Zöhre Ana if he did not help her:

> I read *ayet*s and I make *tılsım*s, while she claims to speak with God. I don't send patients to Zöhre Ana. Zöhre Ana sends patients to me. She cannot save those suffering from *cin*s, from *periler* [fairies], from magic spells. But, with God's permission, with God's *ayet*s, I can save them. That is, my healing of people is a matter of praying and worshipping. For instance, this *tespih* [strand of prayer beads], I'll pray with it throughout the night—after one in the morning, or three, until sunrise. I'll then perform ablutions—I'll wash my arms, my head, my nose, my face, my arms, my feet, my ears. And whenever I'm sitting, I am holding these prayer beads in my hand and reciting Allah's names. I'll do this a thousand times, five thousand times, even six thousand times. Zöhre Ana cannot save patients. She's a liar. You are a more virtuous person than Zöhre Ana. I

cursed Zöhre to her face. And I'll do it again. What sort of *ana*
[mother] is this? An *ana*? That bitch is no mother.·

In addition to capturing the limits of Ibrahim's tolerance for other healers,
as well as the sorts of internecine struggles for patients that one finds within
such local ecologies of religious care, Ibrahim conveys the particular importance of regular prayer, vigilant self-care, and proper ritual practice in the
therapeutic work of the *cinci hoca*.

In other words, Ibrahim would have to hone his piety through prayer,
proper ritual conduct, and virtuous intent if he hoped to be an effective
healer. The continual reading of the Qur'an and recitation of prayers
throughout the day, for instance, were undertaken with the aim of readying
him both technically and ethically, ensuring that *ayet*s were properly recited
during healing rituals and that the reciter was sufficiently "clean" and "virtuous." "Every day, after I complete full ablutions, and put on clean clothes,
I read *ayet*s until the evening," explained Ibrahim. "As I continually recite
prayers, [the inside of the house] will begin to fill with divine radiance
(*nur*). There is a light. It's like rays of sunlight. And, oooohhhhh, there are
things. Your eyes, your eyes squint in the light. And angels speak. They say,
'We're here. We're watching you. What is your wish? What is your intent
(*niyet*)?'"

The demands of this ethical laboring would require Ibrahim to carve
out space and time within a chaotic and cramped home life for daily prayer
(which he regularly completed at home), repeated bathings, elaborate rituals intended to protect him against the malevolent forces surrounding
patients, and the ongoing recitation of numerous prayers throughout the
day in order to attune his piety toward therapeutic ends. Achieving this
pious attunement, however, meant that Ibrahim had to overcome the
immediate conditions of his ritual practice. In looking back over notes from
our conversations, I am struck by the frequency of the scene of me sitting
back on the couch while Ibrahim—wedged between the couch, a chair, and
an entertainment center—completed one of his daily prayers, as his son
paced around in front of a blaring television set and his wife stepped over
his kneeling body repeatedly as she moved between rooms. In addition to
these immediate challenges, Ibrahim also confronted the inertia of a bodily
history that worked against such pious demands. Not only did he rarely
perform prayers before entering prison, but a life of physical labor had left
his body persistently exhausted and regularly in pain.

While Ibrahim argued that leading a pious life—especially in terms of prayer and moderation—would have salubrious effects on an individual, his reflections on the role of piety in his ritual practice suggest that the *cinci hoca* works at a distinctive intersection of the pious and therapeutic. On the one hand, Ibrahim was careful to differentiate the sorts of self and social transformations that coincided with leading a pious life from the sorts of transformations in people and the world that the *cinci hoca* sought to incite through specialized ritual expertise. In this regard, Ibrahim did not regard his cultivated piety as therapeutic in and of itself. His ongoing pious labor was instead conceived as activating the therapeutic potential of his ritual techniques. Ibrahim's account of the *nur* filling his home is indicative of this dynamic. In contrast to Zöhre Ana's story of saintly calling—in which she is caught unawares by the sudden appearance of a divine light in her home—Ibrahim had to call forth the *nur* through a set of bodily and ritual practices of ethical self-care. On the other hand, in addition to regarding his cultivated piety as setting the conditions for therapeutic possibility, Ibrahim also considered it to play a defining role in mediating a set of inter- and intracorporeal relationships at the center of his therapeutic practices—as the following example illustrates.

*   *   *

Fadime had brought her twelve-year-old niece to Ibrahim because of her persistent nightmares, her sudden and recurrent daytime fears (that someone was going to grab her, that something bad was on the verge of occurring), and an overall state of anxiety that was interfering with her school work and her friendships. Fadime and her niece came to Ibrahim without the knowledge of the child's mother and father. The father despised *cinci hoca*s. The mother distrusted them. Yet the child's condition worried the aunt. At their first meeting, while Ibrahim spoke to Fadime about her niece's problems, and simultaneously offered me a lesson on the duties of Islam and his therapeutics, he interrupted himself mid-sentence:

> Look, she is yawning. Look. Do you see that? And her feet are crossed. And her arms are crossed. They're knotted [bound, *bağlamak*, meaning here that she is under a spell]. This is an ensorcelled (*büyülü*) person. It's impossible for a *büyülü* person to sit comfortably. Their legs are knotted, their arms are bound, they are yawning,

they sit like this [as Ibrahim tightens his body, draws in his arms,
crosses his legs]. But we'll take care of this. We can solve this.

For Ibrahim, this attentiveness to the bodies of others was a critical tool for
discerning the presence of unwelcome *cin*s. Moreover, among the many
bodily signs to be read by the *hoca*, it was the yawn—of either *hoca* or
patient—that was particularly telling.

Although a more elaborate treatment regimen would have to wait until
later, Ibrahim administered Fadime's niece a set of palliative prayers to help
her temporarily. After a few minutes of reciting *ayet*s in her right ear,
Ibrahim noted (to me): "She's beginning to yawn, and she's beginning to
tear up, and she is sitting like this [drawing his arms against his chest,
hunching over]. This happens as soon as I start reciting prayers. When I'm
praying over water, or praying over salt, or a thread, when I begin doing
this, at those times she yawns." As in other sessions, Ibrahim was reading
the patient's yawning and bodily discomfort as evidence of the efficacy of
his prayers, in that the *cin*s afflicting the patient were growing uneasy.
While in this instance it required Ibrahim's prayers to incite the girl's yawning, simply his presence—if properly prepared through continual prayer
and ethical self-care—was frequently sufficient: "When they get close to
me, when they see me—like when a criminal sees a cop—they become
anxious. The person will suddenly begin weeping. When they see me, they
begin to weep. Or when a person with epilepsy comes, they'll faint—their
eyes will roll back, they will clench their hands, and they'll fall over."

Alongside its significance for reading the moods of others' bodies, a
cultivated piety also facilitates a *hoca*'s ability to remain attentive to the
signs of his own body. "For instance," Ibrahim explained, "if a patient
comes to me who is unclean—if, for instance, they are menstruating—I
will feel a sign (*işaret*) in my heart. Or if a man comes here who had sex
with a woman but has not washed himself—if he's unclean, that is—my
stomach swells up. Or if there's a *cin*, and the person is afraid, I too feel
fear. I feel this. I feel what's inside of those who come here." In addition to
inciting others' bodies to speak, Ibrahim's pious preparations also served a
second therapeutic function, in that they rendered his own body receptive
to the signs of others. This technique of reading the signs of another within
one's own body was of particular value to Ibrahim, given the *hoca*'s basic
distrust in the ability of patients to speak the truth of their own condition.

Like one's eyes, as Ibrahim was apt to say, the language of the body does not deceive.[6]

The utility of this repertoire of bodily signs—the yawning, contorting of limbs, and other indications of bodily discomfort—extends well beyond a diagnostic significance. For instance, Ibrahim relied on his skills of reading bodies and moods—of patients, himself, and even others in the same room—to continually modify his treatments. Although books such as *Kenzü'l-Havas* offered precise instructions for treating specific problems, actual treatments required considerable adjustment and refinement. Over the course of treating any one patient, Ibrahim would experiment with an assortment of ritual techniques until he discovered—by reading their influence on patients—the most effective. Ibrahim's skills at reading bodily signs also played an important role in determining when treatments were either complete or had crossed a significant threshold. For example, Fadime's niece's yawn—which was accompanied by a tensing and contorting body—indicated the initial disturbance of an afflicting *cin*, suggesting that Ibrahim was on the right therapeutic track. In contrast, the long exhaling yawn that one encounters toward the end of treatment regimens was commonly read as an indication of spells being broken and *cin*s relinquishing control of the patient. "They become relaxed like this [opening his arms, sitting back in the couch]. It's like when clouds move off of a mountaintop, when the sun comes out. The feeling of suffocation, depression, goes away. The fear goes away. That is, a person becomes comfortable. Like a person who has just stepped out of the sea. A person who wonders to God why life has been as such. The world becomes beautiful. Everyone is so good."[7]

I would never learn whether Fadime or her niece experienced such a releasing yawn. Ibrahim's initial prayers were indeed promising. The child yawned and described a sense of release. Based on this initial success, and on his reading of Fadime's niece's bodily response, as well as Fadime and himself—along with the information he gathered regarding the child's mother's maiden name, the child's date of birth, astrological sign, and element—Ibrahim would recommend an extensive set of prayers. The girl would also need a *muska*. After Ibrahim gave them an estimate for the total cost of his treatments, Fadime and her niece left, promising to return the following week—at a time Ibrahim determined was optimal for the prayers. That same afternoon, while I was still at Ibrahim's home, he received a call from Fadime asking if she could purchase the materials for the *muska* herself—hoping she might cut some of the costs for the treatment. Ibrahim explained that this was possible, but he could get the materials at a better cost and, moreover, he knew exactly where to get them and how to determine if their quality was up to his specifications. The conversation evolved into an argument. Fadime felt that the costs were excessive. Ibrahim felt she was getting a bargain. Although they would eventually settle on a payment plan, Fadime and her niece never returned. I was never able to learn if Fadime cut off the treatment because she was not able to afford it, because she distrusted Ibrahim, or because she became frightened by either Ibrahim's powers or a foreign anthropologist's presence.

At this point, I want to be clear about the site at which piety and healing is understood to intersect within the practices of the *cinci hoca*. As we have already seen, the piety of the patient is not imagined as the locus of therapeutic efficacy. While Ibrahim might hope that his treatments would propel a given patient toward leading a virtuous life, and while there are certain forms of conduct one should avoid, the piety of the patient was not necessarily regarded as a precondition for therapeutic success. In other words, the sorts of subjective transformations associated more generally with piety—those deliberative practices of ethical cultivation and self-fashioning that aim to encourage a set of bodily, affective, and rational capacities associated with the ideal virtuous subject—are not the same transformations that are to occur through the *cinci hoca*'s ritual expertise. Rather, Ibrahim's ongoing labor to sustain an ethical and virtuous self is conceived as a catalyzing force within a broader repertoire of therapeutic techniques. Piety, in this respect, is both a set of practices and sensibilities that form the conditions of the *cinci hoca*'s therapeutic efficacy and a specific practical technique used to discern the *cinci hoca*'s effects on others and the world.

*   *   *

When I think about the prominent role played by ideals of piety and pious sensibilities in transforming religious and public life in contemporary Turkey, the far-reaching political implications of Islamist political activism, or the ways Islamic forms of sociability and public visibility are reworking secular ideals of citizenship and the public sphere—that urgent talk of "Islamist politics," of the feasibility of "democracy" in Muslim societies, of religious "liberties" and rights of "free speech"—I find myself returning to Ibrahim's living room, and this encounter between Ibrahim and Fadime. In a small squatter home on the outskirts of Ankara, a healer who began to learn his trade in prison as he tried to imagine a new career at mid-life and continues to struggle to eke out a living on a meager retirement attends to a poor woman concerned about her niece's nightmares and their effects on her schoolwork. I think about Ibrahim's desire to help the young girl, and the continual efforts of prayer, thought, and conduct that are required of such an ethics of care. I also think about other patients, who similarly expected of Ibrahim a visible piety that could attest to these therapeutic abilities. I return, that is, to a specific example of piety forming and circulating within the uncertainties and indeterminacies of social lives.

Although piety may be a quality that has forever been coupled with figures such as the *cinci hoca*, the attributes considered to exemplify it are notably inconstant. The virtues associated with piety, the meanings ascribed to these qualities, the motivations and aims of pious conduct, and the distribution of people who are able to embody piety are both historically contingent and embedded in wider fields of social action. The model of piety embraced by Ibrahim, for instance, is inseparable from those wider developments in the Muslim world commonly characterized as the Islamic Revival, in which authorized forms of Islamic knowledge, sociability, and ethical practice are increasingly brought to bear on the organization and flow of everyday life. These formulations of pious religiosity and their accompanying ideals of Islamic sociability have in turn been envisioned by an expanding number of people—in Turkey and elsewhere—as both the basis and the effects of a coinciding political discourse, one closely associated with the electoral successes of pro-Islamist political parties.[8] Given these religious, political, and social interconnections, the forms of religious practice enacted in Ibrahim's living room cannot therefore be regarded simply as antiquated religious "habits" that exist independent of modern ideals of pious religiosity—as pious critics of the *cinci hoca* commonly assert. Rather than artifacts of an irreducibly local and undifferentiated "tradition," his formulation of a therapeutics of piety speaks toward a decidedly contemporary set of translocal discursive and material conditions. In other words, the forms of piety we encounter in Ibrahim's ritual labors, in his practices of bodily care, in his interactions with patients, and in the continual iteration of prayer are deeply indebted to a host of large-scale visions of collective political and ethical life.

Although indebted to conventional formulations of piety and virtue—Ibrahim similarly approaches piety as a set of deliberative practices of ethical self-fashioning through which one's inner dispositions and desires can be reformed—he also regards this ethical labor as making possible and actively facilitating a distinctive set of therapeutic relationships. Specifically, if he engages in these practices of ethical self-fashioning with appropriate desire, his piety can become the condition of possibility for an intercorporeal economy of signs, where his refined piety (as well as the surrounding environment) can compel other bodies to speak, just as it allows him to read the signs of these bodily effects in himself. Framed in these terms, we can thus conceive of the practices of the *cinci hoca* as a site of intense corporeal and ethical entanglement, where an ethics of piety enters into an ethics of care, which itself takes shape through an aesthetics and ethics of entrepreneurial professionalism and economic rationality. It is here, I argue, that the therapeutic practices of the *cinci hoca* bring into view a fugitive configuration of desire, ethics, and bodily capacity that is indebted to yet exceeds the sorts of potentialities associated with conventional formulations of piety, especially those that traffic under the labels of "orthodox," "juridical," or "authorized" Islam.

These observations offer us a number of important lessons. When one attends closely to the realities in which these forms of religiosity grow—as when Ibrahim, struggling to secure a modest living while he fulfills his lifelong dream of helping others, attends to a young girl whose life has been unsettled by persistent nightmares and daytime fears—we are reminded of the fragility of such pious modern ideals. Although many secularist critics may imagine every outward sign of piety as leading unambiguously back to a unified anti-secularist and anti-democratic Islamist political movement —as was the case for many residents of Hürriyet—the practices of *cinci hocas* such as Ibrahim demonstrate the ease with which piety circulates as a sign within the complexity of local moral worlds, capable of supporting any number of visions of moral worth, community life, and therapeutic as well as political possibility. Here, I would suggest that the disdain the *cinci hoca* attracts from those who embrace such models of modern piety turns less on the *hoca*'s transgression of some abstract legal principle than it does on the skill with which the *cinci hoca* is able to perform his piety—the skill, that is, with which the *cinci hoca* reveals the instability of pious forms as he appears to subordinate an ethics of piety to the signs of piety.[9] Indeed, as these forms of piety work their way through ritual practices and therapeutic relationships—as the signs of piety enter into an interpersonal ethics of care—the *cinci hoca* seems uniquely skilled at intensifying these instabilies.

The Banality and Vitality of Religious Life

An overarching aim of this chapter has been to consider the ways that different modalities of religious healing—with their distinct aesthetic assumptions about possible configurations of authority and the capacity for subjective change, the relationship between power and visibility, the force and materiality of language and text, the limits of the sensible and common sense, and so forth—necessarily articulate within and bring into view large-scale projects of world and subject making in distinctive ways. Whereas Chapter 3 highlighted the sorts of expressly secularist political assumptions and sensibilities that run through Zöhre Ana's saintliness, this chapter examined the economic and ethical entanglements of the *cinci hoca*'s ritual expertise. Of particular importance have been the unanticipated ways market forces and pious ethics are able to cohabitate within the *cinci hoca*'s therapeutic practices.

In tracing the career of a *cinci hoca* who worked in a setting that no longer provided institutional support for the form of religious authority he claimed, we examined his turn toward commercial models of entrepreneurialism in an effort to both fashion a viable model of religio-therapeutic professionalism and anticipate pervasive critiques of economic exploitation closely associated with the figure of the *cinci hoca*. We followed these micropractices of secularist differentiation and world-making as they folded into a series of ethical labors (on both himself and others) that sought to create the grounds for an intercorporeal and interpersonal economy of signs—which were, together, the preconditions for therapeutic possibility. Here we came upon contingent alignments of commercial aesthetics, business ethics, and pious virtue that emerge from and work out through the sorts of therapeutic exchanges that sustain the *cinci hoca*'s labors. Much as Zöhre Ana relies on secularist forms as evidence of her saintliness, *cinci hoca*s like Ibrahim plunder idioms of piety and markets as signs of popular wonder.

Although this and the previous chapter can be read as a sustained reflection on formations of Islamic religiosity and religious subjectivity that fall outside the purview of orthodox or juridical Islam, and thus outside the purview of a great deal of contemporary scholarly engagements with Islam, my aim here should not be misconstrued as a desire to recuperate or celebrate the figure of the *cinci hoca* in the model of an idealized subalternity. I am not arguing that the *cinci hoca*'s derision is necessarily unjustified, nor do I want to suggest that we can find amid such exilic forms of religious life any coherently elaborated models for a more just political, economic, or ethical order. While they may disrupt a range of unspoken assumptions regarding the political ordering of society, they offer no clear escape. In fact, Ibrahim has taught us quite the opposite.

Just as Zöhre Ana spoke to the domesticity of secular principles of political rule and the intimacy of the forms of violence they keep alive, *cinci hoca*s like Ibrahim exemplify the generative force of capitalist forms and the sorts of economic abstraction they rely upon. This is by no means unique to Turkey. In settings throughout the world, it has become commonplace for "traditional healers" to organize their expertise in the model of a small business—to market their services, to issue receipts for services rendered, or to offer consultations with clients over email and cell phones. At least in our case, however, the commercialism of Ibrahim's practice does not represent some sort of parody of capitalist forms—at least any more of a parody than commodities already are. In contrast to arguments concerning comparable forms of religious practice elsewhere (Taussig 1983, 1987, 1993; Comaroff 1993; Comaroff and Comaroff 1999, 2002; Meyer 1998; Kendall 2008), I read Ibrahim's commercial aesthetics as something more than a fantasy born of capitalist relations through which the at once alienating and magical qualities of commodities are manifest and commented on. In fact, I would suggest that Ibrahim's commercialism is a decidedly more mundane commentary on the banality and domesticity of capitalist forms.

Although they may be banal in their ubiquity, capitalist forms do not circulate without resistance. As we have seen, *cinci hoca*s like Ibrahim are regularly derided for subordinating prayer, piety, and bonds of religious obligation to the vulgarity of abstract financial transactions. In anticipation of and response to such resistance, we find *cinci hoca*s struggling to develop an alignment of commerce, ethics, and ritual practice that can both address the suffering of others and remain sufficiently inoffensive to patients, reporters, and tax collectors alike—a struggle that I have described as the *cinci hoca*'s micro-practices of secularist differentiation. Given the ease with which value and virtue run together in the sorts of therapeutic settings that concern us, however, such practices of secularist differentiation require remarkable effort to sustain. And it is when they fail—when circuits of religious obligation align too closely with circuits of market exchange, as they often do—that preexisting ambivalences about the religious healer can rapidly transform into anger, revulsion, and accusations of fraudulence.

In the hands of *cinci hoca*s like Ibrahim, however, such ambivalences are transformed into generative frictions.[10] Extending the previous chapter's concern with those exilic formations of saintly language capable of drawing and holding an audience in conditions organized against such possibilities, this chapter has examined the possible configurations of piety, markets, and value that the therapeutic labors of the *cinci hoca* give rise to. Here, the practices of the *cinci hoca* have emerged as a crucible of vitality and relatedness in which competing discourses—forced together under pressure (of secular state policy, of Islamist mobilization, of market ideologies)—incite one another and, at times, precipitate unexpected stabilities. It is to this vitality of relatedness that I now want to turn, as we widen our attention to the experiences of suffering and loss that seek an audience amid healers such as Ibrahim and Zöhre Ana.

Chapter 5

A Malaise of Fracturing Dreams:
The Care of Relations

To arrive at Zöhre Ana's *dergâh* in the afternoon was to enter a space defined as much by its air of quiet anticipation as by the intense desperation and determined yet fragile hope of those waiting there. By this point in the day, visitors had been waiting hours to meet Zöhre Ana, the living saint who figured so prominently in our earlier discussion. Spread throughout the *dergâh*'s open cement courtyard, clutches of visitors—often families escorting ill or disabled relatives—passed the time in idle conversation. Others spent the afternoon wandering the grounds—drinking tea in the tea salon, taking in the rose garden, and looking over the items for sale in the gift shop. In thinking about the forms of suffering that passed through this setting, innumerable scenes of visible despair come readily to mind: an elderly woman is carried through the crowd and offered a spot on a bench; a child periodically overcome by spasms settles into the shade of his mother's skirt; a young, childless couple stand silently together; a middle-aged woman hobbles across the courtyard; a man with a large abscess on his neck sits in a corner; crutches, walkers, and wheelchairs in various stages of disrepair fill out the thin band of shade that, for at least a few hours, runs along the courtyard's outer wall. This was a space Zöhre Ana's followers considered open and public, a space born at the gathering of therapeutic desires, injured bodies and relationships, and secularism's politics of aesthetics.

The precise time when Zöhre Ana might receive visitors was impossible to predict. For this reason, visitors often arrived early, knowing still that an audience with Zöhre Ana was not guaranteed. On most days, however, at some point in the afternoon, word of Zöhre Ana's car arriving at the building would pass excitedly through the crowd. Dispersed groups would begin gathering, the more frail being ushered into the waiting room. Once the crowd was assembled, one of Zöhre Ana's assistants would offer a brief introduction—recounting a selection of her miracles and providing newcomers with instructions about how to conduct themselves properly in her presence. Visitors then passed into the large room, or *cemevi*,[1] where they again waited for Zöhre Ana's entrance. When she arrived, and after the routine recitation of an opening prayer, visitors—singly or in small groups—would begin making their way on hands and knees up to Zöhre Ana. From there, events moved quickly. As visitors approached Zöhre Ana, they kissed either her feet or the ground immediately in front of her, continued past, and exited the room. While the line's progression was occasionally slowed by exchanges between Zöhre Ana and visitors, these interactions were typically brief and didactic. Within an hour, the building and the surrounding compound would be largely empty.

Although the forms of affliction and histories of failed medical care encountered at Zöhre Ana's *dergâh* might suggest as much, this was not a site of despair and resignation, an institution where those deemed to be unproductive burdens on families were discarded (see Biehl 2005). Despite the intensity of suffering and the inescapable presence of death's proximity found there, the *dergâh* was a site of intense hope that overflowed with the potential for new life and new ways of inhabiting life. It was a space wherein forms of care that consumed other people's lives privately—especially the lives of family members—became focused and, for at least a short while, recognizable to others. This also makes Zöhre Ana's *dergâh* a space familiar with those intimate forms of familial violence that often take hold in such situations, where a trip to the *dergâh* can count as doing "enough" to justify doing little else.

In this chapter, I am interested in tracing the complexity, density, and indeterminacy of lives that move through Zöhre Ana's *dergâh*, and through which Zöhre Ana's presence moves. Building on the previous discussion of the efforts of religious healers to cultivate forms of therapeutic and religious authority in thoroughly inhospitable conditions, I raise here a set of complementary questions regarding the possibilities of listening, truth, and desire that take shape in the presence of such healers. What forms of social and subjective experience become possible within spaces like Zöhre Ana's *dergâh*—or Ibrahim's living room for that matter, or the porch of Feride the *kurşuncu*? What are the potential effects of forms of religious speech and practice that emerge from and gesture toward a space between the juridical orders of religious law and the law of the state? How do experiences of suffering and recovery unfold within the idioms and forms of secularism's politics of aesthetics, with its investments in the organization of sensibilities and forms of sociability, its structuring of the limits of the sensible and community life, and its corresponding regimes of value, truth, and ethics?

To begin addressing such questions, we must acknowledge at the outset that there are no typical stories of healing and recovery to be found here. Thousands of singular stories converge at Zöhre Ana's *dergâh*, in Ibrahim's home, or on Feride's porch. Rather than effacing such singularities, I want to build my discussion precisely within this multiplicity of stories. Appreciating the social forces that give rise to this complexity will give us important insights into a distinctive character of the forms of religious and therapeutic experience taking shape here, insights that tell us about something more than the uncontainability of stories, the polyvalence of signs, or the infidelities of signification. By following closely lives as they moved beyond discrete ritual encounters circumscribed by Zöhre Ana's *dergâh*, one enters onto a remarkable variability of stories of healing that speak to the indeterminate and distributed complexities of social ties and intersubjective relations that give life to both suffering and therapeutic possibility. The following discussion is therefore built on the premise that we have much to learn by approaching healing and recovery, or simply the experience of a healer's presence, through idioms of relatedness.

This turn toward experiences of healing through idioms of relatedness represents an important point of opening in my analysis, an opening that completes a major arc of this book. Where earlier chapters introduced a series of discursive and material forces constraining healers' ability to draw and compel audiences, and subsequent chapters detailed the efforts of healers to work within and capture these constraints in fashioning their own projects of subject and world making, this and the following chapter engage the emergent forms of possibility for inhabiting the world that take form in relationships between patients and healers. In developing this discussion, however, we must be careful to hold at a distance the emancipatory assumptions commonly coupled with visions of opening and new possibility. These relationships—as *distributions* of possibility and new becoming—are also sites wherein alternate possibilities become foreclosed, which means in turn that these relationships can just as ably wound as they can heal. In order to appreciate the significance of these mutual capacities of wounding and healing, given the sorts of social complexities that must be considered to make such an argument, I will focus closely on the experiences of a woman I refer to as Hüsniye and the relationships that assemble around her. Although her experiences are, as with any life, unique, she nonetheless happens to have a great deal of company, and there I suggest hangs a larger tale.

Gender, Labor, Freedom

Hüsniye's parents struggled to cultivate a sense of independence and critical self-awareness among their four children. They were of the generation that joined the mass exodus from the countryside in the 1960s, a generation that had cut its teeth on the wondrous promises made in the name of nation, capital, and the secular modern. Hüsniye was six months old when her parents settled in Ankara. Like many others, they squatted a piece of land on the outskirts of an expanding city and began anew a life of laboring in the hopes of creating a better chance for their children. Beyond struggling to provide the financial means for such a life, Hüsniye's father took particular care in fostering a sensibility among his children that would serve them well in the future he saw on the horizon. He spoke passionately about the basic equality of all people and the fundamental importance of freedom and justice. Unlike his own parents, his children were not to be blindly subservient to what he saw as regressive mental and social habits, of both the past and the village. He impressed upon his children the value of education and independent thought. Hüsniye's father imposed his vision of freedom and reason on his daughters with exceptional vigor, knowing that the obstacles before them were particularly substantial.

In the late 1970s—the period of intense political polarization that led up to the 1980 coup, when the borders between Hürriyet and Aktepe were marked by gunfire and tanks rolled through their streets—Hüsniye, as her parents had hoped, completed secondary school and entered the workforce. On arriving at the Ministry of Education, where she would work as a typist for several years, she expected to meet others who shared her values. Foremost, she expected to meet co-workers who would judge others based on their abilities, rather than by markers of class, religion, and gender. This, after all, was the vision of work that she was raised on, and that had accompanied her through her schooling. Work was a space where the divisions that fractured daily life (leftist, nationalist, Islamist, Alevi, Sunni, communist, socialist) were to be subordinated under broader, less contentious categories of "worker," "citizen," and "fellow human."

"When it became known that I was Alevi," Hüsniye recounted, "a co-worker began standing in the middle of the office saying to me the most backward things about Alevism. 'Alevis don't do prayers, they don't fast, they do *mum söndürmek* ["to extinguish the candle," a component of the Alevi *cem* ceremony that figures prominently in non-Alevi fantasies about ritualized immorality; in this case, Hüsniye alludes to widely circulating rumors about ritualized group sex that is said to occur during the *cem*, at the point in the ceremony when the lights are extinguished].' He didn't necessarily have bad intentions. Maybe he was just jealous. But we argued over this." "At that time," she continued, "I wasn't particularly knowledgeable about religious matters. In spite of this, I defended myself. At least in terms of correcting his factual errors. In that I'm the kind of person who loves to read, I felt it necessary to research this further. I told my [Sunni] friend that I'd research Sunnism and if Sunnism proved itself to be logical, I'd become a Sunni." As she went on to explain, "I began to read, I began to investigate. One should examine the data, and one should make judgments according to this data."

Although she took her research into Sunnism seriously, she would never find in it a logic that warranted abandoning Alevism. "I wasn't a very religious person then, and I'm still not . . . but I have much respect for this topic. People possess the freedom to choose for themselves whether they are going to have a religion or not." "My father had a saying," she went on to explain, "'Keep the ones that are straight, toss out the ones that are warped' (*Doğru olanı al, eğri olanı at*)." This incident with her co-worker would have a lasting effect on Hüsniye. It both woke her up to the lived limits of the humanist and secular democratic ideals that her father had instilled in his children, especially in the workplace, and confirmed to her the value of secularism as an ethics of life for negotiating new societal arrangements.

Although the horizon of freedom and gender equality her father imagined would never quite arrive for Hüsniye, she considered herself fortunate when she married her husband a few years later. They were both "children of the *gecekondu*," their families were from nearby villages in central Anatolia, and they had arrived to Ankara at similarly young ages. Like Hüsniye and other Alevis of their generation, her husband-to-be spoke of his love of learning, his commitment to justice and equality, and the larger political significance of their relationship. Their marriage was to be based on mutual respect and tolerance; their home life was to be "open" and "free"; they were to relate as equals; and she was to continue pursuing her own professional ambitions.

The first betrayal of this political ethics of love and companionship would come with the realization that her husband's respect for her work was born of the financial advantage of two incomes. Several years after their marriage, Hüsniye's husband would move into a substantially higher paying job at a major petrochemical corporation. Coinciding with this financial improvement, and not long after the birth of their second child, he began to tighten his control over Hüsniye. He compelled her to quit her job so that she could, like his co-worker's wives, stay home and care for the children. "I was left between four walls," Hüsniye recalled, "My husband wasn't around. He was drinking a lot and coming home in the middle of the night. I had no one to share my problems with. In the building, there wasn't one friend with whom I could talk. My neighbors were of a somewhat lower cultural level. They spent their days baking pastries and, behind each other's backs, they gossiped about people. That was not for me." Over time, he increasingly limited her opportunities to socialize outside the apartment building, eventually forbidding even visits to her own relatives.

"I'm staying at home, cleaning, taking care of the home, working like mad. And then, on top of that, there are the children, and they are small. I'm bringing them food, I'm making pastries. I'm in the most closed of places. I have no friends. I have no one to cheer me up and to share my daily trials and tribulations." With this restriction of her social life, Hüsniye's husband also became increasingly indifferent and disparaging. "He would accuse me of lying around until the evening. Does a housewife lie down? Being a housewife is the most difficult of professions. I'm cleaning. I'm looking after the children. I'm watching as they come and go. In my husband's eyes, it was nothing. He kept saying that if I were hardworking, everything would be harmonious. I really needed to *deşarj* [lit., to discharge]." During this period, Hüsniye's husband would also begin to physically abuse her.

Hüsniye began to wear under the friction between the ideals of freedom and equality that she was raised with, the educational and economic opportunities that she had experienced, and the patriarchal demands and societal expectations concerning motherhood that now defined her marriage. While she would discover great pleasure in the additional time with her children that this new life offered, she nonetheless experienced these changes as a descent into a form of domesticity that was intolerable, a capitulation to her husband's demands that set the course of her suffering. It is difficult to express the extent and depth of Hüsniye's despair at this point in her life. She described it as her original *hayal kırıklığı*, a phrase I translate, with perhaps excessive literalness, as "a malaise of fracturing dreams." Although the phrase's conventional translation, "disillusionment," conveys an important aspect of Hüsniye's emotional state, it fails to adequately capture the affective and experiential texture of her condition at that time—a condition defined by the relationship between a series of destructive events and an enduring sense of despair that both enclosed and ordered these events into a succession.

Although her confinement and marital conflict defined the immediate context of this malaise, it nonetheless grew amid multiple contingently aligned processes that escaped her immediate grasp, such as ideologies of progress and freedom that animated a history of liberal secularist reform; their specific articulation and expression within an intertwined history of urbanization and economic reform; persistent models of motherhood and familial obligation that remained tightly bound to an idealized vision of domestic life; economic and political reforms that made a woman's participation in the formal economy into a sign of gendered liberation; ideals of neighborliness and class distinction; and a range of intersecting religious ideals that gave the preceding a distinctly moral valence. In the latter case, it is important to recall the ways that Alevi moral principles of justice, tolerance, and (gender) equality intertwine with Kemalist ideals of secular citizenship and a coinciding history of secular modern reform. For Hüsniye, these processes, ideals, and histories converged in such a way as to generate a seclusion that left her vulnerable to her husband's abuse and set the stage for a series of further devastating breaks.

Saintly Mediations, Openings, and Double Labors

No specific event or trauma incited Hüsniye to visit Zöhre Ana. That would come later. Her initial motivation emerged at the chance confluence of several developments: her research about Sunnism sparking an interest in "religious knowledge," which led her to books about the lives of saints; the succession of betrayals and mounting tensions born of isolation that began to weigh heavily on her; and finding in Zöhre Ana a culturally authorized pretext for gathering with friends and leaving the house without attracting her husband's suspicions. It was during this period of feeling socially confined—her intolerable descent into an unwanted domesticity—that Hüsniye began visiting Zöhre Ana's *dergâh* regularly.

As often as possible, Hüsniye recruited a neighbor, relative, friend, or former co-worker to accompany her on visits to Zöhre Ana. On each occasion, after gathering at her apartment to talk over tea and pastries, they would set out on the series of buses and mini-buses that took them across the city to Zöhre Ana's *dergâh*. The anticipation, as Hüsniye described, would build as she moved through the city, intensifying to an almost unbearable level as she stepped off the last mini-bus and approached the *dergâh*'s front gates. Once inside, "I was so happy. So very tranquil. The need to release my tensions that I had been so intensely feeling was gone." Such moments of delight and release, as I came to understand them, stood as focused expressions of a wider integration of Zöhre Ana's presence into Hüsniye's life.

As Hüsniye recounted the history of her relationship with Zöhre Ana, I was struck by the way Zöhre Ana developed into something much more than a figure of personal devotion. She took hold not as an object against which a life was defined, but as a presence that grew within and transformed the very marrow of social life itself—in the forms of interpersonal, bodily, and psychological relatedness that comprise the infrastructure of social being. With her turn toward Zöhre Ana, Hüsniye's suffering was drawn into and remade by Zöhre Ana's presence and the multiple forms of relatedness that gathered around her.

As time passed, for instance, passages and prayers from Zöhre Ana's books began taking a regular part in conversations within the household and between neighbors, relatives, and friends. Likewise, images of Zöhre Ana assumed a prominent place in Hüsniye's home. "I hung them everywhere. There were several in the salon, and in the kitchen. They were everywhere. And everyone was obliged to show them respect." Mirroring Zöhre Ana's multiplying likeness within her home, family life also became punctuated with recurrent references to the sayings and deeds of Zöhre Ana. Hüsniye began to "try out" the language of Zöhre Ana and her followers in exchanges with her husband, much as she attempted to use the language of Zöhre Ana as a means of resolving arguments with relatives and friends. Meanwhile, Hüsniye's dream life came to be peopled by figures from Zöhre Ana's *dergâh* and she began judging her own conduct through what she imagined as Zöhre Ana's eyes.

With this extension of Zöhre Ana's presence beyond the confines of the *dergâh*, visiting her became a recurring opportunity to gather neighbors and relatives in social outings organized by a shared sense of devotion. Although its make-up would change regularly, this group of fellow travelers became a relatively stable set of affirming relationships in Hüsniye's daily life. These relationships would expand over time to include a number of new friendships she developed with other visitors to the *dergâh*. Hüsniye also came to consider a number of Zöhre Ana's assistants as among her closest friends, a group she referred to as her brothers and sisters. "I have some real genuine friends there. There's Ali Ekber, who's been a friend for a long time, whose family I know well—a real honest man, a real Anatolian man (*Anadolu erkeği*). He is someone who leads a virtuous life. He's like a brother. We have a lot of love for one another. And there's Haydar, who is also like a brother. And Özgür. And others, I have so many friends there."

Hüsniye also felt that her relationship with Zöhre Ana was deepening as the ties forged through visits to the *dergâh* expanded. "When my husband was showing no interest in me and being so neglectful," she explained, "Zöhre Ana was my biggest support. Ana was everything to me—my partner, my friend, everything. Ana gave me so much support. When I went to Zöhre Ana, all my problems seemed like nothing. My outlook on life became extremely good. I wasn't sick at all during that period." Meanwhile, Hüsniye came to look forward to the feelings of solidarity and mutual support she experienced at the *dergâh*. She particularly cherished the experiences of collective devotion—the presence of others close by as she knelt in anticipation of Zöhre Ana's arrival, the feeling of being together with others in Zöhre Ana's presence, and the multiple senses of intimacy that she was able to discover in Zöhre Ana's *cemevi*. It would be in these networks of relationships and relatedness that formed around Zöhre Ana where Hüsniye would find a place and a language for release, or *deşarj*.

As Hüsniye grew into these relationships, she began to imagine new possibilities for herself. Although this took innumerable small forms—in how she approached her housework, how she responded to her husband's anger, the pleasure she derived from reading to her children—its most substantial realization came with the reassertion of her professional ambitions. After five years at home, with encouragement from her friends at the *dergâh* and drawing inspiration from Zöhre Ana—as a model of a modern, professional woman—Hüsniye returned to work. Rather than office work, as she had done previously, she decided to open a small deli (*mandıra*) in the neighborhood. Despite the exhaustion that came with opening and operating the business, she was overjoyed to be working again. For Hüsniye, this newfound freedom (to work) brought a sense of purpose to life that had been missing. In a gesture of gratitude, she named the new business "Ana's Deli."

As was often the case, however, Zöhre Ana's effect on people's lives was both ambiguous and indeterminate. Although this will become clear soon enough, I want to point out here that Hüsniye's return to work was not an escape from the pressures of her home life. If anything, they intensified. While I was never able to find out what compelled her husband to relent, Hüsniye's return to work was contingent on an unspoken bargain. To be allowed to work in the store, she would have to perform a double labor common at such an intersection of economic desire, ideals of gender equality, and gendered norms of domestic labor. As Hüsniye recounted, "I would go to work at 7:30, work until late in the evening, and then return home to take care of the children. I resigned myself to this." For her husband, neither labor was sufficient. "I was at the store all day, and did the house smell? Was I able to set aside time? Was I able to relax? Was I able to enjoy doing anything? Stress, stress, stress." Hüsniye's husband became more abusive with time and their relationship grew more acrimonious. "He doesn't speak to me about anything at all. When I explain my problems, he blames me, he insults me. He calls me an idiot, says I'm a birdbrain. He doesn't take me seriously."

The Care of Relations

As I gathered stories that resembled Hüsniye's, I came to recognize how rare it was for accounts of healing to be organized by a straightforward desire for diagnosis. These were not stories of dramatic rupture and ensuing chaos that sought resolution through the certainty and order of diagnostic categories.[2] Nor was healing to be found exclusively in the opening of one's story to others and the making of one's suffering public—as in the common psychotherapeutic premise that rehearsing one's past can have therapeutic effects, or in the more circumscribed semiotic sense of either giving public meaning to private symbols (Obeyesekere 1981)[3] or the orderly symbolic expression of the otherwise inexpressible (Lévi-Strauss 1963). In this instance, conceptualizing healing as a problem of meaning seemed to offer limited help in making sense of Hüsniye's experiences.

In tracing the forms of care and subjective experience that passed through Zöhre Ana's *dergâh*, I also came to realize that the therapeutic effects of such forms of healing could not be fully appreciated by attending exclusively to the isolated characteristics of individual listeners or even the interactional dynamic of discrete ritual events. Indeed, the analytic tools with which I had entered the field—approaches that stressed the centrality of embodied and performative processes to healing encounters, approaches to therapeutic efficacy that emphasized what I would describe as a model of command and event—proved insufficient when it came to making sense of stories of suffering and healing as they traveled through the social ties that comprised patients' lives. While these approaches were indispensable in helping me recognize the intercorporeality of the *cinci hoca*'s diagnostic and therapeutic practices, they provided little guidance in analyzing the ways healers' therapeutic work extended into the interpersonal densities of people's social existence. Rather than phenomenologically rich accounts that centered on transformative encounters with individual healers, these stories of suffering, healing, and being healed found their homes within, and moved slowly through, a world thick with relationships. As I trailed into this social and narrative density, I would find my attention being drawn less to specific therapeutic encounters between patients and healers than to the dispersed sites of exchange and fields of relatedness that healers worked through as they labored—often remotely—in the folds of social life.

With Hüsniye's story of fracturing dreams, both her suffering and her efforts at recovery were irreducibly distributive, in both their sociality and temporality. Her experience of Zöhre Ana's care, for instance, worked its way through the multiple social exchanges that organized Hüsniye's everyday life, the vast majority of which existed outside the immediate physical presence of Zöhre Ana. Like others, Hüsniye employed a widely shared therapeutic idiom that emphasized the transactional and interpersonal qualities of her experiences, an idiom that relied on a vocabulary of obligation, indebtedness, exchange, and relatedness to characterize the forms of care she found at Zöhre Ana's *dergâh*. In what we have heard from Hüsniye thus far, for instance, we find both her malaise and her care taking shape through networks of relatedness that involve her husband, family members, neighbors, ço-workers, Zöhre Ana, Zöhre Ana's assistants, other visitors to the *dergâh*, and numerous less sustained social ties that coursed through her daily life. Moreover, these interpersonal relationships are themselves embedded within and mediated by contingently aligned relationships among institutions, texts, objects, images, dreams, memories, *keramet*, and so forth. We also cannot lose sight of the ways that I too would be drawn into and begin to move through these fields of relatedness.

By considering the sorts of stories that tend to pass with particular frequency through such therapeutic settings—whether they be accounts of a husband's alcoholism or a child's seizures, of a mother's depression or an aunt's cancer, of an elder's declining vitality, or even in those instances when healers such as Zöhre Ana are the last resort in a chain of medical care that has left little hope and few options—we also gain unique insight into how a healer's expertise is embedded within arrangements and assemblages of relations that vary in intensity across multiple temporalities. With Hüsniye, the social distribution of Zöhre Ana's care spanned and varied across years of interactions among Zöhre Ana, her followers, other visitors, and assorted objects, images, and recordings purchased at the *dergâh*. Again, there was no discrete moment or tangible encounter that encapsulated her experiences with Zöhre Ana, just as there was no single origin to her suffering.[4] Here we can appreciate not only how the experience of suffering grows within and even expresses certain configurations of social relatedness (Kleinman and Kleinman 1991; Kleinman 1988, 2006), but specifically how figures such as Zöhre Ana work their way through as they reconstitute, redirect, or even sever those interpersonal ties that are the conditions of experience. Approached in this way, the experience of Zöhre Ana's presence is inseparable from the experience of these relationships through time.

*   *   *

It is important to recognize that figures such as Zöhre Ana are rarely the sole therapeutic presence within these circuits of religious care. Visitors to Zöhre Ana's *dergâh*—especially those with severe illnesses and chronic conditions—will have almost certainly traveled the region widely seeking the assistance of numerous healers. Before continuing, I want to consider briefly this heterogeneity of care. In addition to further introducing us to the range of problems treated by religious healers, this will also illustrate the distinctive instability of these therapeutic relationships.

There was nothing like the appearance of a *muska* at the *dergâh* to bring to light the multiple circuits of care that commonly pass through such settings. One afternoon, for instance, I met a Kurdish woman who had just been publicly scolded by Zöhre Ana when a *muska* was discovered around the neck of her oldest son. As we talked, I learned that he had been taking anti-psychotic medications for years (which I had already surmised from my brief conversation with him) and that she had, for years, been seeking at great expense every possible treatment for him. In asking more about this particular *muska*, their exchange with Zöhre Ana came into view as but a fleeting instant within a sprawling history, as well as geography, of familial care. It was a history that revealed the lengths to which she had gone in pursuing help for her son, as well as the extent and depth of the family's despair. This was one of many such accounts that I would hear over the course of my research: families traveling throughout the country—visiting shrines, tracking down *cinci hoca*s, trying various remedies suggested by neighbors and relatives, consulting neighborhood pharmacists, waiting days outside hospitals rumored to be uniquely skilled at treating particular problems—with the hope of easing one's suffering.

In such instances, it was almost always the case that several circuits of therapeutic care were actively and simultaneously maintained—regardless of the theological or epistemological differences in the forms of healing involved.[5] Put otherwise, these accounts—as well as the fields of social relatedness in which they were embedded—operated in what Byron Good (1994) and Cheryl Mattingly (1998) have described as the "subjunctive mode." Patients and their caretakers cultivated investments in multiple stories about the origins and prognosis of affliction, keeping future possibilities both in motion and in tension with one another—as they alternatively passed through clinics, hospitals, families, the tombs of saints, the homes of *cinci hoca*s, and Zöhre Ana's *dergâh*.[6] It is important to point out that these multiple investments—at once narrative, social, technological, and financial—are typically premised on both what was deemed as potentially effective as a treatment in a given set of conditions and the limited access of the unemployed and working poor to quality care in the formal health-care system. This, in part, explains why such circuits of therapeutic care are particularly dense in neighborhoods like Hürriyet and Aktepe.

*   *   *

With Hüsniye's assistance, I came to see Zöhre Ana as not only a point at which thousands of stories converged, but also a node through which innumerable circuits of care and indebtedness passed. Moreover, as the figures who peopled Hüsniye's stories gradually wove together over the course of our conversations, I began to think of her life less as a succession of events than as a series of relationships that were continually arranging and rearranging themselves across space and time.[7] In particular, I was drawn to the varying and often discordant forms and effects of Zöhre Ana's presence within the shifting fields of relatedness that constituted Hüsniye's life.

Although Zöhre Ana was persistent in these accounts, she was not a singular force or object of devotion but an ever-shifting presence that incited an array of effects over the course of Hüsniye's ten-year relationship with her. In this respect, Hüsniye's experience of care was less about Zöhre Ana's meaning (as an image, icon, or symbol) than it was about the interpersonal and intersubjective conditions of meaning making.[8] And it was through Zöhre Ana's effects on these conditions that Hüsniye was able to discover new potentialities within relationships. That is, as Zöhre Ana's presence wove into the social ties that made up her life, Hüsniye was able to find a new voice to speak of herself and speak to others, especially her husband.[9]

It is here that I would come to appreciate Zöhre Ana and her *dergâh* as a site of multiple exchanges, in the diverse meanings that one can attribute to this term: as a conversation, a juncture, a point of gathering and dispersal, a transition, an argument, a site of transactions, substitutions, reversals, and commerce. With that said, we should not exaggerate the benevolence of these sites of exchange and networks of therapeutic relatedness. If we can find in them the grounds for re-imagining future possibility, we also can find in them the foreclosure of possibilities, as well as opportunities for new injury. It is to the ambiguous play between healing and wounding that I now turn.

Wounds and Perverts

In her writings on political violence in India, Veena Das argues that the relationship between outbursts of dramatic communal violence and everyday socialities of community life should be thought of in terms of continuity, rather than exceptionality: "violence was not set apart from sociality," she writes, "rather, the agency of the violence rendered the social as an entity to be 'made' rather than that which was given" (2007: 149). Explosive violence, Das suggests, is not to be regarded as an exception to a pre-given everyday or an otherwise tranquil community life. Nor can they be reduced to one another. As Das puts it, "To say that the extreme violence was continuous with everyday life is not to say that it was the same, but rather that the everyday provided the grounds from which the event could be grown" (149).

Das's reflections on the relationship between extraordinary violence and everyday social life offer a productive vocabulary for approaching the dynamics of affliction being treated by the religious healers I interviewed. Beyond an immediate relevance for thinking about the role of everyday violence in constituting the forms of suffering that these healers address, Das also helps us make sense of the ways affliction and suffering grow within the weave of everyday life. Given our familiarity with Hüsniye, it is worth returning to her account as a means of examining affliction as an extension of the everyday, rather than its radical exception.

Although I have already spoken at length about Hüsniye's relationship with Zöhre Ana, I have yet to mention that Hüsniye's first attempts to visit ended unsuccessfully. Three times she received leave from work, recruited a neighbor or relative to accompany her, and traveled across the city to only be rebuffed at the gates of Zöhre Ana's home. On the third occasion, angry at being turned away, Hüsniye began to yell at a group of Zöhre Ana's assistants. On being ordered to leave, she learned that the assistant to whom she directed her most intense anger was a relative of Zöhre Ana. That night, she dreamed of Zöhre Ana for the first time. "I was standing there in front of Zöhre Ana, shaking uncontrollably. She began to reprimand me for being so selfish and conceited. I was shaking uncontrollably, I was that frightened." Before she was able to make a fourth trip to the dergâh and apologize to Zöhre Ana and her assistants, she became entangled in a series of events that left her deeply wounded.

After resigning from work to care for her children and before opening her store—during a period when she was feeling particularly isolated—Hüsniye enrolled in the Anatolia University, a government-sponsored distant learning program that would allow her to continue her education from home. Hüsniye recalls the significance of the day she received notice from the post office that her course materials had arrived: "When they gave me my books, I was really emotional. We had seen such poverty while growing up. My father was a very well-intentioned person, but he was trying to raise four children on the salary of a civil servant. There was the feeling that we were being crushed by poverty." While her childhood of *gecekondu* poverty anchored this sense of gratitude, this past also persisted into the present as an open wound of sorts, which left her perpetually vulnerable to the suffering of others. "Because I know the feeling of being crushed by poverty, I can see it in others. And when I see this suffering in the look of others, I feel the pain."

"At the post office, I saw a man who was clearly enduring incredible hardship. I looked at him, he looked at me. We looked at each other . . . and then they handed me my books and I left." She thought nothing more of it until she received a phone call the next day from a man claiming to have met her while she was at the post office with her children. As she recounted the man's words, "'I saw you yesterday, with a young girl, at the post office. I know who you are and where you live.'" He began calling every day while her husband was away at work. Each time, the caller—the telephone "pervert" (*sapık*), as she described him—would speak at length about her beauty, the moment when their eyes met at the post office, and the intense connection they shared. Although she tried to deal with the *sapık* on her own, he continued calling over the following weeks and Hüsniye eventually decided to tell her husband.

Rather than contacting the police, her husband and his sister's husband decided to take the matter into their own hands. Developing an elaborate plan of surveillance and retribution, they purchased a tape recorder and proceeded to script conversations for Hüsniye to enact as she spoke with the *sapık*. After several failed attempts to convince the *sapık* to come to their apartment, they arranged a secret rendezvous in downtown Ankara. "That night, I'm standing on a dark side street, my husband and his friends are spread out along the street, hiding and waiting. I'm standing there, wondering who this person is. A man walks up and winks at me, and I nod my head, and he comes alongside me. At that moment, my husband grabs him. And off we went," Hüsniye now giggling at the retelling, "to the police station."

At the police station, Hüsniye's husband and his brother-in-law played back the tapes to the police. As they listened together to the recordings of her flirtatious role playing, Hüsniye began to see the unfolding events

differently. In contrast to the initial thrill and intrigue of luring the unsus-
pecting *sapık* into their plot, she came to see herself as having been manipu-
lated and drawn into a male fantasy of sexual retribution. Her husband
would also begin to see these events differently. Back at home, he accused
her of bringing these events on herself. Just as Hüsniye had grown suspicious of her husband's motives, he suggested that her flirtatiousness had
been suspiciously authentic and that she derived excessive amounts of
enjoyment from the role playing. These events would mark the beginning
of a period of regular physical abuse. As Hüsniye described, "I can't express
to you how sad I became. I loved my husband so much. I admired him so
much. At this point, I shattered. I entered into this malaise of fracturing
dreams."

Despite the immediacy of her husband's violence, Hüsniye would locate
the source of this shattering in Zöhre Ana. She tied all these events—the
stalking, the harassing phone calls, the role playing, the police station, the
beatings—back to her encounter with Zöhre Ana's relative at the *dergâh*.
"This event with the *sapık*, in my mind, definitely exploded because of the
incident at Zöhre Ana's that day. To what degree this is correct, I can't
know. But that's my assessment." And Hüsniye's husband was quick to
accept this assessment. Rather than acknowledging his own culpability in
these events, such an explanation shifted blame back on to Hüsniye's own
"difficult" behavior. Soon after, he would join Hüsniye on another visit to
Zöhre Ana's *dergâh*, this time to make an offering and plead for forgiveness.
The brother-in-law and a number of neighbors would also accompany
them. Unlike the previous trips, Hüsniye was finally able to meet Zöhre
Ana. "I was really moved. I cried and cried. I was affected in a really different way by the prayer that she offered me. I can't even explain the feeling
of joy that accompanied it. We were in a state of wonder as Zöhre Ana
spoke."

A period of calm descended on their home following the visit, a period
during which Hüsniye felt respected and appreciated by her husband. This
calm, however, would be short lived. Within months, Hüsniye's devotion
to Zöhre Ana was creating new conflicts in their relationship. Although he
was willing to visit Zöhre Ana and make an offering following the *sapık*
incident, he did not like the frequency with which Hüsniye visited Zöhre
Ana. Nor did he like Zöhre Ana's growing presence in the household. In
an effort to undermine Hüsniye's regard for Zöhre Ana, he sought the
assistance of an Alevi religious leader, or *dede*, whom he knew to be

opposed to Zöhre Ana's saintly claims. As Hüsniye described the *dede*'s visit, "When the *dede* came over, I was preparing to go visit Zöhre Ana with my sister-in-law and neighbor. I asked the *dede*, 'If you'll grant us permission, we'll go to Zöhre Ana.' As soon as this left my mouth, he began to swear at us. 'Why do you believe in her? She's not a *dede*. She's no child of a *dede*. She's no descendant of Muhammed. It's reprehensible that she claims to be such an *evliya*. It's sinful (*günah olmak*).'"

Hüsniye came away from this conversation feeling even further broken. "Here is where I suffered a tremendous *hayal kırıklığı*," she explained, "At that moment, I felt such hatred for my husband." Although she would visit Zöhre Ana anyway, and although the *dede* would receive his due from Zöhre Ana (becoming, according to Hüsniye, paralyzed and wheelchair-bound within a year), this encounter with her husband and his *dede* confirmed in Hüsniye the sense that her life was taking shape as a succession of devastating breaks.

Behind this radical break was another story, one that I was only able to piece together slowly over the course of our conversations. In fragments, I would learn that her husband's brother-in-law was a particularly poisonous (*fesat*) person. I would learn that the reason he seemed ever-present in the *sapık* events was that he and his wife were living with Hüsniye at the time. He had recently lost his job and his apartment, and was staying with them while he looked for work. I would learn that this was a recurring problem, that he drank heavily and was regularly unemployed. I also gathered that her husband's brother-in-law was impressed, like the police, by Hüsniye's flirtatious role playing. Like her husband, as well, he harbored a suspicion that she had invited the events onto herself. As Hüsniye eventually explained, he grew increasingly flirtatious over a period of several months, until one day—while everyone was away from home—he attempted to rape her.

Although Hüsniye would not offer any more details, she said: "Like that, I entered into a depression. I can't explain to you how bad it was. I went to Zöhre Ana, but I couldn't look Zöhre Ana in the face. I didn't want her to see." Despite Hüsniye's efforts, Zöhre Ana did see. "Zöhre Ana mentioned this topic in front of everyone. She said to the crowd that there are those among us today who will be attacked even by their own relatives." Hüsniye, rather than experiencing Zöhre Ana's words as a reassuring acknowledgment of familial injustice, felt deeply ashamed. Even though Zöhre Ana did not identify her by name, Hüsniye explained that, "This was my destruction. Then I fell ill. I stopped going to the store. I withdrew into a cloud . . . a heaviness entered into me." Within a year, the store would be out of business and her husband's brother-in-law would be dead, having been stabbed in an altercation outside a bar.

By this point, Hüsniye wanted desperately to escape her marriage. Her relationship with her husband had transformed into something that bore only a vague resemblance to her initial hope for loving companionship and mutual respect, a relationship that had been imagined at the outset as the possible grounds of a just world. Zöhre Ana, however, refused to allow Hüsniye to separate from her husband. "I wanted to leave him several times," she explained. "I was so serious that I had gone to my father. I had retained a lawyer. And once more I consulted Zöhre Ana. Even though I didn't tell her what was going on, she knew. She knows everything. She told me that she never wants people to be separated." At home, her appeal to Zöhre Ana for marital advice only attracted more violence. There was, of course, a cruel irony at play here, in that Zöhre Ana was refusing to allow Hüsniye to escape the very violence Zöhre Ana had played such a large part in inciting.

*   *   *

The stories Hüsniye shared with me about Zöhre Ana spilled forth with such fury that they seemed to possess neither ends nor limits. The ever-multiplying accounts and recollections that, together, filled up our relationship expressed an intense passion for conversation. I would later recognize this passion for conversation as an instance of a more encompassing love for relating with others. This love was a defining sensibility in her life, one that left her perpetually open to both the possibilities of the world and the suffering that accompanies relationships repeatedly betrayed: passionate stories of courtship and marriage alongside accounts of her husband's recurrent brutality; a fondness for work and the new friendships working made possible being ground under economic and familial demands; parental love interweaving with the violence of *gecekondu* poverty; the welcoming of relatives into one's home only to have one's hospitality viciously violated. Throughout these accounts, I was struck by an enduring sensibility that structured Hüsniye's engagement with life, a sense that the world was fundamentally innocent and that people, despite their tendency toward betrayal, were ultimately good.

In following the play of wounding and healing that runs through Hüs-niye's relationship with Zöhre Ana, we begin to appreciate the protean qualities of Zöhre Ana's presence. On the one hand, Zöhre Ana was a presence that facilitated Hüsniye's work of inhabiting a world fractured by disillusionments and broken relationships. She found a sense of recognition in Zöhre Ana, a feeling that her suffering was being acknowledged and taken seriously by another. Zöhre Ana's presence oriented relationships and bodies together toward a common object of devotion and, in the process, enabled others to gather around Hüsniye. Meanwhile, Zöhre Ana's images and language colored moral bonds that held together families and extended networks of neighbors, co-workers, and kin. These bonds, however, were not ties of unalloyed hope and compassion. Zöhre Ana's presence would repeatedly, and capriciously, transform into a menacing and destructive force. Fear and violence run continually through the relations of obligation and indebtedness that bind people to Zöhre Ana and to one another. In Hüsniye's case alone, we find a dead brother-in-law, a paralyzed *dede*, a stalking pervert, a fractured marriage, and a succession of emotional breaks. To this I would add the violence of Hüsniye's continual blaming of herself for her own suffering, a turning on oneself that both Hüsniye's husband and Zöhre Ana colluded in.

As this suggests, the defining effects of Zöhre Ana's presence in Hüsniye's life came not through moments of "healing" or "recovery," but instead through a series of mutually conditioning experiences of wounding and retribution. While Zöhre Ana may be best known as the mender of wounds, she appears in these instances to be equally capable of inflicting fresh injury. As the book's opening vignette illustrated—where a family becomes divided when the father comes to no longer accept her saintly authority—Zöhre Ana just as easily forges and intensifies social ties as she leaves them severed and in ruins. And perhaps this is one lesson to draw from Hüsniye's account, that recovery is to be found—perhaps, at times—in the very infliction of new wounds, which might well be a return to the site of an earlier wounding.

Care and the Vitality of the Ordinary

In searching for a language to speak about the distributive role of Zöhre Ana in Hüsniye's life and the implications, as well as limits, of thinking such entanglements through an idiom of the therapeutic, I want to return to Das's reflections on the relationship between violence and the ordinary. Das, rather than locating healing and recovery in transcendent moments of release or escape, grants primacy to the everyday. "There is no pretense here," she writes, "at some grand project of recovery but simply the question of how everyday tasks of surviving—having a roof over your head, being able to send your children to school, being able to do the work of the everyday without constant fear of being attacked—could be accomplished. I found that the making of the self was located, not in the shadow of some ghostly past, but in the context of making the everyday inhabitable" (2007: 216). This unassuming gesture toward the everyday is intended to draw our attention away from a narrow pursuit of dramatic moments of radical transformation or personal insight and toward the socially distributed work of recovery laboring within the seeming banalities of everyday life. It shifts our gaze, as Das puts it, "to the inhabitation that comes not from the knowing subject but from the subject as engaged in the work of stitching, quilting, and putting together relationships in everyday life" (161).[10] It is here where we can conceive of Zöhre Ana assisting people like Hüsniye in their efforts to make the everyday inhabitable, as she offers one the possibility of reimaging the limits of past wounds.

As my attention became drawn to these relations of care as the interpersonal grounds of therapeutic possibility, I would find myself working against the grain of much contemporary scholarship on both religious and therapeutic experience, which locates the persuasiveness of religious or therapeutic speech in the embodied and performative qualities of speech encounters (between patients and healers, saints and supplicants, speakers and listeners, and so forth). Earlier, I referred to this as an approach to therapeutic efficacy that relied tacitly on a model of command and event. That said, I do not want to underestimate the significance of bodily processes for therapeutic experience (see Csordas 1994, 1995; Desjarlais 1992; Kapferer 1991; Levi 1999). Indeed, there was no shortage of somatic themes among the accounts of those seeking the assistance of healers—of bodies becoming warm at the site of a healer's touch, the feeling of goose bumps (*tüyleri ürpermek*) in the presence of a healer, or one's body trembling uncontrollably when touched or looked at by a healer. Hüsniye's repeated depiction of her visits to Zöhre Ana as the transformation of a heavy and lethargic body into a light and buoyant body, for instance, was a prevalent idiom through which experiences of healing were narrated. Recalling Ibrahim's treatment of Fadime's niece as well, it is difficult to ignore the way that yawning, as a somatic expression of the presence of *cin*, enrolls the entirety of one's body—the contortion of one's face, the twisting of arms and shoulders, and the pressing of legs outward.

As I attempted to situate moments of intense bodily experience within people's lives, however, I came to conceive of them as sensible thresholds within a far longer trajectory of life that, in turn, took form within dense fields of social relatedness and the otherwise unexceptional flow of the ordinary. This is not to suggest that bodily experience is merely an expression of relatedness, or that healing can in any way be disentangled from one's embodied orientation to the world (Csordas 1994). There is certainly a complex set of exchanges at play here, as when Hüsniye described her embodied sense of release and buoyancy as tracking alongside an altered orientation to her interpersonal relationships, within which she felt more open and compassionate toward others after her visits to the *dergâh*. Rather, it is to emphasize the complexity of social ties and intersubjective relations through which meaning is made and bodily experience thematized. After all, there was no single event or encounter that could enclose Hüsniye's experiences with Zöhre Ana, much as there was no single origin to Hüsniye's suffering—her sense of life as a succession of breaks and a malaise of fracturing dreams. It is for these reasons that I suggest we think again about the conventional ways anthropologists conceive relationships between language, experience, and the body—relationships, put otherwise, between command, event, and life—when speaking about therapeutic efficacy.[11]

Although Hüsniye's story could be told as an account of the importance of Zöhre Ana's meaning for her visitors and followers—placing special emphasis on the resonant Alevi symbols, icons, and idioms that Hüsniye found at Zöhre Ana's *dergâh* and in her ritual language, as well as the specifically secular modern form of Zöhre Ana's saintliness—this would be to obscure the ways suffering and healing take shape through the interpersonal densities of people's social existence. Robert Orsi's reflections on the sociality of Catholic devotionalism in the U.S. (2005) seem particularly useful in clarifying this point. "In individuals' and communities' experience of [Mary]," he writes, "the Virgin draws deeply on the whole history of relationships, living and dead, present and absent. She borrows from and contributes to memories, needs, fantasies, hopes, and fears. . . . To tell the story of any person's bond with Mary, it is necessary to recount the story of all his or her relationships, from childhood to adulthood, and to locate Mary in her dynamic place among them. The Marian devotional world is an interpersonally crowded one" (2005: 60). Although one should proceed with great caution in drawing comparisons between Islamic and Christian conceptions of sainthood, Orsi assists us in recognizing the socially and temporally distributive qualities of the forms of care realized through Zöhre Ana's presence. Put otherwise, in taking seriously my interlocutors' emphasis on the transactional registers of healing and recovery, over the performative and embodied qualities of therapeutic events, I have emphasized the ways these meanings are made tangible in a world crowded with interpersonal relationships, which are themselves the intersubjective grounds of meaning making and therapeutic experience.

If my argument returns healing to the density of social relationships, it is not a field of social relating that we can regard as a passive or stable stage on which lives unfold. As Hüsniye makes abundantly clear, these relationships are continually forming and reforming over time—as they enter into novel settings, encounter unforeseen situations, resonate in unexpected ways with past relationships, and give rise to new visions of future possibility. As such, there are no straightforward accounts of Zöhre Ana's effects on people's lives. Zöhre Ana is an unstable figure and her presence cannot be reduced to or contained by single qualities or effects. And in this forming and reforming of relations, her presence multiplies and diversifies. In addition to Zöhre Ana the *evliya*, we find Zöhre Ana the friend and confidant; Zöhre Ana the image on the wall and ideal to which one strives; Zöhre Ana the speaker and disembodied textual voice; a voice of reason and of one's conscience; a person in whom one seeks solace and a force that one fears; a person who works to repair betrayed bonds as she instigates new fractures; an object of devotion and an excuse to get out of the house; a creator and destroyer of social worlds; and a site of both great anxiety and *deşarj*. All these varying forms and intensities, in turn, enter into and mediate multiple forms of relatedness—among family and relatives, to herself and her past, between colleagues and neighbors, employers and physicians, and across generations past and future.

Given the densely interwoven complexity of these fields of relatedness, it is worth reminding ourselves of the dramatic asymmetries that comprise them and how differently they can appear depending on where one is located. If one visited Zöhre Ana on any given day, Hüsniye might well be one of the scores of people spread throughout the *dergâh*'s open cement courtyard, passing the time in idle conversation in anticipation of Zöhre Ana's arrival. She could be one of many people making their way on hands and knees up to Zöhre Ana, kissing her feet, waiting for Zöhre Ana's touch, continuing past, and leaving the *dergâh* to return home. For the disengaged observer, little of this fleeting exchange would suggest the richness of social experience it realized. Little would indicate the encompassing fullness of Zöhre Ana's presence in Hüsniye's life. Even in our case, I have been able to capture but a fragment of this complexity. There are many aspects of Hüsniye's story that I do not know, or do not understand. Why, despite my efforts to talk about her parents' reaction to her husband's abuse, did conversations always shift away from them? Why does her father disappear from her story? And why was she willing to tell me all this? What did she mean when she said that God had sent me to her and that "your presence rescued me from the edge of the precipice (*beni bir uçurumdan kurtardı*)"? What was I to her? Perhaps more time together would have resolved these questions. But perhaps not. Perhaps only further questions would arise, as we entered into unanticipated constellations of relatedness. In either case, if I were to formulate an argument about the locus of therapeutic efficacy, this is where I would begin. Rather than seeking out those moments of ascendance or dramatic rupture, I would seek to make sense of the explosive vitality that inheres in the mundane indeterminacies and intimacies of social relationships.[12]

In light of this book's overarching concern with the entanglement of healing and secularism—as overlapping projects of world making similarly invested in the constraints and affordances of subjectivity, the ordering of interpersonal relationships, the limits of sensibility and bodily experience, and the imagining of possible futures—what, then, does this approach to the therapeutic teach us about secularism's politics of aesthetics, and vice versa? How do the large-scale projects of political, economic, and ethical world making associated with secularism bear on Hüsniye's experiences of suffering and healing? Foremost, Hüsniye's case makes abundantly clear that we cannot read outward from the signs, idioms, and forms of secularist aesthetics to the qualities of one's experience of suffering and recovery. Although relationships are necessarily embedded in conditions born of particular places and times, the ways relationships and conditions inform one another is rarely straightforward. As Rancière would put it, "there is no criterion for establishing an appropriate correlation between the politics of aesthetics and the aesthetics of politics" (2004: 62).

While such experiences of suffering and care may be inextricable from the world making projects of "secularism"—or "Islam," or "market capitalism," or "neoliberalism"—I have resisted the urge (an urge that is resisted far too rarely these days) to read Hüsniye's life as but a symptom of large-scale assemblages of political, economic, and medical power. I have resisted, that is, the inclination to render their influences as self-evident and reduce the complexity of subjectivities to the effects of the machinations of structural forces. To lean on the eloquence of Kathleen Stewart, "I am trying to bring them into view as a scene of immanent force, rather than leave them looking like dead effects imposed on an innocent world" (2007: 1).[13]

While it is not reducible to them, the machinations of large-scale structural forces are readily apparent in the continual undoing and repairing of Hüsniye's life. Her struggle for autonomy and gendered equality, for instance, became caught up within patriarchal demands for domesticity. Ideals of freedom and independence were recoded within familial bonds as sexual promiscuity. A neglectful relationship and a passion for relating entered into a workplace imagined as a de-gendered space of collegial interaction, itself a product of the meeting of secularist ideology and economic development. Her experience of spousal abuse came to stand as an instantiation of those forms of intimate violence that tend to grow within particular configurations of gender and economic possibility. At the same time, we can readily find traces of secularism's world and subject making aspirations in many of the attributes that drew Hüsniye toward Zöhre Ana—as when Zöhre Ana's saintly embodiment of Kemalist models of womanhood redoubles her desire to work (which, in a way, also confirmed her own father's love), as well as the multiple additional ways she embodied a saintliness that realized, rather than opposed, secular modern ideals.[14]

This emphasis on the experience of Zöhre Ana's presence as an experience of relations and relatedness, however, suggests an additional way to conceptualize the entanglement of healing and secularism—one that draws attention not only to the meanings of saintliness in secular modern conditions, but also to the sorts of relationships that give meaning to life. It is useful at this point to recall the specific hostilities that the religious healer attracted in Turkey's history of secular reform. As described earlier, in their efforts to subordinate religious to political authority in state institutions and more tightly regulate religious expression in the emerging nation, secular reformers of the early republic struggled to undermine forms of religious authority deemed threatening to the state. For these reformers, the figure of the religious healer represented a collection of regressive and outmoded sensibilities and habits of thought that were viewed as detrimental to the nation's development. Moreover, the networks of disciples and followers associated with these figures were not only regarded as potential sites of political opposition, but also actively suppressed as an aspect of a wider assault on those elements of social life deemed to run contrary to the forms of sociability and obligation the state was seeking to cultivate as the social basis of its authority.

The relationships that form with and through Zöhre Ana must be situated within such a history of secular reform, with its forcible and at times violent subordination of religious authority to political will. The aesthetics of relating that characterized Hüsniye's relationship with Zöhre Ana (those varying forms, roles, and intensities of Zöhre Ana that worked their way through the folds of her social life) was necessarily embedded in secularism's politics of aesthetics, and its organizing of sociabilities and constellations of social relatedness within the limits of the sensible. In this regard, while an important element of the animosity that Zöhre Ana and her followers attracted certainly involved accusations of credulity, her repeated arrests and continual surveillance, I would suggest, grow out of this specific aspect of secularism's history. They betray, that is, a political paranoia about forms of social obligation, indebtedness, and relatedness seen as threatening the state's efforts of making and remaking the interpersonal grounds of its own reality.

This paranoia is of course exaggerated. In fact, there is a distinctive instability or fragility to these interpersonal bonds of religious obligation and therapeutic possibility that makes them particularly ill suited for building the sorts of political opposition that the state fears. For every flash of exceptional ability or inclination toward ritual expertise that takes hold and forms a social density that endures through time, there are many more that do not. This tendency toward dissolution and fragility, as I argue in the next chapter, will offer us a final lesson on the entanglement of therapeutic power and secularism's politics of aesthetics.

Before turning to such a lesson, however, I want to return briefly to the hagiographic. I raised the question of the hagiographic in a previous chapter as a methodological problem. How does one write about a person such as Zöhre Ana, who never seems to be "offstage" and whose sainthood is premised, in many regards, on the departure of this "person" from the stage? How, in other words, does one write about those who are dead but not yet entombed? In Hüsniye's account, we come upon another means of responding to such questions, a response grounded not in the literary mode but in the genre of living. "Hagiography," Orsi writes, "is best understood as a creative process that goes on and on in the circumstances of everyday life, as people add their own experiences of a saint to his or her vita and contemporaries get woven into the lives of the saints" (2005: 113). In Hüsniye's case, Zöhre Ana's hagiography continues to be lived.

When we last talked, Hüsniye described feeling deeply depressed. She felt lost, that her husband was no longer attracted to her, and that she was of little worth to others. In the hope of bringing purpose back to her life, she had decided to return again to work. With this in mind, Hüsniye visited the *dergâh* and silently wished, as she waited to see Zöhre Ana, that she would be able to find a job. Soon after, she was hired, again, as a typist in a government ministry. As I prepared to leave Ankara when the research for this book was finishing up, I called her office. One of her co-workers answered and said that Hüsniye wasn't at work. "You know," he said, as he lowered his voice, "she has psychological problems."

Chapter 6

Healing Secular Life: Two Regimes of Loss

Niyazi Berkes, the celebrated historian of Turkish secularism, in a discussion of secularist historiography during the early years of the republic, writes:

> The secularist historiography brought to attention also a facet that was either ignored or rejected previously—the Turkish national spirit shows itself at its best within Islamic religiosity not through orthodoxy, but through the unorthodox varieties of Islam. This could be judged from the survivals of the national culture wherever and whenever non-orthodox Islam prevailed among the Turks and from the extinction of any trace of national tradition where and when orthodoxy reigned. Amazingly abundant and variegated, the mystical literature (the only literature besides the folk that may be called Turkish), heterodox sects, heretical movements, and the like became objects of interest [among early republican historians] not for purpose of theological controversy, or to provide a nationalist basis for a religious reform, but for a secular purpose—for the recovery of national culture. (1964: 501)

The challenge facing these early secularist historians, as described by Berkes, would be familiar to post-colonial and post-independence nationalist movements elsewhere. How does one formulate a model of nationalism that at once concedes to a universal modernity and asserts a national singularity? The response that Berkes details would also be familiar: a turn to the historian to unearth elements of one's own past that can confirm the cultural uniqueness of the emerging nation.

The bind for these historians of the Turkish nation—unlike the post-colonial historian—was that there existed no distinctly pre-colonial past to mine for evidence of national authenticity. While the emergence of the Turkish Republic in 1923 bears many of the marks of colonial liberation and post-colonial nation-building—an anti-imperialist war of independence, the consolidation of a sovereign territory through nationalist exclusions (of ethnic, linguistic, and religious difference), a zealous reinvention of itself based on a selective appropriation and tacit recognition of European dominance,[1] and a tendency toward top-down, authoritarian state projects of national development that portrayed modernization as an unambiguous process of progress and enlightenment—the Ottoman state that preceded the republic was a sovereign political entity, not an external colonizing force.[2] The response of the historians described by Berkes was to rummage through the abundance and variegation of the present for remnants of a past that had escaped the homogenizing forces of both Ottoman governance and Ottoman forms of Islamic orthodoxy. The struggle for nationalist liberation was thus to be fought on two fronts—against Western imperialism, on the one hand, and "orthodox" Islam, on the other. The secularist historian's role would be critical here, for it was he who would labor in the interstices of society, amid religious practices and textual traditions existing at the margins of religious law and state authority, in order to recover the nation's lost spirit.[3]

Over the course of my fieldwork, as I listened to stories of loss, suffering, and healing taking shape through the presence of religious healers, I was time and again struck by the unexpected affinities between the therapeutic desires of patients and the scholarly labors of these early secularist historians. I was struck, in particular, by the corresponding ways in which the two approached the present. For patient and historian alike, much of what was readily available in one's surroundings was to be distrusted; little if anything escaped the destructive influence of large-scale political, economic, and religious forces. Yet, for both, the present harbored forms of latent potentiality—one therapeutic, the other political—that needed to be recovered in order for a different future to become imaginable. Indeed, it seemed as if the problematic identified by Berkes was not merely historiographical but therapeutic as well.

Noting this affinity is not to suggest that healing was conceived simply as mining one's past for a new justification for the present, in the sense that national liberation was envisioned as a process wherein a forgotten past could be unearthed and used to support contemporary political ambitions. Rather, I was struck by the way the two projects of world and history making related to the present through a corresponding structure of loss. That is, in stories of healing and being healed where the figure of the religious healer assumed center stage—stories largely set outside the network of state-authorized health clinics and hospitals—one finds a repetition of the historian's desire to rummage through the folds of a corrupt present in the hopes of recovering elements of a lost past that can set the course for a new future.

This was not the case in all interviews, to be clear at the outset. Nor should we expect as much. The reasons that bring people to healers and the sorts of experiences these relationships make possible, as Chapter 5 demonstrated, are always multiple and dynamic.[4] Such corresponding structures of loss, however, did appear to converge with particular regularity in stories that recounted the failing of a healer's abilities—where healers gave up their practice, patients were unable to find relief, devotees rejected the authority they so intensely desired, or patients came to doubt the very possibility of healing. Of the many types of stories I gathered over the course of my fieldwork, I am therefore concerned in this chapter with stories of redoubled loss, where experiences of personal loss and suffering join with a foreclosure of therapeutic possibility as a healer's abilities are recognized as absent, ineffective, or lost. Rather than the positive formulation of religious and therapeutic authority that marked previous chapters (as in its form, presence, circulation, recognition, and experience), this chapter attends to the sense of loss and absence that inhabits the intensities of therapeutic experience. I argue that accounts of therapeutic foreclosure not only express a feeling that the ability of healers to convene and bind an audience is fragile, but also bring into view a more pervasive structure of loss embedded in and enabled by secularism's politics of aesthetics.

In an effort to explore such a redoubling of loss, I juxtapose two accounts of loss below. The first narrates this foreclosure of therapeutic possibility as a confirmation, if not a celebration, of a history of secular nation making; the second introduces the forms of mourning that can coincide with the recognition of a healer's diminishing abilities. By attending to the play of loss and possibility that each story gives voice to—stories that I came to recognize as indexing two regimes of loss—we will encounter a set of divergent yet interdependent assumptions regarding the possible force of the past on the present, which are at once distinctive understandings of the therapeutic possibilities of the world. In so doing, this discussion will offer a final set of lessons concerning the possibilities, as well as violences, of secular political rule in the interpersonal intimacies of therapeutic care.

Late Secularist Historiography of Loss: Celebrating Lost Life

When I first met Aydın, he had recently retired from the small grocery and general store he had owned and operated for more than three decades. Aydın grew up in a village in the central Anatolian province of Çorum and moved to Hürriyet in the 1960s, among the first wave of Alevi settlers. I was introduced to Aydın by Ali's son, whom we met in Chapter 3. Ali had taken his father to see an *ocaklı* because of his father's persistent feelings of exhaustion and unhappiness following heart surgery. It was through Ali that I met Feride, a local *kurşuncu*, who had also treated Ali's other son several times when he was a small child. When Ali's son mentioned my research to Aydın, Aydın insisted that we meet. He had an important story to share with me—a story about his childhood in the village, his friendship with a *hoca*, and a life-defining incident with a *muska*.

According to Aydın, for me to understand the significance of this incident, I first had to receive a lesson on the history of the *cinci hoca*. Such lessons were common over the course of my research. The meaning of the present, as my friends and neighbors repeatedly insisted, was only appreciated by situating it within the sweep of history. It was in Aydın's impulse to explain the *cinci hoca* by recourse to history that I came to appreciate Aydın as a late secularist historian of the exilic. To honor Aydın's skills as a historian and storyteller, and to illustrate the complexity of these sorts of narratives, I have included below an uninterrupted translation of a large portion of our conversation.

> The *cinci hoca*? These practices are not as widespread today as they were in the past, in the time of the Sultans. In the time of the Sultans, matters were governed by Islam, through Shari'ah. Originally, this was based on the religion of the Prophet Muhammed. Later, however, Caliphs appeared. They were like the mullahs of Iran. And then *kadıs* [judges of Islamic law] appeared, and *müftüs* [scholars of

Islamic law], and so on. A common legal system was then set up, one that reflected the time. It was like a constitution, much as with today's European Union. Everything was to be governed by religious law. But this was not the original religious law of the Prophet Muhammed and the religion spread by [the first] Muslims. They distorted every aspect of it. Every one of these mullahs who appeared after the Prophet contradicted one another.

If just anyone says that drinking coffee is unlawful (*haram*), does drinking coffee become unlawful? They actually struggled against coffee drinking for some time. Then, after time passed and they were convinced that coffee was permissible (*helal*), tea appeared. "Oh, tea, it looks like wine! Ehh, tea is the color of wine!" So it was declared *haram*. Later, however, they would allow tea drinking. But then this new technology called "radio" appeared and they proclaimed, "Oh! This is the work of Satan. Listening to the radio is a sin. Satan is inside this thing." It too became *haram*. This is how they talked. Thereafter, they were opposed to all technology. This [opposition to technology] is not something that the Prophet would have agreed with. These were fabrications of their own imaginations.

Meanwhile, they created an environment where women could no longer speak out or escape the four walls of their homes. "Oh! That is a sin, this is a sin. . . . it's a sin for a woman's hair to be uncovered, it's a sin for a woman to go to school, it's a sin to write a letter, it's forbidden to hold a man's hand . . ." According to them, a man could take seven wives if he wanted. Oh please, is this acceptable? Does this make any sense? If there are 10 million men, there are 10 million women. For every man there is a woman. This is a fact of nature. And if I take seven wives, that leaves seven bachelors. Is this proper? No, it is not. You are taking someone's share.

Atatürk, the great original thinker of his times, did something about this. [During the final years of the Ottoman Empire,] Europe, England . . . and even New Zealand were all about. They were coming from all sides. Turkey was done with. Everyone was planning to take their share. At that time, Atatürk was an inspector general in the military. He was sent to Samsun, and that was where he began his work. The British were coming to Istanbul. And the French. The Italians were coming from the southeast. The Greeks had made it as far as Ankara. Against all of these, Atatürk established an island. He drew borders. And then he proclaimed, "This is Turkey." He then brought the law from Sweden to Turkey. He took Sweden's constitution and said, "Turkey, without question, will become a democracy. It will become a republic. It will be secular. This state will not be governed by religion. If religion is allowed to govern the state, Turkey will not advance."

On this subject, Atatürk had opponents. Again, it was those *hoca*s [meaning, in this case, religious leaders more generally]. Those people with beards (*sakallılar*). Most of them were Sunni Muslims. They opposed this. They said, "Oh! Is this possible? We can't abandon Shari'ah." Atatürk responded, "Oh, I'll deal with this. We are going to establish a republic." When he proclaimed this [before those gathered at the Sivas Congress[5]], they established the republic. The assembly agreed, and they established the republic. We owe everything to Atatürk.

Thanks to Atatürk, whatever subject you want to research—chemistry, physics, biology—you can study. The presence of every type of technology in Turkey is because of Atatürk. He established tractor factories. He brought airplanes. All of our sugar used to be imported. All of our textiles as well. Everything used to be imported. Atatürk laid the foundation for all of our first factories.

But his life was cut short. Before he died, he said, "Do not change this republic." For some time, Atatürk's republic continued moving forward. And then [Adnan] Menderes came.[6] When Menderes's party was elected and he established his government, the call to prayer (*ezan*) was sung in Turkish. They changed this. Menderes, as the head of the government, changed the call to prayer back to Arabic. Can anyone read Arabic? Nobody understood it. And then, those who had nostalgia for the old system began to develop a great interest in Shari'ah. "Let's bring back the old Ottoman system," they said. "Let it be again like it was in Ottoman times. Let's govern again with religion. Let's bind everything to religion."

They began to set up *imam hatip* schools [for training government-employed religious personnel]. In these *imam hatip* schools, they taught their lessons entirely in Arabic. They began introducing Atatürk to their students as a bad person. They said he was an infidel (*gavur*). They said that he was a Christian. Then they talked about how he drank rakı and how rakı and wine are forbidden in Islam. And so on, and so on, and so on. They raised these small children listening to these things continuously. And this spread throughout Turkey. The children believed this, because their brains had yet to fully develop. They couldn't recognize if it was true or not. So those [wanting to bring back the Ottoman system] who worked in the state tried to undermine the power of the military. They wanted to bring about a revolution, like Khomeini did in Iran. They wanted to bring back the Shari'ah of the Ottoman era. But Atatürk's system had already become established. It was established. It was open to technology.

Now, this *cinci hoca*. With a doctor, patients are examined. Their blood is analyzed. The doctor runs tests. The doctor will administer the treatments in the sight of the patient. The *cinci hoca*, however, will make two pieces of paper with old writing [Arabic], tell the patient to soak them in water, and hope that God will allow the *muska* to succeed. This is how it was in the old Ottoman times. It was that sophisticated. For this reason, many people were dying. Many people were dying of tuberculosis. They were dying from smallpox. They were dying from cholera. Meanwhile, in Europe and in America, scientists were researching all of these diseases and had developed technologies to treat them. Turkey was alone in not being able to use them. An effect of this was that the number of religious conservatives (*dinciler*) increased. And today we have the Hezbollah, who are ready to cut off the head of anyone who is not a Muslim.[7] Come on, is this really possible in Turkey? Everyone is Muslim. I mean, there isn't anyone who isn't Muslim.

Now, as for this matter of the *muska*, I don't believe in them at all.

In the old days, in the villages, people used to use antiquated plows. There was no tractor in my village. It was a poor village. The people of Anatolia, before Atatürk, were poor. Before technology arrived, we used these antiquated plows. In the mornings, you would get the oxen from the stable and take them to the field, where you'd find the plow and the chain for the plow. You'd seed the field by hand. If God sent enough rain, then there would be abundant wheat. If not, you had nothing. In short, we lived with very little.

In our village, there was a large room where people gathered. Older people and important people from the village gathered there, people the same age as my father and grandfather. They would tell stories to young children like myself. They would talk about how they saw *cinler* and *şeytanlar* [spirits and demons] gathered down by the stream, celebrating as if it was a big wedding. The *cinler* were celebrating and dancing (*halay çekiyorlar*). I was a child, right? I believed everything. You know, grown ups would never lie, right? And they would just keep telling these stories, without pause. And I kept listening. I kept listening and I kept growing. I grew up listening to these stories.

Now, in my village, there was a *hoca*. This *hoca* would lead prayers. He would explain religious matters. And he wrote *muska*. The *hoca* had a little book with prayers in it. People would come to him and explain their problems—a stomachache, a toothache, back pain—and he would look it up in the book and write a *muska*. You see, there weren't any doctors back then. That is what we did.

When I was still young, maybe fourteen or fifteen years old, I became friends with the *hoca*. I spent a lot of time with him. He taught me how to read and write in Arabic. And then one day, my mother became ill. She said "Go to the *hoca*, have him write a *muska* for me." But the *hoca* wasn't in the village. He had apparently come here, to Ankara. So he wasn't able to write the *muska*. I went back to my mother and said, "The *hoca* is not here." "He went to Ankara," I said. "The *muska* can't be written." While I was taking care of her, she said to me, "I haven't been able to sleep at all. If the *hoca* could have written the *muska*, I'd be comfortable. I'd be able to sleep." I kept waiting for the *hoca*. After a week, he still hadn't returned. And my mother, every day, she remained sleepless. She was sick to the point where she couldn't sleep.

I then went to my room, hiding from my mother, and wrote a *muska*. Just like the *hoca* would have, I wrote three *muska*. I told my mother that the *hoca* had returned and had written these three *muska*. One of the *muska* was put under the bed where she slept. One *muska* was placed in a glass of water, which my mother drank. And one was burned inside of the room. The match was struck and the *ayet* in the *muska* went up in flames. After that, my mother recovered. How she slept! She felt so comfortable. In the morning, she said, "I haven't been able to sleep at all for a week. But now, my illness has passed." This was my incident with the *muska*.

When the *hoca* came back. I told him that I had written a *muska* for my mother and that I had told her it was from him. And that she got better. "How is this so?" I asked the *hoca*. "How is it with these *cins*? In all honesty, those stories you hear about *cins*—those stories about people looking in a glass of water and seeing a *cin*—are they really seeing a *cin*? If so, show me." And the *hoca* responded, "There is definitely no such thing." So I asked my father: "Those spirits and demons that you described to me, those ones celebrating and dancing by the stream, did you see them?" My dad said, "No son. I did not see any such thing." He then explained that people were either describing their dreams or making it up. I asked the same question of my grandfather. He too said that he had never seen any spirits or demons.

I then asked the *hoca*, "Why then do you write *muska*?" This is what he told me. "In the time of Sultan Suleyman, oooh thousands of ages ago, there was a book that was written. It contained prayers that benefited people. It also contained mathematical formulas. We write *muskas* according to this book and give them to sick people. And either the *muska* does them well, or they die. If a person has a tumor, for instance, a brain tumor. While the tumor may be the original cause of the illness, the *muska* bolsters their morale (*moral bulmak*). Thereafter, the *muska* may do them well, or they may die, or they may remain the same." This is what the *hoca* said. He was a *hoca* who always spoke the truth. Our village *hoca* was an enlightened *hoca*. He wrote *muska* for the same reason that I wrote the *muska* for my mother. If my mother believes in them, then she will recover. It's psychological that is. In my opinion, it bolsters one's morale.

Readers by this point should find many aspects of Aydın's account familiar. We are reminded, for instance, that the figure of the *cinci hoca* does not belong to the order of the secular nation. For Aydın, the *hulufas* who corrupted Muhammed's message, the *imam hatip* schools that brainwashed children, and contemporary *cinci hoca*s who deceive their patients are all varying iterations of a commonly regressive social and historical force associated with Islamic orthodoxy. In each, those claiming to speak in the name of Islam not only corrupt the essence of Muhammed's original message, but also suppress individual autonomy and distort Atatürk's political vision of secular modern liberation. From Aydın, we learn, again, that integral to achieving this personal freedom and national liberation is the eradication of the conditions that sustain the practices of the *cinci hoca*.

Aydın's account should also be familiar in the way it positions a recurring set of nationalist juxtapositions across a recognizable temporality of the nation. A series of mutually conditioning distinctions—Ottoman/republican, theocracy/democracy, ignorant/enlightened, rural/urban—organize Aydın's historical narrative. These distinctions, in turn, are mapped across a temporal partition demarcated by the birth of the republic and the life of Atatürk, such that events in Aydın's narrative gain their meaning as they are positioned in relation to this partition—as occurring "before" the War of Independence (in an undifferentiated "time of the Sultans") or "after" the republic was proclaimed (in an age with technology, medicine, and history). For Aydın, the practices of the *cinci hoca* fall squarely on the side of the former. As a relic of an outmoded era, again, the *cinci hoca* does not belong to the temporal order of the modern nation.

Although we will return to consider the ways that Aydın characterizes the *cinci hoca* as indexing a set of pre-modern religious and social potentialities capable of persisting latent within secular modern conditions, I want to first draw attention to the structure of loss embedded in Aydın's historical narrative. In his account, we find a story that stages the loss of a distinctive worldly capacity, both personal and collective. On the one hand, this is a story of a lost or foreclosed future for Aydın. A generation earlier, this incident with the *muska* might well have marked the beginning of his career as a *cinci hoca*.[8] On the other hand, this is a story that foretells the failing of a community's common sense, a transforming distribution of the sensible that can no longer breathe the same life into a particular conception of the world—one where *cins* are ever-present both in one's surroundings and in one's stories. It is useful to keep in mind here the way that the autobiographical and historical are mutually embedded in Aydın's account, such that this period of his life is portrayed as rehearsing in miniature the story of the nation's liberation.

In both instances, for Aydın, these were not forms of loss that deserved mourning. Quite the opposite. They were to be celebrated, for with their passing came new possibilities for a more just, rational, and free world. For Aydın, they marked the condition of his and the nation's liberation.

Importantly, I am not suggesting that Aydın experienced these incidents as moments of personal, let alone national liberation. The intensity with which he narrated the story's conclusion—where he confronts his parents and other village elders about the existence of *cins*—suggests that feelings of anger and betrayal, rather than emancipation, defined his experiences at the time. Ascribing emancipatory implications to these events would thus come later. In this regard, Aydın's account shares the teleological conceits of Berkes and his secularist historians, where past events are read as leading ineluctably to the liberation of the nation and the birth of the secular republic. In other words, the sense of both loss and emancipation that Aydın describes seems to be as indebted to the events themselves as to their later recounting.

The point I am struggling to make is that the sense of loss that characterizes Aydın's story resides not within the event itself. Rather, the event only gains the quality of loss in its subsequent narrativization. Slavoj Žižek captures this argument well when he writes: "the paradox to be fully accepted is that when a certain historical moment is (mis)perceived as the moment of loss of some quality, upon closer inspection it becomes clear that the lost quality emerged only at this very moment of its alleged loss. . . . [N]arrativization occludes this paradox by describing the process in which the object is first given and then gets lost" (1997: 12–13). The significance of this point concerning the coincidence of emergence and loss will become clearer as we juxtapose Aydın's account against the next section's complementary story of loss, one that portrays in more detail the unfolding dissolution of a healer's ability to gather and hold an audience.

Archeology of Loss: Mourning Lost Life

Just as there was widespread contempt for figures such as Zöhre Ana the *evliya* or Ibrahim the *cinci hoca*, there was also no shortage of people willing to attest to their extraordinary powers. On my visits to Zöhre Ana's compound, for instance, followers would regularly offer me a large ledger—one of many being stored in the foundation's offices—that compiled hundreds of written testimonials detailing the miraculous cures brought about by Zöhre Ana. As I pored through the testimonials, I would repeatedly find myself overcome by their uncanny familiarity, feeling as if I were looking at the earliest recorded versions of the stories that I now heard with such consistency and passion circulating among visitors and followers at the *der-gâh*. While such testimonials interested me in their regularity, they were also lifeless stories; little remained of the ambiguity, indeterminacy, and uncertainty of the experiences they narrated. These therapeutic narratives seemed to operate for a single purpose, to confirm Zöhre Ana's wondrous powers.

In contrast to the testimonial, I also found myself drawn to a genre of story that depicted a more ambiguous relationship to Zöhre Ana, stories that could be situated somewhere between the strident rejection of all forms of religious healing and the certainty of Zöhre Ana's testimonials. These were accounts that chronicled a process whereby a healer's powers, initially recognized, came to be regarded as absent or no longer effective. These were not stories of deception, such that the patient suddenly realizes that he or she had been duped and that the healer was and had always been a fraud. Indeed, in the way they recount an initial intensity of desire and hope that experiences a gradual process of disillusionment, the language of "fraudulence" and "authenticity" seemed particularly unhelpful in analyzing these narratives.[9] In addition to extending our discussion of the dynamic nature of relationships that form between healers and those seeking their assistance, these accounts also bring into view a distinctive configuration of loss that will be the focus of this section.

Where the declining fortunes of the *cinci hoca* was cause for Aydın's celebration—as the condition for his and the nation's liberation—the story that I want to examine now inspired a countervailing sense of loss. Rather than regarding such figures as the *cinci hoca* as embodiments of a regressive religio-political sensibility in need of being eliminated, this account portrays the religious healer as representing a repository of religious capacities and worldly possibilities that are endangered by the destructive forces of secular modernity. As such, I regard this second story of loss as a sequel to the first. In it, the disappearance of religious healers and the increasing restriction of the language of suffering to the clinical and biomedical—which Aydın's life embodies and his story celebrates—becomes narrated in a gesture of mourning, as something vital and important being lost. These countervailing regimes of loss, as I will argue, suggest distinct ways of relating past to present, which also suggest distinct understandings of the therapeutic possibilities of the world. In this regard, if Aydın can be considered a late secularist historian of the exilic, I would characterize the subject of this section, Nihal, as a late secularist archeologist of loss.

*   *   *

When Nihal first visited Zöhre Ana in 1984, Zöhre Ana was still receiving visitors in the modest, single-story *gecekondu* home where she had received her first visions. Nihal had completed university a few years earlier and had been working since. At the time of our conversation—now forty years old, and with two young children—Nihal recalled that there was no specific illness or problem that prompted her first trip to Zöhre Ana. As with Hüsniye, she was interested in meeting the woman about whom she had been hearing rumors. Unlike many of the early visitors to Zöhre Ana, Nihal was not Alevi. She considered herself to be nominally Sunni—in the sense that, while familiar with the obligations associated with Sunnism, she was not raised in a religiously observant household. If pressed, Nihal would characterize herself as a secularist, although she did not care much for the label. After a handful of sporadic visits to Zöhre Ana, Nihal began to attend weekly gatherings held at the *dergâh*. She eventually became a regular participant. Nihal's relationship with Zöhre Ana and her participation in the events at the *dergâh* would trace the major period of Zöhre Ana's emergence and the consolidation of her saintly authority.

As with many of Zöhre Ana's regular visitors, Nihal's relationship with Zöhre Ana was not defined exclusively in therapeutic terms. At the time of her initial visits, Nihal was drawn to Zöhre Ana because she felt that something important was missing from her life. In her efforts to describe this feeling, Nihal drew attention to the intensity of experience that characterized these early visits to the *dergâh*. Sitting near Zöhre Ana, she described, was like "being close to the sun," close to "something very natural," "something very fundamental." "It was as if everything was there, and I was nothing. When Zöhre Ana came, she gave one look and saw everything." Nihal described feeling distinctly present and intensely close to Zöhre Ana at these moments.[10] There was a sense of intimacy and immediacy, in other words, that she was able to discover in Zöhre Ana's presence. For Nihal, the intense feelings of warmth and naturalness that she found in Zöhre Ana's presence represented the kinds of experience that she felt was missing from her life, and for which she was continually on the lookout. They embodied forms of "primitive" (*primitif*) experience, as she put it, that had become increasingly difficult to realize in the material, technological, and ideological conditions of modern life. Moreover, they were forms of experience that orthodox Islamic practice—with its emphasis on legal reasoning, textual interpretation, and restrained emotionality—actively suppressed.

As with Hüsniye, Nihal's experience of Zöhre Ana was inseparable from the experience of the relationships through which Zöhre Ana's presence moved and the interpersonal ties within which Nihal's experiences (of warmth, intimacy, and immediacy) grew. That is, there was a sociality in Zöhre Ana that Nihal found deeply compelling. She recalled fondly, for instance, the contagious quality of emotions while in Zöhre Ana's presence, of an intense feeling of agitation (*gerginlik*) sweeping the room, of a crowd swaying in unison and spontaneously bursting into tears. For Nihal, these gatherings, at their most intense, represented a dissolving of myriad individuals into a collective, swelling individuality. Moreover, this collective intimacy, as Nihal saw it, was both an extension of and a basis for the collective ethic of mutual caring and hospitality that animated social life around Zöhre Ana's home.

Rather than describing her encounters with Zöhre Ana as an experience of escape or transcendence, to recall the discussion in Chapter 5, Nihal's feelings of "closeness," "warmth," and "naturalness" suggested a descent into an intimate relatedness with the world. This was not a relationship, however, that was always reassuring. For Nihal, in order to understand Zöhre Ana one had to appreciate the relationship between this intimacy and the forms of fear that Zöhre Ana's presence could evoke in visitors. As Nihal put it, alongside feeling close to Zöhre Ana, and having a sense of release much as Hüsniye had, "seeing Zöhre Ana awakened in me a sense of dread (*dehşet*) and a sense of fear (*korku*)." Others depicted a similar reaction. Malik, a twenty-year-old visitor to Zöhre Ana, described it in these terms: "The first time I saw her, I was shocked. Truly, she knew my illness. She told me what my illness was. At that I trembled (*titremek*). I felt a real presence." Hüsniye also comes to mind: "I was with a friend, we sat and Zöhre Ana was looking at us. We weren't able to meet eyes, and my head began spinning. I wasn't able to look at her eyes. But how happy I felt inside. I felt indescribably happy. The world was mine. I was flying." For Nihal and others, then, this co-present sense of excitement and fear represented a defining phenomenological register of one's experience of Zöhre Ana's presence, much as yawning and the uncontrollable contortion of bodies characterized one's experience of the *cinci hoca*'s ritual expertise.

Nihal's recollections, however, were fundamentally elegiac. "If only you could have seen Zöhre Ana in those times," she explained. "That was a different era. A different era for Turkey." When Nihal and I met, some fifteen years since she first visited Zöhre Ana and nearly seven years since her last trip to the *dergâh*, she had little remaining interest in her. She described the sense of intimacy and presence that had drawn her to Zöhre Ana becoming increasingly difficult to achieve over the eight years of visiting the *dergâh*—as Zöhre Ana's accumulating wealth became more and more visible, as those controlling access to Zöhre Ana started choosing "milder" illnesses to increase the chances of displaying her curative powers, as the intimate intensity of gatherings gave way to regularized "performances" that self-consciously emulated folkloric performances, as a hierarchy of devotion came to separate her "followers" from "visitors," and as jealousy between followers began to poison friendships. Her last visit to Zöhre Ana would come in 1992.

Before considering in detail the factors that contributed to Nihal's waning interest in Zöhre Ana, I want to acknowledge the powerful explanatory narrative that awaits her account of disillusionment, as well as Aydın's story of personal and national enlightenment. That is, both would appear to exemplify the story, most famously told by Weber (1958), of the world's inescapable "disenchantment" and "secularization" at the hands of the rationalizing and calculating forces of modernity and capitalism. If held at a sufficient distance, we could indeed conceive of Nihal's disenthrallment as the world's enchantments succumbing to the advances of the secular modern, much as we could read Aydın's refusal to become a *cinci hoca* as signaling the demise of a particular conception of the world's wonders. Although this story has its appeal—one that Nihal herself was drawn to, as we will consider later—I want to examine here the ways that the complexity and texture of loss described by Nihal continually escaped such a narrative frame.

In particular, I want to consider the story of her waning interest in Zöhre Ana—this loss of worldly possibility commonly narrated as disenchantment—as it relates to a form of loss that structured her relationship with Zöhre Ana from the start. As I listened to Nihal's account of her early visits to Zöhre Ana and the intimate intensity of the gatherings, I was struck by the way that she engaged the present as if something of it was missing, an engagement in which she sought to recover or reclaim a lost potentiality. Making explicit the way these two forms of loss rely on one another will offer us an important lesson on the relationship between loss and secularism's politics of aesthetics. Toward this end, I want to think further about the specificity of Nihal's experiences with the assistance of Georges Bataille, a thinker whose reflections on religion and modernity offer a productive means for approaching the configurations of loss, desire, and secularism being described by Nihal.

The structure of experience that Nihal describes, at least during the early years of Zöhre Ana's career, encapsulates for Georges Bataille the substance of religious experience (1989). For Bataille, religious experience—or, in Bataille's terms, the "plethoric" experience of the sacred—is characterized by an experience of the world as continuous, indivisible, and without interruption. Such a world, or what he describes as the "order of intimacy," is one that lacks autonomy and self-consciousness, of oneself as well as one's relations to others. To relate to the world in this way, for Bataille, becomes possible through the overcoming of the discontinuities of a world fragmented by innumerable divisions, divisions that separate things from things, and people—as objects in the world—from other objects and things.

The ability to experience the world as continuous and without interruption, however, for Bataille, has become increasingly difficult over time. In particular, the possibilities of "plethoric experience" have grown all the more difficult to achieve (they have become evermore interrupted, that is) with the explosive proliferation of things and their increasing organization under a logic of utility in the expansion of industrial capitalism. As Bataille writes:

> From the start, the introduction of *labor* into the world replaced intimacy . . . with rational progression, where what matters is no longer the truth of the present moment, but, rather, the subsequent results of *operations*. The first labor established the world of *things*. Once the world of things was posited, man himself became one of the things of this world, at least for the time in which he labored. It is this degradation that man has always tried to escape . . . man is *in search of a lost intimacy* from the first. (Bataille 1988: 57, emphasis original)

In such a set of conditions—where existence becomes ever more interrupted by things, operations, and rational progression—meaning becomes perpetually mediated and experience deferred. "Reality," as Bataille put it, "never resides in the moment" (1989: 42).

While this process may close one off to "plethoric" experience, the introduction of difference into the world in the form of discontinuity is also what makes the subject possible. It is through such worldly discontinuity that the individual becomes a distinct thing amid a world of things, which is at once a subordination of things (e.g., tools) to people and, thus, people to the use of things. Because the subject's possibility relies on the discontinuities of the world, Bataille further argues, religious experience is necessarily ambiguous. "Undoubtedly, what is sacred attracts and possesses an incomparable value, but at the same time it appears vertiginously dangerous for that clear and profane world where mankind situates its privileged domain" (1988: 36). It is, as Bataille describes, "what causes one to tremble with fear and delight" (1989: 129). Approached in these terms, religious experience is then the disruption, through a move of reclamation, of the world's discontinuity so as to reintroduce an immediacy of experience and "to regain an intimacy that was always strangely lost" (1989: 129). It is to tear the subject, as a thing, out of the infinite chain of relations that bind things together, as discontinuous objects. It is to relate, in other words, without difference, distance, or duration.

If we can set aside its evolutionary framework,[11] Bataille's formulation of religious experience—as the reclaiming of a lost intimacy, an experience of continuity amid a discontinuous world of things and work—captures well the sorts of desire that brought Nihal to Zöhre Ana. It was in Zöhre Ana's presence, for instance, where Nihal was able to experience those forms of intimacy and continuity that she felt were missing from her life, those forms of experience that had grown increasingly interrupted by Turkey's secular and capitalist development. Again, for Nihal, sitting near Zöhre Ana was like "being close to the sun,"[12] "close to nature" (*doğallara yakın*), and close to "something very fundamental." In Zöhre Ana's presence, Nihal also discovered an immediacy of experience and presence capable of binding words, things, and people in a way that was normally elusive. "When I was with Zöhre Ana, it was as if everything was there, and I was nothing." In addition to offering us a useful vocabulary for speaking about Nihal's experience of Zöhre Ana's presence, I am specifically drawn to Bataille because of the framework he provides for thinking this experience in tandem with Nihal's ensuing disillusionment and both the complexity and temporality of loss we find there.[13]

This becomes distinctly apparent when we consider the specific reasons Nihal stopped visiting Zöhre Ana, of which there are three. First, and like others, Nihal was critical of the financial component of the expansion of Zöhre Ana's ritual practices. A particularly troubling aspect of this expansion was the transformation of the informal networks of reciprocity that surrounded Zöhre Ana's home in the early days into a local economy that would find a home in the small, and then large, gift shops her followers operated, where visitors could purchase items blessed by Zöhre Ana. For Nihal, the growth of this economy and Zöhre Ana's coinciding accumulation of wealth were inversely related to her saintly powers. For example, when I asked Nihal about the price of the apples sold at Zöhre Ana's *dergâh* in the past—apples that were understood to promote fertility, and were being sold for 10 million lira (U.S. $20) when I was regularly visiting—she gave me a confused look. "The first times I went to Zöhre Ana's, nothing was being sold. When I was there, being that people were coming from central Anatolia, they were bringing apples from their own gardens to be blessed. They now sell them for 10 million? This means she is finished. When she had this power (*enerji*) to heal, there was no money . . . she accepted no money from visitors in the past. Now the *enerji* is finished. Now, she is filled with money. Her power has now apparently transformed into money." For Nihal, in other words, this conversion of *enerji* into money meant not only that Zöhre Ana's powers could circulate, with things, in the economy that formed around her, but also that, like money, they could be squandered over time.

Interwoven with her scorn for the economies gathering around Zöhre Ana was a related criticism regarding the institutionalization of her religious and therapeutic authority. While institutional structures were present early on, Nihal noted that these structures had formed spontaneously and reflected traditions of saintly devotion common throughout Anatolia. Moreover, they were understood to be at the service of Zöhre Ana's *keramet*. Over time, as Nihal described, this spontaneous organizational structure transformed into an elaborating bureaucracy. With this came the proliferation and strict enforcement of rules regulating interactions with Zöhre Ana, as well as one's conduct while on the *dergâh*'s grounds. As Nihal explained:

> When I was visiting her, they had only recently begun to formalize things. When I first began going, for example, she didn't see herself as one of the Twelve Imams. There wasn't such a thing. Later we noticed that she started regarding herself as one of the Twelve

Imams. Then began the effort to formalize the rules for the *dergâh*. Before, there really weren't rules. Everyone, to one another, through word of mouth, explained about Zöhre Ana. Later, slowly, they began creating all of these rules concerning relations with her. And you were forced to follow the rules. When she first appeared, there wasn't so many rules and so forth at the *dergâh*.

For those who visited Zöhre Ana during this period, there was a shared sense that the emerging class of "followers" were beginning to act like bureaucratic functionaries, as they exercised their own authority through the seemingly capricious and arbitrary enforcement of rules and regulation of visitors' access to Zöhre Ana. This would be the period when Hüsniye would be received with such hostility by Zöhre Ana's assistants. In Nihal's case, the increasing number of conflicts with Zöhre Ana's assistants left her feeling that she was becoming entangled again in the precise sorts of bureaucratic rationalities that were endlessly frustrating in her daily life. Although institutional forms may have been at the service of Zöhre Ana's *keramet* initially, Nihal's account charts the gradual subordination of Zöhre Ana's *keramet* to the needs of the institution.

Paralleling the encroaching economic rationality of therapeutic exchanges and the increasing regulation of conduct and relations, the closest of Zöhre Ana's followers also began to talk about Zöhre Ana's "philosophy" (*felsefe*). The basic Alevi moral injunction—"be the owner of your hand, tongue, and loins" ("eline, diline, beline sahip ol!")—gave way to a more elaborate set of ideas and sayings associated with Zöhre Ana's *keramet*. Again, Nihal: "In the past, there was definitely no 'philosophy.' The exact opposite. That is, it was primitive (*primitif*), an original essence (*kaynaklanan bir cevher*). And that was very important for me. Zöhre Ana had the demeanor of a child, of a meek villager. What kind of philosophy could there be? What could a villager's philosophy be?" Although they would never gain the coherence of a formal doctrine, selections of Zöhre Ana's ideas and sayings would nonetheless, in the ensuing years, become systematized, codified, and transcribed into texts—to be sold at the gift shop.

Nihal began regularly visiting Zöhre Ana with a desire to reclaim a form of experience that she felt was missing from the present ordering of society, a sensibility that could be discovered and reclaimed in spaces that eluded the homogenizing forces of both secular modernity and orthodox Islam. While not all visitors were drawn to Zöhre Ana with the same desire, Nihal illustrates a familiar form of relating to her, as well as to other healers. İsmet, the self-described amateur anthropologist I introduced in Chapter 3, for instance, was attracted to Zöhre Ana for similar reasons. Like Nihal, he described being continually on the lookout for forms of religious life that had survived the destructive forces of secular modernity. Like Nihal, he saw in them the remnants of a form of experience that was at once essential and more *primitif*. The same could be said of Gülay's father, Ümit, whose story of familial conflict opened the book. Although I would never learn what led to his rejection of Zöhre Ana's authority, and the subsequent divisions in the family, the Ümit I knew—who was intensely devoted to Zöhre Ana—described being drawn to Zöhre Ana for these precise reasons. Like Nihal, İsmet, and others, he was able to discover with Zöhre Ana—in the interstices of state and religious law, at the economic and religious margins of society—an immediacy and intimacy of experience that he regarded as endangered in the modern present, a form of experience that was able to fill out the emptiness of the contemporary.

With time, however, Nihal's experiences with Zöhre Ana grew more and more remote. Rules of conduct came to mediate her relationships with Zöhre Ana and other visitors. Zöhre Ana's representatives increasingly interrupted, if not blocked, her desire to interact with Zöhre Ana. Zöhre Ana's speech began to dissipate into books and slogans. The spontaneity of the early years succumbed to formalized institutions. Zöhre Ana's *keramet* became invested in objects, which became commodities, which were sold in the gift shop. In short, a proliferating number of rules, objects, texts, and operations came to insert themselves between Nihal and Zöhre Ana. The developments and innovations that allowed Zöhre Ana's presence to extend in tangible and material ways beyond the *dergâh* were the very developments and innovations that undermined, over time, Nihal's relationship with Zöhre Ana. As Bataille would put it, the immediacy and intimacy of experience that she initially found at Zöhre Ana's *dergâh* became ever more mediated, interrupted, and bound within the limits of a discourse of utility.

As this begins to suggest, I have found Bataille's reflections on loss, religious experience, and modernity to be particularly useful in making sense of the specificity and temporality of loss experienced by Nihal. In so doing, they also help us gain a clearer understanding of the distinctiveness of the two regimes of loss represented by Aydın and Nihal. For Aydın, his choice not to become a *cinci hoca* and his revelations about the "ignorance" and deceptions of his parents' generation marked the death of the idea of the *cinci hoca* in his life, a loss that also marked the condition of possibility for his personal and the nation's liberation. It is a story of loss, moreover, that was told squarely from within the frame of a secular nationalist historical narrative, by a person who identifies with the narrative's victors.[14] As such, Aydın's account articulates a relationship between past and present that diverges in important ways from Nihal's account. His is a story of vanishing and foreclosed possibilities, of a past that has been abandoned and laid to rest. It is a passing, as well, that is to be celebrated.

For Nihal, in contrast, this loss of worldly possibility is to be mourned. With Bataille's assistance, we are able to recognize in Nihal's shifting feelings about Zöhre Ana a complex play between loss and possibility that suggests a unique set of assumptions regarding the force of the past on the present and the nature of historical transformation. For Nihal, the sorts of capacities represented by the religious healer need not disappear for the individual to be set free, the nation to be liberated, or society to be modernized. She does not narrate a story of foreclosure so much as a story of mounting obstacles—where particular capacities of experience become difficult to achieve within contemporary conditions. In Nihal's formulation, the prevalence of religious healers in past eras spoke not to widespread ignorance or a lack of scientific reasoning, but to the presence of a set of conditions that made such forms of experience more easily achieved—where the ability to overcome the discontinuities of life so as to experience the world without difference, distance, or duration was more available.

Although such distinctions may appear inconsequential, they in fact take us a long way in making sense of the ways that these contrasting structures of loss are each embedded within secularism's politics of aesthetics. This is most apparent in the distinctive temporalities that order their respective accounts of loss. For instance, while Aydın's account of the loss of a worldly ability was able to find a home within a larger story of national liberation, the structure of loss narrated by Nihal presents a more complex and challenging picture, a form of loss not easily secured within the coordinates of the nation's historical time. As such, it was not a loss that could so easily be mourned, that could find an orderly expression in the narrative of the nation. My point here is an extension of our earlier conversation about Zöhre Ana's saintly language as a site of return, where the ability of deceased *evliya*s (such as Atatürk) to comment on the present disrupted secular nationalist assumptions regarding the ordering of time—where history is written as a progressive succession of events, in which the present continually surmounts the past. While Nihal's story of disillusionment was certainly indebted to the temporality of the nation—her desire to experience the *primitif* and her interest in "original essences" assuredly took part in a larger discourse of nostalgia for a simpler, agrarian past (in which the villager had no pretenses to philosophy)—it is also a story that struggles to escape the temporality of secularism's distribution of the sensible.

This dynamic is particularly evident in the configuration of loss and history that we find in Nihal's account. While both Nihal and Aydın depict the healer as a figure of the past—such that a visit to a healer is a brush with the past, a traversing of time that coincides with entering into a healer's presence—they nonetheless conceive of this relationship with time along divergent lines. Simply put, Nihal narrates a past that continues to thrive in the present. Although the sorts of worldly possibility represented by the religious healer are endangered, their passing is not a prerequisite for the progression of time. In this respect, despite the sense of disillusionment Nihal expresses, we can also regard this as a hopeful relationship with the past. Eng and Kazanjian, in their reflections on the relationship of loss and mourning to the politics of history proposed by Walter Benjamin, capture this point well when they note: "According to Benjamin, to mourn the remains of the past hopefully is to establish an active and open relationship with history. . . . We might say that as soon as the question 'What is lost?' is posed, it invariably slips into the question 'What remains?'" (2002: 1–2). Nihal's attraction to Zöhre Ana seems to be organized by just such a question—what remains?

Although Nihal may narrate her sense of disillusionment and loss in a gesture of mourning, the past that she gives voice to is not closed off to the present. While the past, for Aydın, is in a sense resolved—the death of a worldly capacity had to occur so that something new could come into existence—Nihal conceives the past as suffusing the present. It lives in the contemporary as a latent potentiality of experience, one that endures in those pockets of social life that have escaped the destructiveness of the twin forces of modernity and religious orthodoxy. Framing Nihal's experiences in these terms helps us understand why she does not narrate her disillusionment as a crisis of faith or a decisive rupture in her life—as with Aydın, whose world was turned upside down. For Nihal, while Zöhre Ana's demise is to be mourned rather than celebrated, this loss does not pass without hope, for the vitality of the world represented by Zöhre Ana will assuredly reappear again elsewhere—in a remote village, in another *gecekondu* neighborhood, or in some other setting that has yet to succumb to the discontinuities of the modern world.

Conclusion: Healing Secular Life

Whence there arises that quality of time immemorial associated with the irregularities of history, as if they harked back to a beginning without a past, the dark recesses of an insecurity, a latent "singularity," revealed in the continuous plurality of events. But how valid is this impression, too quick to relate the facts to an atemporal neutrality? Can we so easily exile panic from history—make it into something outside or below history, or history's law? (de Certeau 2000: 1)

At this point, we arrive at the other end of the journey that began at Anıt-Kabir, where a group of Zöhre Ana's followers confronted the caretakers of the tomb of the nation's founder. We arrive, however, not with an unyielding devotion that might embolden one to confront the guardians of Atatürk's burial site, but with an abiding sense of loss that shadows one's desire for a seemingly endangered form of religious and therapeutic possibility. In this space of both exile and loss, we similarly come upon an additional means of approaching our larger concern with the entanglement of therapeutic power and secularism's politics of aesthetics. To elaborate on this point, I return to the figure of the historian that opened this chapter.

As Niyazi Berkes observed, the work of the secularist historian of the early republic was to lay claim to a past in all of its abundance and variegation in an effort to discover the grounds for a new national spirit. For these historians, however, the basis for a new national spirit was not to be found in the immediate past, but in those social and religious formations that escaped the homogenizing forces of Western imperialism and Ottoman Islamic orthodoxy. The unique skills these historians offered thus revolved around their ability to discern in the complexity of contemporary conditions the traces of such lost traditions, those persistent social vitalities surviving in the interstices of religious law and state authority. In this, we find not only a quest for an affirmation of national singularity, but also a sense that it has always been there—just under one's nose—waiting to be *re-discovered*. Their task was, after all, as Berkes described, "the *recovery* of national culture" (1964: 501). As such, the historian's work was envisioned as a reclaiming of the latent potentiality of the past in order to return meaning to the present and, in turn, chart a new future.

In the forms of desire animating Nihal's story of loss, as well as the wider collection of stories of foreclosed therapeutic ability of which her account is indicative, we find a repetition of the secularist historian's desire to mine the margins of a corrupt present for salvageable elements of an unscathed past. For many of Zöhre Ana's visitors and followers, to experience her presence was to experience an endangered worldly capacity, which was simultaneously an experience of loss. It was "to regain," as Bataille put it, "an intimacy that was always strangely lost" (1989: 129). In these mutually conditioning experiences of loss and reclamation, we can thus conceive of the historian and the patient as sharing a common objective: to rummage through the abundance of the contemporary world for remnants of a lost past in the hope of reordering relationships between former limits and future possibilities.

In this play between loss and recovery, I find myself returning to my fellow anthropologist, İsmet, and his insistence that Zöhre Ana represented something new: "Of all the *hacı, hoca, üfürükçü*s, or *muskacı*s that I had seen, she was quite different. She showed a more modern form. . . . She showed a new form." But is this truly something new? Indeed, how does one know when one sees the new? In trying to answer such a question, we confront an impasse familiar to the late secularist historian of the republic. How to be sure that what one sees is a manifestation of a surviving worldly possibility to be reclaimed, rather that a corrupted element of the present traveling in the guise of an unscathed past? "Is this the outbreak of something new," as de Certeau asked of the possessions at Loudun, "or the repetition of the past?" "The historian," he rightly points out, "never knows which. For mythologies reappear, providing the eruption of strangeness with forms of expression prepared in advance, as it were, for that sudden inundation" (2000: 1).

Rather than trying to resolve this impasse, I want to step back to reflect on the sorts of historical conditions within which such questions can arise. And here I want to suggest that we have something important to learn about Nihal's experience by returning, as well, to the sorts of historical conditions within which Georges Bataille's thinking on religion and loss took shape. The aspect of Bataille's work that has concerned us in this chapter—namely, his interest in unmediated "plethoric" experience—was one shared by a number of prominent European philosophers writing in the aftermath of World War II. Especially among phenomenologists working during this period, there was a widespread interest in formulating a pre-linguistic and irreducibly sensual substratum of human experience. This was a period, for instance, when we find phenomenologists such as Maurice Merleau-Ponty writing about "preobjective" experience and Edmund Husserl exploring the "origin of geometry." In addition to reflecting this phenomenological trend, Bataille's concern with the ever-proliferating mediation of experience under industrial capitalism also worked within a larger historical imagination that read history as a process of ongoing destruction and disenchantment. Indeed, as Habermas has noted, "Weber's interpretation of the Protestant ethic can be integrated without strain into [Bataille's] perspective" (1984: 99). In other words, while Bataille was unique in the way that he combined the themes of death, the sacred, and eroticism in his philosophical and literary writings, his conceptual work was nonetheless inextricable from the postwar European political, economic, and intellectual milieu within which he lived.

Two points follow from these observations. First—and one that perhaps goes without saying—the early secularist historian's vision of the past and its relation to the present was, as with Bataille's work, based on a historically specific conception of the world and its history. It was a style of thought founded on an idea of society, history, and religion indebted in large measure to a European history of secularism and to the universal concept of religion (Asad 1993) and homogeneous, empty time (Benjamin 1968; see also B. Anderson 1991) that it presupposed. In our case, the desire to restore meaning to the present by reclaiming past cultural elements that escaped the corruptions of the modern was born of a historical imagination itself constitutive of Turkey's project of secular modernity. This past, rather than being recovered from the folds of the present, was being called into existence by the historian's work of discernment. These "traces," "remnants," and "survivors" of a pre-Ottoman past were, in other words, the effects of a field of modernist vision.

By drawing attention to the historical specificity of Bataille's thinking, I am not attempting to diminish the analytic force of the concepts he introduced. In fact, and this is my second point, they become all the more powerful. In an incisive reflection on the tendency of anthropologists to deploy the "'theoretical quick fix' of philosophers names" as "nonsituated" and decontextualized surnames—engaging, in other words, the thought of philosophers in a way that we would never approach the thinking of our interlocutors in the field—Michael Fischer suggests that appreciating the situated specificity of these decontextualized, surnamed philosophers can both limit and strengthen the force of their conceptual work in important ways (2010: 337). In our case, by acknowledging the historical context of Bataille's work (even if to a very partial extent), it is possible to conceive of his ideas as sharing a plane with those of Nihal, İsmet, Hüsniye, and others. Here, recall Nihal's characterization of Zöhre Ana's presence as being "primitive," "fundamental," and "natural." Recall as well the way that İsmet described Zöhre Ana's uniqueness in terms of her ability to manifest an ancient religious capacity (again, as something *primitif*) within the inhospitable conditions of secular modernity. My point here is not that all these people are merely versions of Bataille, or that these varied sensibilities are but anachronistic expressions of a postwar French conception of the "sacred." In addition to prompting challenging questions about their shared histories (we must keep in mind that, as Berkes's historians would assuredly note, early secularist reformers of the Turkish republic were deeply indebted to a French history of *laïcité*, within which Bataille must also be situated), this historicization of Bataille allows us to better appreciate the way that the sense of loss expressed by Nihal and others is embedded within the structures of a historical imagination that is both indebted to and enabled by secularism's politics of aesthetics.

Put otherwise, it is the feeling of something having been lost that is itself born through the consolidation of a historical imagination that can support such a distribution of the sensible. By recognizing this coincidence of loss and emergence, we can thus appreciate Nihal's repeated disillusionments with Zöhre Ana as rehearsing the impossibility of the desire that originally drew her to Zöhre Ana. The series of obstacles and mediations that interrupted her desire to descend into the intimacy of the world—the formalization of bureaucratic structures, the circulation of commodity forms, the codification of regulations, the appearance of texts and philosophies—continually turned her back to the corruptions of a surrounding discontinuous world. As Zöhre Ana's charisma became routinized, as Weber (1964) would put it, she was carried back to the routines of the world.

Nihal's account makes vivid a sensibility that spanned interviews: a sense that the desire for intimacy, on the one hand, and its experience, on the other, were separated by a seemingly insurmountable gap. Much like the secularist historian who runs the risk of revealing the fiction of his or her endeavor by looking too closely at the evidence, the patient continually runs the risk of exposing his or her desire for unmediated experience as but an illusion of a discontinuous world. Although certainly not shared by all, I would suggest that this distinctive configuration of desire, intimacy, and loss represents a certain underside of secularism's politics of aesthetics. This, then, is what I meant earlier when I described this chapter as an inquiry into the redoubling of loss buried deep within the types of therapeutic desires that gather around exilic forms of religious life, an aesthetics of loss that is inseparable from secularism's politics of aesthetics.

I want to make clear, again, that Nihal's experience of loss, much as Aydın's account of foreclosed therapeutic possibility, is not present in all of the stories of healing and being healed that I gathered over the course of my research. As I argued in the last chapter, there are many ways to experience a healer's presence—a presence that is necessarily multiple, given the shifting nature of the social ties through which this presence moves. As such, the preceding discussion has no pretenses of making universal claims about "religious experience" (as was the case with Bataille), let alone about "Muslim experience." The piety of Ibrahim the *cinci hoca*, for instance, certainly represents a contrasting modality of religious experience, one that is less concerned with the immediacy of unmediated experience than it is with a purposeful project of ethical self-fashioning. Much the same could be said of Aydın. Although, like Nihal's, his is a story of loss and foreclosure indebted to Turkey's history of secular reform, it is a story that expresses a distinctive relationship between history, subjective capacities, and the possibilities of the present world. While not generalizable, I am nonetheless arguing that Nihal's account does indicate a widely acknowledged set of sensibilities regarding religious experience. Much as Ibrahim's approach to piety reflects particular arrangements between prevailing trends in Islamic legal interpretation and modern forms of state authority, Nihal articulates an alternate model of religious subjectivity born of a different arrangement of subjectivity, modernity, and Islam—one distinctively located within secularism's distribution of the sensible.

Conclusion: Fragments

The preceding chapters reflect my continuing effort to make sense of the urgency with which the theme of secularism circulated through the stories of loss, healing, and being healed I listened to over the course of my research. What began as a study of the experiential and embodied qualities of therapeutic processes developed, over time, into an exploration of the vital entanglement of therapeutic power and political life. As such, this book has traced the experiences of religious healers and their patients in settings of urban poverty as they sought recovery and new future possibilities in the interstices of religious and state law. And it was here where I became convinced that the efforts of these healers to articulate voices that could be heard, words that could touch and heal, and forms of relatedness that could reorder past limits offered an important lesson about healing and secularism as interwoven projects of world, subject, and history making.

A substantial challenge of this research has been learning how to listen to these stories of loss and healing—learning, that is, to be attentive not only to what was being said, but also to the unspoken histories, unacknowledged interlocutors, and the multiple shades of speaking and listening that moved powerfully, if not silently, through these stories. In struggling to develop such an attentiveness—a struggle that is incomplete, unfinished, and humbling—I would rely on a wide range of sources. While the time and presence that ethnography (and its funding) afforded would be of primary importance to this project, I also found myself consumed at different points by medical journals of the 1930s, popular periodicals of the 1940s and 1950s, folklore studies from the 1930s through the 1960s, public health pamphlets from the post-war years of the republic, newspaper and magazine articles that spanned the nation's history, health policy and urban development reports of the 1970s, Turkish cinema of the 1980s, television programming of the late-1990s, and those myriad scenes of domesticity, labor, and conversation that ethnography privileges. In searching for an end to this discussion, I find myself returning to four fragments that precipitate out of these varied sources, four spatial fragments that seem to capture the trajectory of the preceding chapters.

Archival

On January 15, 1938, the Ankara Development Directorate approved a request to appropriate block 28, parcel 6 for the construction of a widened boulevard running through what some now refer to as "old" Ankara (Figure 12). This petition is but a small fragment of an enormous trove of such petitions that were submitted during this period. For the new city planner, the streets of Ankara were in desperate need of a rational, modern order. In our petition, the planner's rendering of the parcel contains both an outline of the proposed boulevard's expanded dimensions, as well as the outline of an existing structure that was to be demolished to make way for this expansion, a structure that the document identifies as a "*türbe yeri*"—the site of a tomb or shrine. According to Law 1351, passed in 1928, the Directorate had the right to seize such properties, especially those of religious orders, or *tarikat*s, without payment. Once the request was accepted, the tomb was purportedly relocated.

This first fragment speaks toward the exilic. A dead saint and the surrounding shrine—to which visitors regularly traveled, worshiped, and sacrificed—were cast out of the order of city. Their exile was to be a precondition for a rationally ordered future of Ankara. This moment, as I read it, rehearses the wider and no less methodical diversion of a collection of religious practices and forms of religious authority to the outside of a national order in the name of secular reform and societal regeneration, a civilizational impulse that was felt with particular intensity (or at least manifested with unique explicitness) during the early years of the republic.

As the campaigns of scientific and medical literacy that emerged during this period illustrate, society's secular modern development—according to the nation's early secular reformers—would require an alliance between science and secularism that medicine made possible. In these interdependent projects of societal and medical reform—which were at once projects aiming to undermine inherited models of social authority, habits of thought, and forms of social relatedness—the figure of the religious healer

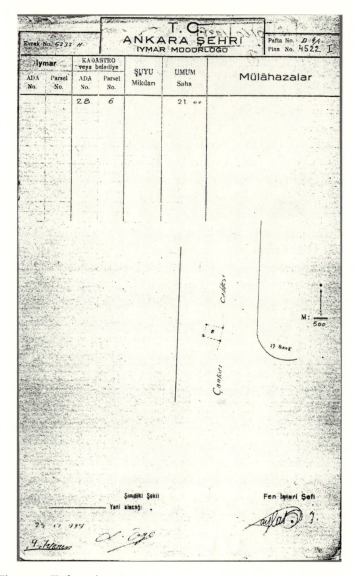

Figure 12. *Türbe yeri*, 1938.

would come to assume a privileged place. It is here where experiences of injury, affliction, and suffering were marked in advance as sites of new and future struggle. And it would be the scars of this past of medical and secular reform that I would time and again encounter as people I spoke with both maligned and sought out the forms of religious and therapeutic possibility that the figure of the religious healer embodied. This book, in a sense, has been an extended reflection on how to listen to and for this history.

An unavoidable and perhaps obvious lesson to draw from this history of secular reform—when approached through the contemporary forms of therapeutic desire that have concerned us—is that these sites of future struggle would, in time, take on a life of their own. While traces of this history would appear and reappear in both the intimacies of therapeutic relationships and everyday conversations about religious healing in the two *gecekondu* neighborhoods where I worked, they nonetheless appeared under unanticipated conditions, which in turn offered their speakers a new language. That is, although the figure of the religious healer continued to play a defining role in inscribing and enforcing the limits of community (which were at once thresholds of reason and sense), the religious healer simultaneously attracted a range of emergent social anxieties and gave voice to a panic about the future viability of the contemporary political order.

The way this first fragment collapses time—the way in which the past (in the form of the dead saint's remains), the present (site of the tomb), and an imagined future (of a rationalized cityscape) share a common plane and set of margins—also brings us back to the commerce between death, healing, and state power that initiated our conversation. Indeed, this is a commerce whose echoes we would encounter repeatedly throughout this book, as it circulated insistently through stories of loss and healing. If we take this fragment out of the context of its submission to Ankara's Development Directorate—which secures our reading of its temporality (first tomb, then boulevard)—the petition introduces again the question that de Certeau helped us pose in the final chapter: "Can we so easily exile panic from history—make it into something outside or below history, or history's law?"

Mythic

Some forty years later, another petition would be approved that permitted the construction of a series of intersecting streets not a mile from the tomb of block 28, parcel 6. The aim would be the same, to further order and rationalize the flow of Ankara's traffic. On this occasion, as the story goes, a group of municipal workers were busy plowing and leveling the underlying Anatolian steppe to make way for the new roads when their bulldozers suddenly stopped working. Try as they might, they could not make the bulldozers restart. After efforts to repair the machinery, a worker noticed fragments of human remains in the freshly turned soil immediately in front of the stalled bulldozers. There was only one explanation. These were the bones of a holy person. The workers refused to continue. After much debate, the bones were excavated and a tomb was constructed on the site. The intersection was redesigned to accommodate the new *türbe yeri*. It is still there today, and it makes for a curious site. Despite its inhospitable location—enclosed by a cage and wedged into a narrow median on a heavily trafficked four-lane road—the saint's tomb continues to receive visitors, offerings, and sacrifices.

This fragment suggests a response to our previous question. No, panic is not so easily banished from history. If we recognize the first fragment as a moment in the larger history of secular reform—an explicit instance of the subordination of religious life to state power, what I have referred to as one of secularism's originary acts of violence—then this fragment reminds us yet again of both the specificity and the limits of Turkey's project of secular modernity. Although we will return to these specificities and limits below, it is first important to make clear the lessons that should *not* be drawn from this fragment and, by extension, the preceding chapters.

Much as we cannot regard the contemporary entanglement of healing and secularism as but a repetition of early republican struggles over the right to tend to injury, so too must we be careful not to read this fragment as merely a straightforward story about the revenge of a pre-modern past on a modern present—where the bones of the holy person seize the machinery of Ankara's modernization. By extension, this story, as well as the forms of religious practice and religiosity considered in this book, offer us no lesson on the "incompleteness" of Turkey's modernization and secularization, to say nothing of the country's "stage of development" or, in an older vocabulary, its "civilizational status." Nor have the preceding chapters taught us anything about an Islamic "revolt" against the modern, which might then be used to further interrogate the extent to which Turkey "belongs" in Europe, or whether Turkey is turning toward the "East." In fact, the preceding chapters sought to disrupt, if not dislodge, the very terms on which such conversations typically unfold.

This is not to say that our discussion has nothing to offer to these debates and conversations, especially those being waged over the proper place of religion within democratic state structures and, more precisely, the possibility of Islam coexisting with secular-liberal models of democratic governance. Indeed, Turkey has emerged as a central setting and stage for these debates. As a Muslim majority region at the margins of European political and territorial orders—a region, indeed, that has figured prominently in a history of European visions of external threat and, as such, played a founding role in consolidating Europe's image of its own orderliness and enlightenment—Turkey has become a prominent "case study" for reflecting on the viability of secularism in the Muslim world. Where a generation earlier Turkey was held up as a model "experiment" in modernization, it is now a "natural laboratory" for studying the life chances of a "moderate" and "tolerant" form of politically engaged Islam, or "Islam-inspired" politics. At the same time, Turkey has also (again) emerged as a prominent screen against which debates concerning the identity of a new Europe are to be played out. In each instance, Turkey comes into view as both a menacing site of gathering alterities (where the Muslim world threatens Europe, where Islam threatens Christianity, where the traditional threatens the modern) and a hopeful bridge to a new, plural, and more tolerant political future.

While there is a justified urgency to these conversations, setting them exclusively at the intersection of formal state politics and authorized forms of Islamic orthodoxy narrows the scope of conversation to such a degree that their utility comes into question. Limiting the conversation in this manner, as I noted at the outset, is to take that which is most visible and most vocal as the limit of what can be said. Beyond the problematic ways in which these debates employ monolithic terms like "Islam" and "democracy," they leave out both the incredible diversity of religious sensibilities that one encounters in such settings and the everyday ways that large-scale political structures are continually being built and rebuilt in the course of social life. The people whose lives and relationships serve as the basis of this book would appear to be inconsequential actors in these larger dramas. While they may be acknowledged as playing a small role—as transnational labor migrants to Germany, or as an anonymous face within a crowd of Islamists—they are most assuredly not at the center of these debates about secularism, Islam, and European identity. And even more foreign to these conversations are the forms of religious practice that I have considered throughout this book. The religious healer is welcomed by neither party in the imagined negotiation between "secular democracy" and "Islam." The healer speaks without political reason, from a time out of joint.

It is clear that the terms of these negotiations need to be rethought. In this respect, my consideration of the entanglement of healing and secularism takes part in an emerging anthropological rethinking of the concept of secularism. Rather than regarding secularism as merely a political principle concerning the relationship between political and religious authority within state structures, this work approaches secularism as an assemblage of thought, policies, institutional practices, and coincident formations of sensibility, sociality, and ethics in an effort to attend to the subjective and social realities of secularism. In our case, instead of approaching scholarly debates on secularism along the conventional path of political doctrines and religio-political movements, our attention was directed toward a heterogeneous collection of less formal, intensely intimate, and constitutively local modalities of Islamic practice. More specifically, we have attended to those religious figures, practices, and sites that flourish with particular intensity around illness, suffering, and misfortune. It was here—among those exilic forms of religious life laboring in the interstices of religious and state law—where we struggled to make sense of the unexpected urgency with which secularism circulated through stories of loss, healing, and being healed.

To learn how to listen to such stories required an appreciation of the specificity of Turkey's history of secular reform. As we learned, this was a history as much about structural differentiation (of religious from political institutions) as it was about control and regulation, such that the removal of religious influence from within the state was to be achieved by subordinating religion to the state, rather than simply their separation. In the process, selective religious institutions would be incorporated into the state apparatus, while those that could not be repurposed to support an innocuous nationalized culture—and especially those that were regarded as potential sites of political opposition—were actively suppressed. At the same time that it provided the political principles for reorganizing state institutions, secularism was simultaneously envisioned as an encompassing way of life for the emerging citizenry of the new nation. As a large-scale project of world, subject, and history making, secularism was promoted as a normative moral discourse concerning one's proper conduct as a citizen, as well as a patient.

Appreciating the specificity of Turkey's project of secular development would begin to explain the unexpected ways that the theme of secularism moved through the stories of loss and healing that I was hearing. After all, the forms of citizenship and subjectivity being articulated in secularist discourse, and specifically its alliance with medical reform, were defined in opposition to the set of social practices and modes of religio-political authority represented by such figures as the religious healer. Yet, as our second fragment reminds us, although cast out of the order of the nation, the religious healer was not so easily banished from history. Indeed, the returns of this history of secular reform, as well as the visions of history that secularism incited, would emerge as recurring themes in our discussion.

Appreciating the specificity of Turkey's project of secular modern development also helped us recognize the extent to which secularism and healing can be regarded as overlapping projects of subject, world, and history making. Here, Rancière's approach to the politics of aesthetics would help us think about the shared aesthetic stakes of both therapeutic processes and secular forms of governance. As we would observe repeatedly, that which is at stake in healing is precisely what is at stake in Turkey's project of secular modern development: the constraints and affordances of human action and subjectivity, the ordering of constellations of social relatedness, the relationship between speaking and recognition, the limits of sensibility and bodily experience, and the building of possibilities for alternate futures and re-imagined pasts. This observation, in turn, would put before us a set of questions that commanded our attention throughout the book: What forms of saintly speech are able to gather an audience today, and what does this tell us about the conditions of speaking and being heard? How does the criminalized voice of the religious healer—which is to possess curative powers—interact with other types of permitted religious, political, and medical speech in modern Turkey? In their desire for such forms of religious and therapeutic authority, how might patients both inhabit and rework ideals of reason, scientific progress, economic productivity, and individual freedom at the center of secular-liberal models of political subjectivity?

Among the many responses that such questions elicited, we would return time and again to the generative intimacy of secular forms of political governance. Even in settings associated with the most radical forms of Islamist activism, we encountered the multiple ways in which the ideals and principles of secularism had settled deeply into the weave of social life as a predictable frame through which people ordered their existence and imagine themselves and their neighbors as participants in a common political community. While we found residents of the two neighborhoods where I lived and worked imagining this participation in distinctive ways, their shared commitment to the basic principles of Turkey's project of secular modernity nonetheless ran counter to ominous warnings foretelling the demise of secularism, or Turkey's "eastward" turn. At the same time that our approach to the relationship between secularism, Islam, and modernity through exilic forms of religious life allowed us to recognize the generative intimacy of secular rule, it also highlighted the instability of secularism's politics of aesthetics. This is not an instability, however, that foretells, necessarily, the end of secularism. Instead, it is an instability that acknowledges the ways that secularism is sustained through a continual process of world making and re-making.

Before we speak further of the fragility of secular truths, I want to point out an additional reason for introducing this second fragment. Over the course of my fieldwork, I would hear many versions of the story recounted above. Although the setting would change, its basic outline remained the same. To gather together these various iterations of a common story, as I want to suggest here, is to invite us to imagine differently the topography of the city. Rather than a rationalized cityscape now and again ruptured by the appearance of the long-buried remains of an ancient presence, this corpus of stories suggests an "underground existence," as de Certeau would put it, that has never actually left and continues, however obliquely, to organize events. Earlier I cautioned the reader against reading this fragment as a story of the revolt of the past against the modern. I reject such a reading because the forcible suppression of these forms of religiosity during the early years of the republic did not result in their eradication, only to have them exact their revenge at a later date. Rather, they merely moved out of the state's field of vision, as it were, into the folds of social life. If, for a moment, we give priority to the *türbe* in our vision of the city's landscape—allowing the city's more recent construction to recede into the background, bringing into relief the numerous tombs scattered throughout the city as a living network of devotion, indebtedness, social obligation that exists within the order of the city—we can imagine this fragment as posing a challenging question to its audience: Can one imagine a visit to the *türbe* not as the traversal of a partition of time and the exiting of the city, but rather as a movement across a threshold of relatedness?

Figure 13. Zöhre Ana, Ali, Zöhre Ana, Ali. Used with permission of the Açık Kapı Derneği.

Devotional

The creative exuberance of Zöhre Ana's *dergâh* never ceased to enthrall me. Its layers of ornamentation, its overflowing collections of images and handcrafted objects, its supply of plaques and urns, statues and figurines, paintings and posters seemed limitless. Out of this colossal bricolage of material devotion, I am drawn here to these fragments (Figure 13). The first two—mosaics of tiny, multicolored stones—were, I was told, gifts to Zöhre

Ana made by a follower. Each was clearly crafted with painstaking detail, in that the stones making up the mosaics were individually arranged and glued in their respective frames. In looking at them, I cannot help but appreciate the intense investment of attention and time that went into their production.

These mosaics, as the above shows us, are exceedingly close approximations of the third and fourth images. And these images, in turn, are both iterations of mass-produced representations of Zöhre Ana and Ali that are readily available at the *dergâh* and, in the case of the latter, in Shi'i communities throughout the Muslim world. Beyond the dizzying interreferentiality of these four images (where the image of Ali that appears over Zöhre Ana's shoulder in the third image is a miniaturized reproduction of the fourth image, both of which can be regarded as the inspiration of the second image, which is in turn erased from the first image, which is based on the third image), I am drawn to the way these mass-produced facsimiles of both Ali and Zöhre Ana incite new forms of devotion as they are personalized through their secondary (or tertiary) reproductions. The circulation of forms that this collection of fragments represents—where generic mass-produced images gain personal meaning in their careful reproduction and gifting—offers an additional commentary on the ways that prominent idioms and materialities of Turkey's project of secular modernity are able to circulate through the forms of exilic religious life that we have been considering over the course of this book.

More specifically, the explosive exuberance of Zöhre Ana's *dergâh*, as well as her *nefesler*, offered us an important lesson about both the subjective experience of healing and the social force of secularism. As such, where our concern with secularism's politics of aesthetics brought into view the means through which secularism organized the terrain of the sensible and possible, it also pushed us to think differently about healing. Here, the sorts of questions that might come naturally to a conventionally formulated aesthetic inquiry—Are the images one finds at Zöhre Ana's *dergâh* convincing to visitors? Are Ibrahim's ritual performance persuasive? How does the patient respond to the idioms of secularism appearing in Zöhre Ana's saintly speech?—elicited answers that could only partly account for the multiple and shifting effects of healers on and in people's lives. In an effort to appreciate these multiple and indeterminate effects, I instead directed our focus toward those discursive and material processes and conditions through which certain phenomena become perceptible, speakable, or possible, while others remain imperceptible, unspeakable, or seemingly impossible. While gauging the effects of ritual performances or saintly speech on a healer's audience in discrete therapeutic encounters remains important to such an analysis, I have nonetheless sought to broaden our attention to consider the sorts of aesthetic relations that give life to both suffering and therapeutic possibility.

This would also allow us to listen differently to people's stories of loss and healing. Rather than accounts of healing as moments of sudden, miraculous transformation, we came to appreciate the transactional and interpersonal qualities of these stories—stories that traced the dynamic play of loss and desire for new futures as they moved into and through the density of the social ties that comprised everyday lives. It is in this context that we also came to recognize the healer's presence as a distributive force that works its way through shifting fields of relatedness. The explosive indeterminacy of devotion and adornment that characterizes the materiality of Zöhre Ana's *dergâh* thereby plays itself out in the interpersonal and aesthetic relations that gather and move through the presence of healers. And just as we were able to see how new possibilities for inhabiting the world could take shape in the presence of such healers—as distributions of possibility and new becoming—so too were we able to understand their capacity to inflict fresh and lasting wounds.

Toward this end, an important aim of the preceding chapters has been to bring together two scholarly conversations that are rarely combined. In particular, this book emerged from a sense that the long-standing interest in ritual healing within medical anthropology had something important to say to the more recent anthropological efforts to rethink secularism, especially as these efforts are being worked out in the context of the Middle East. While the meeting of these conversations offered many lessons— lessons that traveled in both directions—I want to emphasize here but the most prominent. Whereas the anthropological engagement with secularism helps us recognize secularism as a dynamic assemblage of ideas, sensibilities, politics, and institutional practices—rather than merely a political principle concerning the organization of state institutions—our focus on secularism's aesthetic entanglement with healing has allowed us to consider the social and subjective reality of secularism in sites not directly implicated in secular state politics, as one finds in the more common study of "Islamist politics," "political Islam," and the like. Moreover, by positioning our discussion at the intersection of therapeutic power and political rule, we were able to track secularism's politics of aesthetics as it worked its way through the social intimacies of subjective experience and transformation. Put otherwise, in the ways that religious forms of healing both bear witness to the historical diversion of the "irrational" to the outside of a national order in the name of secular modernity and also work to transform intimate spheres of bodily and subjective experience, religious healing proved to be a powerful optic for considering the generative force of sociopolitical systems within everyday lives.

At the same time, this book's attempt to integrate anthropology's enduring interest in ritual healing, therapeutic process, and ethnomedicine into more recent debates in medical anthropology concerning subjectivity, governmentality, and biopolitics has allowed us to appreciate the distinct instabilities of secularism's politics of aesthetics. As we observed in both the sorts of returns staged in Zöhre Ana's saintly language and Ibrahim's micropractices of secularist differentiation, for instance, such forms of therapeutic possibility have a unique capacity for confounding the sorts of societal differentiations (between science, law, economy, politics, and so on) that secularism presumes. Our attention to the ease with which healers are able to draw on the idioms and forms of secular rule as signs of popular wonder likewise demonstrated the instability and infidelity of secularism's politics of aesthetics. By approaching this infidelity through themes of loss and healing, we came to appreciate the distinctly fugitive character of these aesthetics, especially at those sites where the state's hold is tenuous and where the grounds of its authority must be continually made and remade with particular diligence.

While some may find assurance in speaking of this in terms of "multiple secularisms," or "multiple modernities," such concepts already presume a coherence and stability that these infidelities belie. Gilles Deleuze's reflections on semiotic regimes seem particularly apt here: "the closer one gets to the periphery of the system, the more subjects find themselves caught in a kind of temptation: whether to submit oneself to signifiers, to obey the orders of the bureaucrat and follow the interpretation of the high priest—or rather to be carried off elsewhere, the beyond, on a crazy vector, a tangent of deterritorialization—to follow a line of escape, to set off as a nomad, to emit what Guattari called a-signifying particles" (2007: 15). Indeed, this is how I came to read the explosive exuberance of Zöhre Ana's dergâh—a pulsing bricolage of vibrating particles ever ready to escape the saintly economy that briefly contained them.

Which brings us back to my interest in what I earlier depicted as an "Islam without movements." While our concern with the entanglement of healing and secularism has allowed us to attend to forms of religious practice and experience that fall outside common accounts of Islam and politics, we do not find here any coherently elaborated designs for a new social or political order. These forms of religiosity and religious practice offer neither an explicit model of religious development (other than, perhaps, freedom from affliction) nor any sort of teleology of political liberation (beyond their unique ability to disrupt governing distributions of the sensible). Although some may take root, forming a social density that can endure through time, others may well falter or fade away, to only have their densities of relatedness dissipate and form again elsewhere.

Closings and Openings

At some point during the course of my fieldwork I noticed a pattern to my movements. On the way to health clinics to speak with their staff of physicians and nurses, I somehow always found myself traveling along the paved streets, streets that never really headed to any particular destination, except to some distant place beyond the neighborhood—an elusive "downtown," what had years earlier been a NATO base far outside the city, or more distant destinations of Istanbul and Samsun. When walking to visit healers, however, I recurrently found myself relying on the many paths that crisscrossed the streets, paths that always took you somewhere nearby, and more determinate. Reflecting on this in my field notes, I wrote:

> The alternating networks of movement—streets vs. paths, in this case—seem to reflect something distinct about *gecekondu* neighborhoods. Where one network is paved, defined by (relatively) clean angles and (relatively) clear boundaries, paths crisscross and interconnect roads. And you see this too within alternating networks of legitimacy, authority, and cooperation that make up the local. The streets could be said to represent the state's presence—a veneer of order, permanence, and durability that communicates its coordinated strength. Streets are named, numbered, mapped. In a sense, too, the streets enact the creative-destructiveness of Turkey's project of modernity, a destruction announced in advance by large red "X"s painted on *gecekondu* homes, marking them for demolition to make

way for newer, wider, straighter roads. Artifacts of this destruction can be seen in the precariously standing homes that have been severed in two—half run through with road and sidewalk, half still occupied (Figure 14).

Paths, on the other hand, travel with the landscape—between homes, along ledges, behind property. Paths don't seem to need names. One could argue that they interconnect streets, but that would be the city planner talking. Paths don't merely take up where the street ends, where the state's presence leaves off. They are networks of their own that are occasionally crossed by streets. Paths to visit neighbors, to visit relatives, to go to the store, to school, to home. . . . They're not just a means of transportation, nor lines sketched on a map in a municipality office. They hold and circulate meaning and memories in distinctive ways. They represent, from within. Streets, of course, also represent, and their histories and meanings interlock with paths. I'm sure many streets were once paths that have since been paved by the city. Much in the same way that village and religious social networks were, as they still are, used toward political and electoral ends. Paths are networked, streets are gridded.

The health clinics are always on streets, healers off paths.

When I returned to Ankara in 2005, little had visibly changed in Aktepe since my last visit. Ahmet's shop was still there. I slipped back into familiar conversations with Ahmet, his family, and his regular clients. Ahmet continued to work fourteen-hour days, even though business had improved since the economic crisis of 2000–2001. Osman, as well, was still working fourteen-hour days as a shoe repairman. Although Ahmet's nephew was getting old enough to help in the shop, he was only allowed to work a few hours a day. His studies were to take priority. Ahmet was already contributing a significant amount of the shop's income toward his nephew's education. And he had similar plans for his own young children. While a handful of new streets and new apartment buildings had been built in the neighborhood, the changes in the built environment seemed inconsequential in comparison to Hürriyet.

Hürriyet was virtually unrecognizable. Since my departure, there had been an explosion of new construction. The entire main street, with the exception of a few buildings, had been torn down and rebuilt. Four-story

Figure 14. Street, sidewalk, home. Photograph by author.

apartment buildings now lined the main thoroughfare. A new high school had been built. Several of the small corner markets had become *süper markets*. Meanwhile, Ali was married and had a beautiful new daughter. His younger brother, unlike the vast majority of his friends, had done well on the university exam and was now studying archeology at a university on the Black Sea. Kemal, an owner of one of the expanded *süper markets*, told me that Fikret's brother had gambled his money away and was now a laborer in a small town between Ankara and his home village. I learned from Ali that Aydın had moved across the city. Although my long absence made the progress of lives all the more striking, still more jarring, admittedly, were the architectural transformations in the neighborhood. Although I do not want to speculate on what forces can account for the different rates of construction in the two neighborhoods, I do want to note the impact of these developments on one's mobility in Hürriyet.

When I stepped off the bus in Hürriyet, as I had so many times before, I headed off to visit Ali and his family. After orienting myself to the unexpected verticality of the new construction, I made my way down the main road and onto the path that would lead me to Ali's house. Before long, the path came to an abrupt halt in front of a massive, newly constructed cement apartment building. The way that the path ran almost all the way up to the side of the building made it seem as if the building had simply grown, fully formed, out of the ground. As I made my way around the building, and the others nearby, I began to have the unfamiliar feeling that I was trespassing on someone's property. This would be a recurring experience in my time there. The paths that I had spent so much time on before had either become impossible to find or repeatedly disappeared into new construction sites, only to pick up on the other side—until they ran into another new building.

Although these fragments of former paths indicated that something important was being lost in the neighborhood, the explosion of construction that was interrupting their flow spoke at the same time to new possibilities. The recently constructed buildings spoke, that is, to newfound stability in one's housing, and the years of sacrifice and saving that were required to fund their construction. They spoke to new familial arrangements and the opportunity of formerly dispersed families to share a common address. They also spoke to higher rents, the further concentration of wealth in the neighborhood, and the redoubled sense of poverty for the thousands of homes that remained unchanged in their shadows. I would eventually pick my way through the new construction and make it to Ali's house, where I passed the afternoon visiting and becoming acquainted with his new wife and child, before heading off to Zöhre Ana's *dergâh* and, soon after, finding myself in a caravan of cars making its way through the streets of Ankara to the burial site of Atatürk.

Appendix: Genres of Healing

In what follows, I offer a brief overview of the four principal genres of religious healing practiced in Hürriyet and Aktepe. This overview will consider the therapeutic and ritual procedures engaged in by healers, the means through which their therapeutic skills or abilities are acquired, the range of problems they treat, some of the defining features of their clientele, and the sorts of historical and geographic variation one may encounter among different healers and forms of healing.

Kurşun dökme, which roughly translates as "the pouring of lead," involves a lead pouring specialist (*kurşuncu*) who treats patients who have been struck by the *nazar*, or "evil eye." The evil eye can manifest itself in a variety of forms, including but not limited to experiences of fever, sweating, "fright," bad luck, pimples, skin rashes, and nightmares (see Maloney 1976; Çelik 1974; Sachs 1983; see also Herzfeld 1981). Although it is practiced exclusively by women, both men and women seek the assistance of *kurşuncu*s. Women and children (both male and female) are, however, the most frequent visitors. The primary ritual feature of the *kurşuncu* is the pouring of molten lead into a basin filled with water over which the patient leans, with a scarf or piece of cloth over her or his head. While the lead is being poured, the *kurşuncu* recites prayers and commonly states some variation of, "It is not my hand, it is the hand of our mother Ayşe Fatma." After the lead has been poured—which creates a cloud of steam that passes over the patient's face—the *kurşuncu* removes the solidified piece of lead and reads it to divine the source of the evil eye.

Outside this basic ritual formula, there is remarkable variation, particularly in terms of the additional items that accompany the lead pouring and what the *kurşuncu* instructs the patient to do with these items. For instance, a wide assortment of objects can be incorporated into *kurşun dökme* rituals, such as onions, bread, salt, oil, coal, keys, bars of soap, strainers, brooms, forks, and gold rings. In keeping with such material variety, these objects are put to a range of uses. After the lead pouring is finished, for example, the patient can be instructed to throw the water where no one will walk, toss the onion behind oneself without looking, feed the bread to a dog or cat, bury the bread at a crossroads, neither speak to nor kiss anyone for a designated period, and so forth. The ritual techniques of the *kurşuncu* are passed through the female line of a family, thus making relationships between female elders and daughters or granddaughters central to the succession of healers. The actual passing on of the ability to heal is described as *el vermek*, "to give one's hand." In comparison to other forms of healing, *kurşun dökme* appears to have experienced little historical change. Accounts from the late Ottoman and early Republican era describe seemingly identical practices (Lewis 1971).

A second modality of religious healing widely practiced is that of the *ocaklı*. The practices of the *ocaklı* are wide-ranging and overlap with *kurşun dökme*. As compared to *kurşun dökme*, however, this form of healing is defined not by its ritual techniques but by its association with holy or sacred ancestors. The term *ocak*, the root of *ocaklı*, while having many connotations (furnace, hearth, fireplace, mine, political body, guild, fraternity), is associated here with a notion of family lineage. To be *ocaklı*—literally, "with the *ocak*"—connotes persons who have special powers to heal based on their descent from an ancestor to whom miraculous powers were attributed.[1] The *ocaklı* is thus usually linked to a particular tomb, that of his or her dead ancestor, which is generally located near his or her home village. In this regard, while my research focused on the person of the *ocaklı*, the healing power of the *ocak* can also be strongly associated with a place (e.g., a rock, cave, or tree).

The ritual practices of *ocaklı*s vary widely, although individual *ocaklı*s are regarded as possessing considerable specialization in regard to the afflictions treated. For instance, there are *ocaklı*s who exclusively treat warts, rashes, arthritis, shingles, jaundice, or malaria. Particular *ocaklı*s are also known for their ability to cure alcoholism, promote fertility, treat a range of mental disorders, or provide good fortune in general. Ritually, the recitation of Qur'anic verses appears to be consistently present, especially those verses known to have therapeutic power (*şifa ayetler*). While these verses are understood to have specific therapeutic effects regardless of the qualities of the reciter, the *ocaklı* is regarded as uniquely able to facilitate the verse's intent. Beyond this, there are some common but less ubiquitous ritual components to the practice of the *ocaklı*. Drawing or scratching (*çizmek*) on the skin is one such practice, particularly for skin-related ailments. As with the *kurşuncu*, the efficacy of the *ocaklı* is attributed to their inheritance of a special gift or power to heal from an ancestor to whom miraculous or extraordinary powers are accredited. Although, like the *kurşuncu*, the *ocaklı* is customarily a senior member of the family or community, unlike the *kurşuncu* both men and women can be *ocaklı*s. Likewise, both men and women seek their assistance. Similar to the *kurşuncu*, the practices of the *ocaklı* seem to have changed little over time and there appears to be little difference between *ocaklı*s practicing in rural and urban settings.

*Cinci hoca*s are known for their ability to influence or control the world of *cin*, a term commonly translated as "spirit." Although practitioners of this form of healing are frequently referred to as *cinci hoca*s, they may also be described as *üfürükçü*s or *muskacı*s. In the scholarly literature, one also finds practitioners of this form of healing referred to as "Qur'anic healers." Rather than being an inheritance of a divine gift, such as with the *ocaklı* and the *kurşuncu*, the capacity of the *cinci hoca* to heal centers on the acquisition of expert religious knowledge and the mastery of ritual formulas and techniques for the fabrication of ritual objects. Any given treatment is typically the result of elaborate calculations based on the patient's problem or intent (*niyet*), astrological sign (*burç*), defining element (*tabiat*, such as earth, air, water, fire), and a numerical value attributed to Arabic characters used in the spelling of the patient's and/or patient's mother's names (which are, in turn, generated by assigning Arabic equivalents of Turkish characters). These factors combine to determine the form and ordering of ritual procedures necessary for the treatment of specific patients and problems.

These procedures may include not only the appropriate prayers to be recited a designated number of times at specific times, but also instructions for the production of different ritual objects (*tılsım*s). Foremost among the ritual objects produced by the *hoca* is the *muska*, thus the *cinci hoca*'s alternative designation as *muskacı* (a maker of *muska*). The *muska* is a piece of paper over which a Qur'anic verse, a ritual prescription, the patient's name, the patient's mother's name, and/or the object of the spell's intent has been written using Arabic script. The paper is then folded, frequently into a triangle, and put into a pouch. This pouch can be worn or placed on the body of the patient (e.g., around the neck, in one's pocket), or placed in prescribed locations to realize a desired effect (e.g., under a mattress to obstruct adulterous relationships).[2] In determining the ritual formulas necessary for treating any specific problem, *cinci hoca*s are known to rely on such texts as *Havasu'l-Kur'an ve Kenzü'l-Havas* or simply *Kenzü'l-Havas*, both subtitled "Repositories of the Secret Sciences" (*Gizli İlimler Havinesi*). Many *hoca*s nonetheless reject the utility of such books, arguing that they represent overly formulaic manuals that foster the proliferation of self-taught *hoca*s whose limited knowledge is ineffective or dangerous.

The *cinci hoca* treats problems that are typically associated with being struck, harassed, or possessed by *cinler* (pl. of *cin*) or *periler* ("fairies"). These problems can take many forms, the most common being marital and familial conflict (especially adultery), nightmares and experiences of extreme fright (especially among children), seizures (especially, again, in children), sleeping difficulties, infertility, problems at work, and any number of everyday aches and concerns. In addition to treating people who have been affected by *cin*, the *cinci hoca* may also, and more controversially, work to control *cin* in an effort to bring harm upon others. In such instances they are considered practitioners of magic (*büyücü*). Whereas the vast majority of *cinci hoca*s are men, there are instances of female *cinci hoca*s. Similarly, men, women, and people of all backgrounds are known to seek the *hoca*'s assistance.

In speaking about the *cinci hoca*, mention should also be made of the occasional efforts of local imams to treat assorted ailments and problems. While imams, or *cami hoca*s (as they are sometimes distinguished from the *cinci hoca*), would emphatically disagree with being compared to the *cinci hoca*, many imams nonetheless engage in similar ritual healing practices, assign enormous importance to the *şifa ayetler*, and incorporate the ritualized blowing over the patient while reciting prayers characteristic of the *cinci hoca*—which appears to be the basis of the title *üfürükçü*, itself a derivative of the verb *üfürmek* (to blow on someone or something). As might be expected, imams nonetheless identify a number of decisive differences that separate their work from that of *cinci hoca*s. The imam, for instance, does not use the astrological and numerological aspects of the *cinci hoca*'s practices. Other than perhaps writing out the *şifa ayet* for the patient, the imam does not produce *muska*. Last, the *cami hoca* tends to treat minor ailments and does not venture into the realm of magic. Accordingly, in that *cami hoca*s are infrequently utilized as a therapeutic option, they are not typically regarded as representing a distinct tradition of healing.

An *evliya* is a person acknowledged as possessing extraordinary spiritual powers based on his or her possession of *keramet* (Arabic, *karama*), the God-given capacity to perform miracles. The term *evliya* (Arabic, *walī*, the singular form of the plural *awliyā*) is commonly translated as "saint." Although care should be taken in comparing the concept of *evliya* to the Christian concept of "saint," the principal task or duty of the *evliya*, as with the Christian saint, is to intercede with God on behalf of petitioners or supplicants. Unlike Christian, especially Catholic, concepts of sainthood, however, there is no formal system of canonization for determining one's status as an *evliya*. Importantly, while the ability to heal is one of the God-given powers commonly ascribed to the *evliya*, *evliya*s are not regarded exclusively as healers.

Unlike the *cinci hoca*, whose powers are regarded as the product of ritual expertise, the powers of the *evliya* are conceived as an expression of the divine gift of *keramet*. In this regard, the *evliya*'s powers typically arrive without advance preparations or notice. In other words, where the *cinci hoca*'s powers are acquired, the *evliya*'s are granted. Because their efficacy as healers revolves around their ability to perform miracles, itself understood as a consequence of the *evliya*'s proximity to God, training is of little significance for the *evliya*'s authority. Moreover, and unlike the *ocaklı*, the *evliya*'s powers are not necessarily regarded as the result of one's descent from a holy person. Rather, the *evliya* may be the holy person from whom future *ocaklı* will descend and to whom a *türbe*, or tomb, will most likely be dedicated. While one can find the tombs of *evliya*s scattered throughout Turkey, and stories of the miraculous powers of saints circulate widely, [3] living saints are nonetheless rarely encountered. Unlike other traditions of healing found in Turkey—such as those in the neighborhoods where I lived and conducted research—*evliya*s do tend to attract regular visitors and designated groups of followers.

Taken together, these traditions of religious healing treat an astonishing range of problems, disorders, and afflictions. They thereby make up a significant proportion of the therapeutic options available in both Hürriyet and Aktepe. Yet, the vast majority of these healers, although regarded as religious and ritual specialists, would not be characterized as leaders—charismatic or otherwise—of religious sects or movements. With the exception of the *evliya*, most were individuals who, like others, assumed a variety of social positions yet, because of their specialized ritual knowledge, were accorded additional respect.

It is important to note that the above schematization does not exhaust the entirety of therapeutic options available within the neighborhoods where research was conducted. This broad sketch leaves out, for instance, the ready availability of biomedical forms of healing—present in the form of small state-operated health clinics in both neighborhoods, a handful of privately owned clinics, numerous pharmacies, and several large hospitals within easy reach of the neighborhoods. Moreover, in addition to the principally religious-based forms of healing discussed above, one can also find forms of healing that are not specifically religious in character, such as the bonesetter (*kemikçi* or *kırıkçıkıkçı*), the widespread use of herbal remedies prepared by herbalists (*lokman hekimi*), and a broad array of home remedies.[4]

With that said, the ordering and categorization of therapeutic options that I have offered is not without controversy. On the one hand, distinctions between therapeutic modalities are frequently blurred in practice. It is not uncommon for individual *kurşuncu*, for instance, to employ practices associated with the *ocaklı*, such as drawing or scratching on the patient's skin. The imams of local mosques, again, may employ practices popularly associated with the *cinci hoca*. In this regard, although I have repeatedly referred to individuals as "*cinci hoca*s," "*ocaklı*s," "*kurşuncu*s," and "*evliyas*," one should keep in mind that these categorical distinctions can be quite fluid in practice. On the other hand, as I have already discussed at length, many residents of both Hürriyet and Aktepe denied the very possibility of such an ordering, in that they rejected the authority implied by granting these therapeutic traditions a position within an academic order.

Notes

Introduction

1. Quoted in Soileau (2006); see Mango (1999: 435).

2. In that the forms of religiosity discussed here typically fall under the category "popular" or "folk" religion, a few words are in order to specify my conception of "small-scale" religious authority. Peter Brown rightly observed that the categories "popular" or "folk" religion suggest a form of religiosity conceived in subordination to a presumed "orthodoxy," which is thereby implicitly granted the authority to define the criteria of legitimate religious practice (1981). While I recognize the value of such a critique, I will at times nonetheless rely on such categories, for two reasons. First, I use them at different points in order to take part in a set of specific scholarly debates that have formed around religious practices conceptualized in these terms. Second, I have found the processes of subordination described by Brown to be, in fact, ethnographically relevant. In this instance, I invoke "popular religion" as shorthand for those forms of religious life that are excluded from dominant trends in Islamic legal interpretation and that take shape in spaces outside institutions authorized by juridical Islam. I will later refer to these as "exilic" forms of religious life. In either case, I prefer the connotation of "scale" that accompanies a notion of "small-scale" authority, in that it suggests a modality of (therapeutic) power defined not by quantity or intensity, but by a horizontally configured reach of influence.

3. Nguyen and Peschard have described this as the "centrality of therapeutic systems to the political physiology of a society . . . the entanglement of the power to heal and the power to rule" (2003: 459).

4. Ahmet Kuru (2007) would describe this as an example of Turkey's (and France's) "assertive secularism," as opposed to America's "passive secularism."

5. We cannot, of course, reduce politics to a partitioning of the sensible. Accordingly, Rancière is careful to distinguish his approach from concerns with either the "aestheticization of politics" or the "politicization of aesthetics." Where the first concerns what Walter Benjamin (1968) saw as fascism's approach to life as inherently artistic and politics as a form of art, the second concerns the subordination of art to the political.

6. I am indebted here to Anna Tsing's formulation of power as the capacity to convene an audience (1990: 122).

7. By approaching therapeutic and religious authority in aesthetic terms, I intend to examine something quite different than the persuasive and affective qualities of healing as a form of performance, a topic that has received considerable attention within anthropology (Tambiah 1977; Kapferer 1991; Csordas 1994; Desjarlais 1992; Schieffelin 1985; Laderman and Roseman 1996; Laderman 1991; Roseman 1991; Danforth 1989; Joralemon 1986). Where this influential literature privileges the capacity of ritual performance to transform participants through transforming perceptual experience, my concern rests primarily with the ways different forms of therapy take part in a wider "distribution of the sensible." Mention should also be made of Halliburton's (2003) study of the aesthetic qualities of healing in South India. Halliburton's approach to aesthetics in terms of the pleasantness of treatments is nonetheless markedly different from the conceptualization of aesthetics being formulated in this book.

8. While I translate the term *laiklik* as "secularism," some argue that it is better translated as "laicism" to capture the specificity of Turkey's model of political secularism (Davison 1998, 2003; Parla and Davison 2008; White 2002; Berkes 1964). Parla and Davison, for instance, argue against the use of "secularism" because, for them, it suggests a challenge or opposition to the "ideas of religion and God"—"for secularism to exist in full, religion must be removed not only from the institutions of public life but also from the realm of individual conscience and theoretical consciousness" (63). Laicism, in this account, connotes an arrangement of political and religious authority within a state that is not necessarily anti- or irreligious. I find this definition of secularism, and their subsequent distinction between secularism and laicism, thoroughly untenable. Among its many shortcomings, the formulation confuses "secularism" (as a political project) with "secularization" (as a societal process) and simply reproduces a long discredited narrative of modernization in which "secularization" brings about the end of religion and the death of God. A large body of literature would certainly suggest a more complicated understanding of the relationship between secularism, religious practice, and religious experience (see note 9). While "laicism" might have the benefit of being a closer linguistic approximation of *laiklik* and thus better capture Turkey's indebtedness to French models of *laïcité*, I will use the term secularism—although imperfect—as a larger category within which laicism could be included. I will elaborate further on the distinctiveness of Turkish secularism in Chapter 1.

9. For the productive or "positive" qualities of secularism, see Asad (1993, 2003), Connolly (2000), Mahmood (2005), Hirschkind (2006), Scott and Hirschkind (2006), and Asad et al. (2009). Although engaging a substantially different set of concerns, see Taylor (2007) for a related critique of "subtraction stories" of secularism. For the false oppositionality of the theological and political, see LeFort (1988) and de Vries (2006). For the way ideas of "religion" and "secular" emerged out of European colonial attempts to deal with and govern religious and cultural difference, see van der Veer (2001) and Fitzgerald (2007). For a broader consideration of secularism that reflects similar analytic concerns, see Cannell (2010) and the edited volumes by Warner et al. (2010), Jakobsen and Pellegrini (2008), and Bhargava (1998).

10. For critiques of approaching the state as an agentful entity, if not an anthropo-morphized "thing," see Abrams (1988), Taussig (1997), Aretxaga (2001), and, in the case of Turkey, Navaro-Yashin (2002), as well as Alexander (2002).

11. To offer but one example, M. Hakan Yavuz's well-regarded study *Secularism and Muslim Democracy in Turkey* takes stock of the entirety of Turkey's "religious landscape" and identifies but four "actors": "political Islam; the social Islam of the widespread (neo-)Sufi groups; the state Islam of the Directorate of Religious Affairs (DRA); and the radical Islamic groups" (2009: 41–42).

12. Although I will return to this topic repeatedly in this book, anthropologists have developed a rich corpus of analytic approaches to healing and therapeutic processes. Where some anthropologists have, for instance, considered ritual healing as a means to examine the operation of symbolic structures and mythic worlds in the ordering of society and experience (Lévi-Strauss 1963; Dow 1986), others have emphasized the capac-ity of healing rituals to resolve social conflict (V. Turner 1967; Katz 1982). In turn, anthropologists have repeatedly turned to notions of performance and dramaturgy to locate therapeutic efficacy within the capacity of ritual performance to constitute experi-ence and remake selves (Tambiah 1977; Kapferer 1991; Schieffelin 1985); to forge links between music, sentiment, and bodies (Laderman 1991; Roseman 1993); or to rework interactions between cultural sensibilities, emotional distress, and bodily experience (Desjarlais 1992). Where some turn to theories of narrative to explore how patients can be drawn along therapeutic plots (Mattingly 1998), still others engage theories of embodiment and rhetoric to explore how persuasion can work to incrementally alter one's embodied orientation to the world (Csordas 1994). To read this literature chrono-logically, in fact, is to rehearse a remarkably coherent introduction to the major develop-ments in anthropological theory in the past half-century, moving from the structuralism of Lévi-Strauss through the cultural phenomenology of Csordas.

13. Tendencies to privilege text over context in the study of religion, especially with the study of Islam, have been a longstanding point of critique among anthropolo-gists. Stanley Tambiah a quarter century ago noted that "to confine the study of 'reli-gion' to the doctrinal beliefs and philosophical constructs is an unfortunate rationalist Enlightenment legacy that both unduly narrows and pauperizes the phenomenon" (1984: 7). Writing nearly twenty years earlier, concerned specifically with Islam, Clif-ford Geertz captures a similar sensibility when he contends that "whatever God may or may not be—living, dead, or merely ailing—religion is a social institution, worship a social activity, and faith a social force. To trace the pattern of their changes is neither to collect relics of revelation nor to assemble a chronicle of error. It is to write a social history of the imagination" (1968: 19). Each is responding to the prevailing and continuing bias within the scholarship on religion toward the study of religious formations with coherently articulated philosophies, established doctrines, instituted practices, and traditions of textual interpretation.

14. Concern with the religious and political lives of women is especially prominent here. See the works of White (2002), Çınar (2005), Göle (1996), and Saktanber (2002)

for ethnographically grounded examples of this trend. For an excellent ethnographic study of the Fethullah Gülen movement, see Turam (2007).

15. Such an approach becomes less an anthropological engagement with the state than a "state philosophy," in the sense introduced by Deleuze and Guattari—where analytic concepts align with the needs of states: "If it is advantageous for thought to prop itself up with the State, it is no less advantageous for the State to extend itself in thought, and to be sanctioned by it as the unique, universal form" (1987: 375).

16. Readers familiar with this literature will notice that I appear to be working with the much-maligned distinction introduced by Ernest Gellner (1981) between "High Islam" (literate, urban, scriptural, rationalized, philosophical, respected) and "Low Islam" (magical, illiterate, rural, popular). I will not rehearse the numerous critiques of Gellner's work, but say that such distinctions do not hold for the forms of Islam addressed in this book—ones that are, using his terminology, at once popular, urban, and literate.

17. Because I am concerned with these religious formations in relation to healing and recovery, I should be careful to note that this list does not exhaust the totality of therapeutic options available in the neighborhoods. For instance, I will not address forms of healing not commonly defined in religious terms (e.g., herbalists, bonesetters, midwives) and forms of healing that although religious in nature do not include a living healer (such as shrine visitation).

18. For ethnographic examples of such work in Turkey, see Çınar (2005), Göle (1996), and Navaro-Yashin (2002).

19. Giorgio Agamben alerts us to the utility of thinking through the exception, as well as the passion it elicits. "The exception," writes Agamben, "does not only confirm the rule, the rule as such lives off the exception alone" (1998: 16). Quoting Carl Schmitt's *Political Theology* at length, he continues: "'when one really wants to study the general, one need only look around for a real exception. It brings everything to light more clearly than the general itself. After a while, one becomes disgusted with the endless talk about the general. . . . [T]he general is thought about not with passion but only with comfortable superficiality. The exception, on the other hand, thinks the general with intense passion'" (Schmitt 1985, quoted and translated in Agamben 1998: 16). For Agamben, it is the exception—the capacity to suspend law, declare an exception—that constitutes sovereignty. And it is through tracing the biopolitical significance of this form of juridical exception that one can examine the hidden logic organizing the political rationalities of modernity.

20. On the distinction between "belief" and "knowledge," see Good (1994).

21. I have in mind here Michael Taussig's "colonial mirror of production"—a "mirroring of otherness that reflects back onto the [anthropologists] the barbarity of their own social relations" (1987: 134).

22. Much of what I read before beginning my research led me to initially regard these resistances as a consequence of my desire to conduct research on a topic that

was closely associated with gendered spheres of domestic labor, spheres from which men were to be typically excluded. While it would be nonsensical to suggest that gender was an insignificant methodological factor, I nonetheless found that it worked in concert with multiple other factors to shape the limits of my research. I often found, for instance, that my status as a "foreigner" and non-native speaker of Turkish created social affordances that were not available to my male interlocutors. More significantly, I did not find the therapeutic worlds that I moved through to be nearly as segregated as expected. While specific healers may have attracted a predominantly female clientele (as with particular *kurşuncu*), this was not the general case.

23. I have in mind here Kim Fortun's (2001) concept of "enunciative communities."

24. This formulation is drawn from Homi Bhabha's account of the work of mimetic desire in colonial discourse. For Bhabha, the complex mimetic response of the colonized to colonialism was structured by a difference impossible to overcome, such that the colonized were always to be "not white/not quite" (1994). Abdallah Laroui's related discussion of the temporal disjuncture or "time-lag" of (Moroccan) postcoloniality, as described by Pandolfo (2000), seems particularly relevant here. For Laroui, Arab consciousness takes shape through identifying with Western forms of consciousness that are, in their very availability for identification, already anachronistic: "It is as if, in the effort to make sense of itself, the Orient turned into an archeologist and rediscovered superseded forms of Western consciousness. . . . Yet, because of the time-lag effect [*décalage dans le temps*], in contemporary Arab thought the phase of reality for each form of consciousness is already ideological. This explains, perhaps, the lack of freshness and the superficiality that many readers, familiar with European history, feel in reading modern Arab writings" (Laroui 1982: 37; cited in Pandolfo 2000: 123–24).

25. This history also teaches us an important lesson in geography, in that Turkey arose out of the remnants of the multiethnic and religiously plural Ottoman Empire that, at its most expansive, reached across large swaths of the Arabian Peninsula, through the eastern Mediterranean, northward into the Balkans, and westward to present-day Algeria.

26. Fieldwork for this project formally began in 1997, with a brief stay in Ankara, followed by a year of field research in 1999–2000, and a period of follow-up research in 2005.

Chapter 1. Medicine and the Will to Civilization

Epigraphs: Michel Foucault, "Two Lectures" (1980: 83); Ministry of Culture, Republic of Turkey (2005).

1. This first-hand description of Mustafa Kemal's landing draws heavily on, and in a sense seeks to reproduce, Kinross's ingratiating account of these events—even though Kinross was not himself present (1964: 163).

2. For a discussion of Dr. Refik Saydam's influence on the history of medicine and health policy in Turkey, see Yürür-Kutlay (1998) and Demirhan-Erdemir and Öncel (2006).

3. Gökalp embraced Durkheim's notion of the supremacy of society over the individual in order to assert that the nation was to be the natural social and political unit. See Davison (1998) and Parla (1985) for a discussion of Ziya Gökalp's writings on Turkish nationalism.

4. In this brief depiction of the history of Turkish nationalist thought, I cannot do justice to the complexity of ideas and relations that surrounded debates about nationalism during this period. Kadıoğlu (2010), for instance, makes the important observation that there were noteworthy differences between Gökalp's vision of Turkish nationalism—in which religion was to be removed from state institutions and placed within (national) culture as a basis of social solidarity—and those of the early republican elite, who viewed religion as a more negative and ultimately threatening force in relation to the emerging nation. While I do not dispute Kadıoğlu's claims, I would suggest that the broad outline of Gökalp's nationalist vision was nonetheless exceedingly influential in the work of these early reformers, even if they rejected Gökalp's desire to create a "synthesis" of "Turkism," "Islamism," and "Westernism."

5. For these reasons, Turkish secularism is frequently compared to the French model of laïcité, which suggests a subordination of religion to the state, as compared to a separation of religion and state. See Introduction, note 8.

6. For a related consideration of the ways that the concept of religion is indebted to a history of European secular reform, see Asad (1993).

7. See Good and Good (1992) for an anthropological consideration of Greco-Islamic medicine, alternatively labeled "Islamic medicine," "Galenic-Islamic medicine," or "Arabic medicine."

8. For further reading on the history of medicine in the Ottoman Empire, see Aydın (1995, 1996b) and Shefer-Mossensohn (2009). My discussion of the history of biomedical services during this period is focused principally on the Anatolian provinces of the empire.

9. The Faculty of Medicine would be one of the first state institutions to teach European history and literature. Tıphane-i Amire would also provide a setting for the early organization of the Young Turks, among them Dr. Refik Saydam.

10. A contributor to the journal Ülkü, writing ten years after the founding of the republic, describes well the sentiment toward Ottoman healthcare policy: "We will never be able to forget, nor will we ever forget, the degree to which village health services were neglected and how spending even the smallest amount of money from the state's purse on them was withheld in the period before our Republic" (Ülkü 1933: 254).

11. For considerations of the history of medicine during the early republican period, see Sağlık ve Sosyal Yardım, Bakanlığı (1973), Ege (1998), and Aydın (1997).

12. As of 1925, there were 1,631 doctors working in some fashion with the state, and an estimated additional 600 in private practice. Of 326 administrative districts in

the country, only 96 of the district capitals had even a single doctor. By 1946, there were 4,590 doctors, 1,085 dentists, 1,635 midwives, 2,697 health personnel, 475 nurses, 600 village health personnel, and 730 village midwives employed or licensed by the state. These, as well as other healthcare statistics used in this chapter, come from Sağlık Bakanlığı (1996), Aydın (1997), and Zürcher (1997).

13. Recalling this period, Aşık Veysel, the great poet and musician of village life (1894–1973), sang the praise of the new nation and its care in a poem entitled "Hospital": "The afflicted seek remedy in you / You serve the nation, hospital / It bandages wounds of all sorts / Long live the doctors, the glorious hospital . . . / The hospital is a great blessing in Sivas / The sick come and go with ease / My God! Don't leave anyone in tears / In every province let there be a hospital" (Veysel 1985: 194).

14. One must of course be cautious not to reduce biomedicine to solely a site of ideological production or political control. At this juncture, it is also necessary to make a point that is perhaps obvious to many readers. Regardless of tendencies to (mis)construe modernization as Europeanization, the "civilizational" changes promoted by these political and medical reformers should not be regarded simply as instances of imitation. On the one hand, as numerous scholars have demonstrated, all systems of medical knowledge and practice are both constitutive of and constituted by particular cultural contexts (Kleinman 1980; Good 1977, 1994; Rhodes 1996; Kuriyama 1999; Langford 2002), making them unfinished products of cultural history (Gaines 1991, 1992). On the other hand, as many others have observed, we cannot accept an autogenous conceptualization of European modernity, in that notions of Europeanness—as well as ideas of "religion," "culture," "liberalism," and so on—were themselves formulated through the colonial careers of European empire. Instead, this chapter aims to examine the role of medical reform in Turkey's project of secular modernity, revealing some of the inconsistencies, affordances, and unintended consequences that coincided with the expansion of Turkey's medical system. Moreover, by examining figures and practices that are excluded or marginalized from the modern, we begin to gain an understanding of both modernity's shifting boundaries and the ways these figures, in their exclusion, play a constituting role in the staging of the modern. I am reminded here of Timothy Mitchell's observation that modernity is defined by both its universalism as a project (its claims to uniqueness and unity) and its singularity as an always incomplete realization of this project (2000).

15. Following Gyan Prakash's characterization of the role of science in colonial India, the clinic operated as a small-scale "legitimating sign of rationality and progress" (1999: 7).

16. Although this dramatic increase is partly a result of increased licensure, as well as a relatively high rate of population growth, the overall increase in the number of physicians is nonetheless dramatic. These statistics come from Sağlık Bakanlığı (1996, 2002) and Aydın (1997).

17. For a discussion of the Turkish medical system during this period, see Aydın (1996a), Fişek (1981), and Öztek and Eren (1996).

18. For a revealing consideration of the role of the military in introducing modern disciplinary techniques into the Ottoman Empire, which also resituates Turkey's political and social genealogy into the Balkans, see Silverstein (2003). For a thorough discussion of the role of the military and the idea of the "military-nation" in Turkish nationalism and Turkish national development, see Altınay (2004).

19. Although disbanded in 1950 amid accusations of being too closely tied to the ruling political party, a second period of activity began with their reopening in 1963. The zeal and enthusiasm of the 1930s and 1940s, however, would not be recaptured. For an overview of the People's Houses, see Karpat (1963) and Karaömerlioğlu (1998). For a relevant discussion of the role of theater in the People's Houses, see Arı (2004).

20. Adnan Menderes would later become an instrumental figure in closing the People's Houses.

21. The full run of *Ülkü Halkevleri Mecmuası* consists of three periods (1933–1941, 1941–1946, 1947–1950), each with distinct volume and issue numbers (1: 1–17: 102, 1: 1–11: 126, 1: 1–8: 23 respectively). Because the last two periods reflect an ideological shift away from the journal's initial goal of populist, nationalist re-education, my discussion focuses principally on the first period.

22. This echoes closely the work of Reşit Galip (1893–1934), a prominent figure in the development of state theories of Turkish history. Drawing on R. B. Dixon's *The Racial History of Man*, published in 1923, Galip worked to overturn the substantial body of anthropological work that had classified Turks as members of the "yellow" or "Mongolian race." Following Dixon, he placed Turks in the category brachycephalic— what Dixon regarded as an "Alpine type" predominant in southeastern Europe and western Asia—so as demonstrate the "natural" disposition of Turks for European civilization. For further discussion of Galip, see Vryonis (1991).

23. Again, this emphasis on medicine as a means of political enlightenment was not necessarily unique to the Republican era. Sanal, for instance, describes Ottoman anatomists of the 1820s imagining their work as taking part in a larger project of civilizational enlightenment (2011).

24. "This shift from primary to secondary identifications," writes Slavoj Žižek, "does not involve a direct loss of primary identifications: what happens is that primary identifications undergo a kind of transubstantiation; they start to function as the form of appearance of the universal secondary identification (say, precisely by being a good member of my family, I thereby contribute to the proper functioning of my nation-state)" (1999: 90).

25. Lessons about "appropriate" healthy behavior made regular appearances in *Ülkü*. For example, fictionalized accounts of scarlet fever outbreaks in Istanbul instructed readers about the global mobility of disease (as it passed "from China, Java, India, Buhkara . . . to Turkey, Java, China, . . . and Mecca"), the importance of eschewing home remedies and seeking medical care immediately ("Doctor! If the girl's mother and father had not been negligent and if they had reached you in time, maybe

you could have saved her"), and the measures that could be taken to prevent the spread of disease (Nuri 1933: 169–70).

26. Çınar, in her analysis of the politics of clothing during the early republican era and among Islamists in the 1990s, identifies a similar series of processes whereby individual bodies become envisioned as sites of simultaneous personal and national development (2005).

27. In the decades to come, the vocabulary of war and militarism would be repeatedly invoked to assert the state's image as the great protector of the nation's health, as in the pivotal "Malaria Wars" of the early and mid-twentieth century (Aydın 1998).

28. Pierre Bourdieu records a strikingly similar story during his research in Algeria in the 1950s. An elderly Kabyle woman explained to him: "In the old days, folk didn't know what illness was. They went to bed and they died. It's only nowadays that we're learning words like liver, lung, intestines, stomach, and I don't know what! . . . Now everyone's sick, everyone's complaining of something. . . . Who's ill nowadays? Who's well? Everyone complains but no one stays in bed; they all run to the doctor. Everyone knows what's wrong with him now" (1977: 166–67). This story is used by Bourdieu to support his argument regarding the ways objective and internalized structures align within determinate social formations—where the established cosmological and political order is perceived as a self-evident and natural order, such that agents' aspirations have the same limits as the objective conditions of which they are a product. Nancy Scheper-Hughes would later cite the same passage as an instance of medicalization (1993: 196). Remarkably, both take the veracity of this recollection for granted, thereby failing to consider its full complexity. Neither consider, for instance, that the temporality of the narrative—an "old days" without illness giving way to a present overflowing with illness—might itself be indebted to colonialism, as but one instance of a nostalgic reconstruction of a time before colonial rule.

29. A prominent example of this disdain can be found in a series of seventeenth-century scandals that involved Sultan "Deli" Ibrahim's (Ibrahim the Mad's) close relationship with a cinci hoca. See Ahmet Refik Altınay's Samur Devri (1927) and M. Turhan Tan's historical novel Osmanlı Rasputini Cinci Hoca (1938).

30. For an illuminating, and parallel, discussion of the ways the major mystical figures and poets of Turkish history—for example, Mevlana, Yunus Emre, and Hacı Bektaş—were repurposed in Turkish nationalist thought so as to indicate the historical depth of Turkey's humanist tradition, see Soileau (2006).

31. Numerous scholars have considered the ways medicine and public health, particularly in colonial contexts, served to extend governmental control over bodies (see W. Anderson 2006; Arnold 1993; Bashford 2004; Comaroff 1993; Harrison 1994; Prakash 1999). Working under the rubric of colonial, imperial, or tropical medicine, however, this scholarship is exclusively concerned with the relationship of medicine to colonialism. My attention to the relationship between biomedicine and preexisting healing traditions in a noncolonial context introduces a parallel, yet underexplored,

set of concerns—particularly as they relate to my specific interest in secularism. Fanon (1965), Comaroff (1985), and Pandolfo (2000), although still working in colonial contexts, do address the relationship between biomedical and "indigenous" forms of therapy. See, as well, Nancy Rose Hunt's *A Colonial Lexicon* (1999).

Chapter 2. Healing Difference at the Limits of Community

1. *Bilinç*, the root of *bilinçsiz*, literally translates as "sense," "conscious," or "consciousness." In this context, *bilinçsiz* carries connotations of being ignorant, unenlightened, or uneducated.

2. Stacey Pigg, writing about the "question of belief" in shamanism in Nepal, describes a similar process whereby her interlocutors' commentaries on shamanism served to position the speakers within a series of overlapping discourses concerning modernity, development, and national identity (1996). In a related vein, as Katherine Ewing describes in her study of *pir*s in Pakistan, "When talking with people in the neighborhood where I lived . . . I needed only to turn the conversation to the subject of pirs to see ideology in action" (1997: 94). Byron Good's analysis of the status of belief in anthropological analysis (1994) seems to indicate an alternate, if not related, approach to thinking about the ideological implications of speaking about "belief." For relevant discussions of the play between ritual healing practices and the articulation of communal or cultural identities, see Crandon-Malamud (1991), Sharp (1993), Csordas (1999), Tsing (1993), Brodwin (1996), Langford (2002), and Kapferer (1991).

3. I initially demarcated these research sites by the government-defined boundary of the *mahalle* (neighborhood, or district), which are sub-units of the larger municipality. The artificiality of these administrative units would become quickly apparent. *Mahalle* boundaries had little to do with the social boundaries recognized by people residing in each neighborhood. I came to roughly locate my research in areas linked together through regional, village, familial, and social ties that crossed and were never fully encompassed by *mahalle* boundaries. The fictitious names I have chosen—Aktepe and Hürriyet—refer to these social communities.

4. For a discussion of piecework and family workshop production in a comparable neighborhood in Istanbul, see White (1994). For *gecekondu* neighborhoods as a source of domestic service labor in Ankara, see Ozyegin (2001).

5. By 1997, 60 percent of Turkey's population were living primarily in cities, compared to 18.3 percent in 1945 and 16.4 percent in 1927. See Devlet İstatistik Enstitüsü (1974, 1975), Heper (1978), and Hacettepe University Institute of Population Studies (1999).

6. Although both neighborhoods have experienced significant change over the past two decades, Hürriyet and Aktepe were still made up primarily of original settlers, their families, and (former) co-villagers. This differs from the forms of *gecekondu* development described by White (2002) and Şenyapılı (1992) in Istanbul, where early forms of social cohesion dissipated as neighborhoods transformed into heterogeneous urban neighborhoods comprised mostly of renters. In Hürriyet, despite increased construction of multistory apartment buildings, especially in 2000–2005, these new apartments were primarily for the expanding families of the original settlers. Neighborhood

composition also continued to be closely regulated by prominent property owners and real estate agents. That said, these trends do suggest that a significant transformation in community life is on the horizon.

7. Although *gecekondu* neighborhoods are commonly described as "slums" or "shantytowns," they bear little resemblance to their structural parallels elsewhere (e.g., *bidonevilles* in Morocco, *favelas* in Brazil, *barriadas* in Peru, or *bustees* in India). Indeed, debate persists concerning the analytic utility of the concept *gecekondu*, as compared to *varoş*, "suburb" (Pérouse 2004). I nonetheless use *gecekondu* because it continues to wield a powerful social force in the neighborhoods where I worked, as well as in interactions with those who lived outside such neighborhoods.

8. The scholarly literature on urban development in Turkey does little more than confirm, albeit with more subtlety, popular discourse on *gecekondu* life. While scholarly considerations in English remain limited, there is an extensive literature in Turkish that addresses aspects of urbanization and *gecekondu* development. As with other research grounded in traditional models of migration studies that emphasize themes of migrant adaptation and urban integration, these studies tend to portray migration as a unilinear process that moves ineluctably toward the modern/urban (see Yörükan 1968; Karpat 1976; Kongar 1976; Erder 1982; Ersoy 1985; Gökçe et al. 1993; Sosyoloji Derneği 1997). This work also overlooks significant differences within and between *gecekondu* neighborhoods, collapsing analyses under a generic notion of *The Gecekondu*, the title of Kemal Karpat's influential book (1976). In this regard, these studies take part in a wider discursive production of the *gecekondu* that is at once homogenizing and totalizing. Not only does the reader gain limited insight into the lives of migrants and *gecekondu* residents, little effort is made to capture the diversity of experiences and processes the term *gecekondu* subsumes. Notable ethnographic exceptions can be found in the works of Tahire Erman (1996, 1998), Sema Erder (1996, 1997), Jenny White (1994), Ayşe Güneş-Ayata (1987), and Neslihan Demirtaş (2009).

9. For example, the cover of Umut Duyar-Kienast's study *The Formation of Gecekondu Settlements in Turkey* (2005) is a photograph of Mamak. For a history of Mamak Municipality, see Dermirtaş (2009).

10. Indeed, Alevis are a heterogeneous group of Turkish, Kurdish, Arabic, and Albanian-speaking non-Sunni Muslims, and Alevi is used as an umbrella term for various religious groups alternatively called Bektaşi, Kızılbaş, Nusayri, Abdal, Ocakzade, Çelebi, Tahtacı, or Çepni (Erdemir 2005).

11. This brief consideration of Alevism is drawn primarily from conversations with residents of Hürriyet, supplemented by scholarly works such as Birge (1937); Noyan (1995, 1998, 1999); Olsson, Özdalga, and Raudvere (1998); Güneş-Ayata (1992); Bal (1997a, 1997b); Shankland (1990, 2003); Keçeli and Yalçın (1996); Erdemir (2005); Erman and Göker (2000); and Soekfeld (2008).

12. State persecution dates back to at least the sixteenth century when Alevis sided with opposition forces of the Safavid Shah Ismail against Ottoman Sultan Selim I, after which the sultan decreed that the Alevi were to be excluded from Ottoman society.

13. For the Alevis with whom I spoke, the ideals of tolerance, humanist inclusion, and equality are what set Turkish Alevis apart from other Shiʻi communities of the region, such as the Shiʻa of Iran and Iraq, or the Alawi of Syria.

14. For a discussion of the specific ways religious and nationalist politics are played out over women's bodies, see Chatterjee (1993) and Abu-Lughod (1998). See also Malek Alloula's *The Colonial Harem* (1986). To this discussion could be added contemporary European debates about secularism and Islamic forms of sociality occurring under the pretense of headscarves and over, once again, women's bodies. See, for instance, Bowen (2008) and J. Scott (2007).

15. This refers to the solidified piece of lead that is interpreted by the *kurşuncu* with the hope of identifying the origins of the "evil eye," or *nazar*. A piece of this lead is frequently pinned to the patient's clothing, as was the case here.

16. While I can only touch on the topic here, the ways Fikret distinguished himself from his brother Bektaş reflect larger processes of internal differentiation that have become increasingly common within Alevi communities. Sehriban Şahin, for instance, writes about the rising influence of Alevi research-writers in the broader Alevi community (2005). David Shankland writes about divisions between those who view Alevism as a distinct religious faith and those who approach it as a humanist philosophy that offers guiding principles for life in the modern world (1999).

17. Attributing the murder of Hüseyin to "Sunnis," as was common in Hürriyet, simplifies a more complex history. To be precise, Hüseyin was murdered in the Battle of Kerbela at the hands of the Umayyads, who recognized Abu Bakr rather than Hüseyin's father Ali as the leader of the Islamic community following Muhammed's death.

18. In a rare example of research conducted in both Alevi and Sunni urban neighborhoods, Allen Dubetsky described the movement between neighborhoods as a movement across two moral communities (1977). Hüseyin Bal (1997a, b) and David Shankland (1990) more recently conducted comparative research between rural Alevi and Sunni communities. Although these studies offer important insights into Alevi-Sunni relations, they depict communities that are far more circumscribed than what I encountered in Hürriyet and Aktepe. Moreover, the emergence of identity-based political mobilization and its accompanying revitalization of languages of difference as means of gaining political recognition have proven transformative to communal dynamics and identity, especially among the Alevi. The increasing electoral influence of pro-Islamist political parties has also had a significant impact on these dynamics within neighborhoods such as Aktepe.

19. Such comparisons between Alevism and shamanism are by no means isolated to everyday discourse in Aktepe. Irène Mélikoff, for instance, speaks of Alevism as an "Islamized shamanism" (1998).

20. For a discussion of the concept of "progress" in relation to contemporary Islamic practice in Lebanon, see Deeb (2006).

21. I am indebted here to Saba Mahmood's observations concerning the cultivation of bodily and affective dispositions and capacities through practices of ethical

self-making among female participants in Cairo's mosque movement (2005). In this case, I am referring specifically to her discussion of the role of fear, fear of God in particular, in such practices of ethical cultivation. "For many Muslims, the ability to fear God is considered to be one of the critical registers by which one monitors and assesses the progress of the moral self toward virtuosity, and the absence of fear is regarded as the marker of an inadequately formed self" (141). Such fear, in other words, is an affective capacity that one must cultivate through continual ethical practice, such that an inability to feel frightened (of the retribution of God) can be understood as "both the *cause* and the *consequence* of a life lived deliberately without virtue" (141). Suggesting the utility of such an emphasis on ethical self-cultivation, Heiko Henkel (2007) and Rebecca Bryant (2005) have separately employed a similar approach to examine the relationship between (ethical) self-cultivation and modernity in the context of inhabiting urban space and folk musical performance, respectively, in Istanbul.

22. Only once did a conversation in Aktepe draw a causal relationship between Alevism and the practice of religious healing. On this occasion, when I explained to a resident that I was living in Mamak so as to do field research, he expressed considerable confusion about my choice to reside in Hürriyet. To truly understand Turkey, he asserted, I needed to live in a good Muslim neighborhood like Aktepe. After offering any number of reasons for living in Hürriyet (foremost being that I could not find someone to rent me an apartment in Aktepe), he was only satisfied when I explained that my research interests involved religious forms of healing. He understood because Alevism, "as we all know," is a form of "shamanism" (*şamanizm*) and one would of course expect the widespread presence of such healing practices among descendants of shamans.

23. This tendency to view Sunni Islam in normative terms repeats itself throughout scholarly and media accounts of religion in Turkey.

24. This suggestion that the listener had lost the capacity to discern what warranted attention draws on ideas developed in Hirschkind's study of ethical listening and Islamic counterpublics in Cairo (2006).

Chapter 3. Hagiographies of the Living: Saintly Speech
and Other Wonders of Secular Life

Epigraph: Jacques Derrida, "Faith and Knowledge" (1998: 44).

1. For related approaches to secularism as a productive historical, social, and ethical force, see Connolly (2000), Mahmood (2005), Hirschkind (2006), and Scott and Hirschkind (2006).

2. See Irvine (1996) for an illuminating discussion of the multiple shades of participation that make up speech events. See Keane (1997) for an overview of similar topics specifically in relation to "religious language," an overview that also builds on yet extends Goffman's elaboration of participant roles and participation structures within speech events (1981).

3. Gül Baba was a sixteenth-century Bektaşi dervish and companion of Sultan Süleyman the Magnificent. The tomb of Gül Baba continues to be a popular pilgrimage site in Budapest.

4. This emphasis on *keramet* (Arabic, *karama*) as evidence of Zöhre Ana's status as an *evliya* is not shared in all accounts of Muslim sainthood, particularly those based in North Africa. One finds in North African studies of saintly authority, especially in Morocco, a focus on the concept of *baraka*, which Geertz defined as "blessing, in the sense of divine favor" and whose best analog is "personal presence, force of character, moral vividness" (1968: 44). A critical feature of *baraka*, according to Julien, is that it can be transmitted between saints and kin or disciples, thus perpetuating saintly lineages (1970). These studies of Muslim sainthood, typically working under the concept of "maraboutism," are deeply indebted to Weberian formulations of authority and correspondingly match the concept of *baraka* to Weber's notion of "charisma." See, for instance, Gellner (1969), Geertz (1968), B. Turner (1974), and Gilsenan (1973), as well as Cornell (1998) for a more recent appraisal of this body of research. In our case, Zöhre Ana's followers did not regard her sainthood as emanating from or being captured by a notion of *baraka*, or the Turkish approximation *bereket*. Instead, they emphasized her *keramet*, her ability to perform miracles. Her "sense of presence," however, was not *keramet* per se; both, rather, were regarded as signs of her saintliness, frequently glossed as her *evliyalık* or *vilayet*.

5. I can only gesture here toward the sizable scholarly literature that addresses manifestations of sainthood in different Islamic traditions, as well as the complex theological basis of sainthood in Islam (see, e.g., Goldziher 1971; Denny 1988; Smith and Ernst 1993; Faroquhi 1979; Crapanzano 1973; Ewing 1997; Gellner 1969; Gilsenan 1973; Keddie 1972; Cruise O'Brien and Coulon 1988; Hoffman 1995; Basu and Werbner 1998). As many have argued (Cornell 1998; B. Turner 1974; Denny 1988), however, we must take great care in applying the label "saint" to the forms of religious life considered here. "When we use the term 'saint' to apply to Islamic cases of the holiness of persons," writes Denny, "we must do so with the understanding that we are importing a foreign notion that only partially fits the data" (1988: 70). For Denny, the Arabic term commonly translated as "saint"—*awliyā* (plural of *walī*, and *evliya* in Turkish)— suggests one's proximity to God (e.g., being "one of God's friends") rather than an individual's holiness. Approached in these terms, "sainthood" connotes a specific form of relatedness, rather than an individual quality—a distinction we will return to in later chapters.

6. The foundation would later change its name to the Açık Kapı Derneği (The Open Door Association).

7. As with many terms in Zöhre Ana's *nefesler*, *dem* carries several divergent connotations. In this instance, *dem* can refer to blood, breath, spirit, time, and steeping tea. See Soileau (forthcoming) for a thorough discussion of the significance of *dem* in the context of Bektaşi ritual.

8. Maurice Bloch (1974) would depict this in terms of the "illocutionary force" as compared to the "propositional force" of ritual language. In fact, there are many ways to frame Zöhre Ana's saintly speech analytically, particularly in terms of its therapeutic qualities. Tambiah (1977), for instance, drawing heavily on the linguistic theory of J. L. Austin, conceptualizes ritual healing in terms of a performative model of ritual communication. Taussig (1987) and Desjarlais (1992) argue for the potentially therapeutic power of "wild" images in ritual language. In our case, these approaches should be distinguished from those that highlight such processes as the narrative construction of therapeutic plots (Mattingly 1998), the dialogic constructions of performative realities (Schieffelin 1985), or the forms of rhetorical persuasion described by Csordas (2002), Harding (2001), and, in a related vein, Favret-Saada (1980). The extremely limited interactions between Zöhre Ana and her visitors do not allow for the sorts of dialogic exchanges that these approaches emphasize, a topic to which we will return in Chapter 5.

9. To this could be added a discussion of the shifting temporal coordinates of Zöhre Ana's *nefesler*. Given the way people, spaces, and events conjoin here, we could suggest, following Bakhtin (1981), that her *nefesler* exhibit a particular "chronotope," a distinct configuration of time and space that orders her saintly language. For a relevant anthropological engagement with Bakhtin's concept of chronotope, see Lambek's examination of practices of spirit mediumship in Madagascar (2002). For Lambek, performances of spirit mediumship represent settings where diverse historical figures can inhabit the contemporary, thereby articulating a distinct historicity and means by which people can "bear" history.

10. The intertwining of voice, name, and place characteristic of her *nefesler* is particularly apparent in her second book, *Mehtaptaki Erenler* (Saints in the Moonlight). In its basic format, the book represents a prophetic travelogue and guidebook. Organized regionally, *Mehtaptaki Erenler* catalogues her visitations to tombs spread throughout Turkey, accompanied by the *nefes* the respective saint inspired in Zöhre Ana (along with a photograph of her or her family at the tomb). In keeping with her duty as an *evliya*, the *nefesler* associated with particular tombs work to undo historical misperceptions that have accumulated around deceased *evliya*s. Although the prophetic aspect of the book is unique, it draws on a tradition of popular-oriented books describing Anatolian tombs and shrines (e.g., Araz 1966).

11. This is in reference to the setting of the Battle of Dumlupınar, the final major battle of the War of Independence.

12. One of the significant reforms introduced by Atatürk was the replacement of the Arabic script used for Ottoman Turkish with a modified Latin alphabet.

13. Although *hoca* is used widely as an honorific when addressing a teacher or scholar, it is used here to ridicule what Zöhre Ana regards as a regressive and dogmatic form of Sunni religious authority—the form of authority associated with the figure of the *cinci hoca*.

14. Much more could be said about the irony generated from Atatürk's returned presence in Zöhre Ana's saintly language. For instance, a significant set of reforms promoted under Atatürk concerned the standardization of the Turkish language. One of the objectives in these reforms was to make standardized Turkish more comprehensible to the ordinary citizen (unlike the notoriously unintelligible Ottoman Turkish, the administrative language of the Ottoman state), so that the new citizen could fully understand the language of politicians and theologians alike. Atatürk's appearance in Zöhre Ana's *nefesler* would appear to belie this history. He uses anything but the unadorned and easily intelligible Turkish sought after in language reforms. At the same time, the difficulty of comprehending the meaning of Atatürk's statements in Zöhre Ana's *nefesler* could also be regarded as a commentary on the forms of unintelligibility that were themselves foundational to secular reform. After all, the "reformed" Turkish Atatürk used in many of his speeches was, for some time, largely incomprehensible to audiences. Similarly, his acclaimed *Nutuk* speech (which lasted, in all, thirty-six hours and chronicled his vision of the nation's origins) must be translated to be understood by contemporary audiences.

15. See Mardin (1991) and Bozdoğan (2001) for further discussions of the prevalence of religious idioms in early formulations of Turkish nationalism. See also Tapper (1987) for an alternate reading of the relationship between Islamic and secular nationalist ideologies in Turkey.

16. While an intense admiration for Atatürk is assuredly commonplace, especially among Alevi, it is worth pointing out again that he is regarded by the vast majority of people as a political hero, not as an *evliya*.

17. For an excellent analysis of the role of architecture in the nation-building projects of the early Republic, see Sibel Bozdoğan's *Modernism and Nation Building* (2001).

18. In a discussion of the material externality of ideology, Slavoj Žižek argues that architecture holds a unique capacity for communicating truths that cannot be spoken openly. Taking as his example the enormous statues of the idealized New Man constructed atop office buildings in the Soviet Union, Žižek asks: "Does not this external, material feature of architectural design reveal the 'truth' of the Stalinist ideology in which actual, living people are reduced to instruments, sacrificed as the pedestal for the spectre of the future New Man, an ideological monster which crushes actual living men under his feet?" (1997: 3). Žižek's point, of course, is not simply that ideology permeates the material. Rather, he suggests, we find in ideology's materialization antagonisms that the explicit formulation of ideology cannot afford to acknowledge.

19. For a discussion of secular nationalist conceptualizations of the "Kemalist woman," see Bozdoğan (2001). For a broader discussion of the discursive position of women in such secular nationalist visions of gender and modernity, see Sirman (1989), Kandiyoti (1989), and Göle (1996).

20. As in other settings where feminist ideals express a particular set of class possibilities, it must be noted that Zöhre Ana's ability to live up to these ideals and openly

renounce gendered conventions commonly ascribed to women in her class position in Turkey was made possible by the authority and autonomy she gained by becoming a saint.

21. The opening of Zöhre Ana's first book explains: "Nearly everyone knows that the principles of modern medicine began with Hippocrates, who was born in İstanköy or on Kos Island about an hour from our beautiful Bodrum in 460 BC. . . . From that day until now, medical science has, with various fits and starts, progressed. Within the social and technical possibilities of the century we find ourselves in, we have reached an apex. . . . On the one hand, let medical science keep developing. On the other hand, people before and after Hippocrates have used other methods of curing outside of scientific practices" (1991: 5).

22. Zöhre Ana is not exceptional in being a female saint. Though the majority of saintly figures are male, there is an established tradition of women being ascribed such miraculous powers. She was distinctive, however, in terms of the ways gender was performed through her saintliness and the ways her saintliness embodied recognizable secularist ideals of female autonomy and feminine visibility.

23. For a discussion of the ways the idea of the Turkish state takes part in everyday processes of self-definition, community identity, and gender politics in a rural setting, see Sirman (1990).

Chapter 4. The Therapeutics of Piety

1. Unlike accounts of *cins* (or *jinn*) elsewhere in the Muslim world, I did not encounter individuals—let alone *cinci hocas*—developing long-term relationships with individual *cins*, what has been depicted elsewhere through metaphors of "marriage" (see Crapanzano 1973; Masquelier 2001).

2. The use of these texts was not without controversy. While I was on a trip to a village in central Turkey to visit a renowned *cinci hoca*, the *hoca* openly disparaged use of such books. For him, *hocas* who rely on these texts are inexperienced, unskilled, or fraudulent. When I relayed this to Ibrahim, he explained that being a *hoca* in a village was easier. Because the problems village *hocas* address are fewer and simpler, they can rely on memory for much of their daily practice. In cities, according to Ibrahim, one deals with a wider and more complex set of problems, so that it is necessary for *hocas* to rely more frequently on these texts.

3. See Flueckiger (2006) for a similar approach to the importance of words and text in Islamic healing traditions in South Asia. For a brief discussion of debates surrounding the theological permissibility of amulets, see Doumato (2000: 153–55).

4. See Meeker's excellent study of the persistence of local formations of social and political authority in the transition from empire to republic along the Black Sea coast (2002) for an account of this period that similarly features the figure of the *hoca*. Importantly, Meeker is concerned with the title *hoca* as it applies to a religious teacher who has studied formally at a *medrese*.

5. Indeed, as Rudnyckyj (2009) describes in Indonesia, the forms of ethical self-fashioning and bodily discipline they each require can be mutually enforcing.

6. In its broad strokes, such a therapeutic emphasis on interpreting the signs of the body is by no means unique to the *cinci hoca*. Anthropologists and historians of medicine have documented a similar privileging of the body as a source of medical truth in a range of healing traditions (see Leslie and Young 1992; Good 1994; Kuriyama 1999). Indeed, this privileging of the truth of the body over the speech of the patient characterizes a defining impulse of the biomedical sciences. Michel Foucault, in describing the origins of neurology, makes this point well: "Broadly speaking, the neurologist says: Obey my orders, but keep quiet, and your body will answer for you by giving responses that, because I am a doctor, I alone will be able to decipher and analyze in terms of truth" (2006: 304). Despite affinities, however, we must be careful not to presume that the "body" being demanded to speak in these divergent traditions is necessarily identical or that it exists outside the specific historical moment (or even the healing tradition itself) under consideration.

7. Following Csordas's discussion of Catholic Charismatic healing, we can regard the yawn as both a learned cultural objectification and an embodied metaphor of spirit presence (1990, 1994). In discussing demonic discernment, Csordas explains: "Persons do not perceive a demon inside themselves, they sense a particular thought, behavior, or emotion as outside their control. It is the healer, specialist in cultural objectification, who typically 'discerns' whether a supplicant's problem is of demonic origin" (1990: 14). We will return to the significance, and limits, of thinking healing in terms of bodily experience in Chapter 5.

8. There are a number of excellent accounts of Islamist political mobilization in Turkey. See White (2002), Çınar (2005), Saktanber (2002), and Yavuz (2003).

9. I have in mind here Roland Barthes's reflection on the physiognomy of Abbé Pierre, a Catholic priest popular in 1950s Paris for his commitment to helping the poor and disenfranchised. As Barthes writes, "I get worried about a society which consumes with such avidity the display of charity that it forgets to ask itself questions about its consequences, its uses and its limits. And I then start to wonder whether the fine and touching iconography of the Abbé Pierre is not the alibi which a sizeable part of the nation uses in order, once more, to substitute with impunity the signs of charity for the reality of justice" (1972: 48–49). This mirrors precisely the common religious critiques leveled against the figure of the *cinci hoca*. That is, *cinci hoca*s like Ibrahim are denounced for the ways in which they instrumentally embrace pious forms so as to convince others of their legitimacy—of substituting "with impunity," in other words, the signs of piety for the presumed ethical reality of living a purposefully virtuous life.

10. This reading of ambivalence as a generative friction emerges out of Jacques Lacan's re-reading of Freud's psychoanalytic formulation of ambivalence. For Freud, ambivalence referred to instances in which opposing impulses of similar intensity existed within a single subject. Such opposing impulses (e.g., love and hate,

attraction and repulsion) can be at once unbearable and immobilizing. In Lacan, the immobilizing potential of Freud's notion of ambivalence becomes recast as an aggressive tension, a tension that is generative and mobilizes the subject (see Lacan 1988).

Chapter 5. A Malaise of Fracturing Dreams: The Care of Relations

1. In its restrictive sense, *cemevi* refers to the building, room, or site of assembly where the *cem* is performed—the central communal ritual of Alevism. The term may also be used to designate a "cultural center" for Alevis. In Zöhre Ana's case, the *cemevi* is the primary, and largest, interior ritual space where she commonly receives visitors.

2. A long history in the anthropological study of ritual and healing positions "order" on the side of the therapeutic. See the work of V. Turner (1967), Lévi-Strauss (1963), and Kapferer (1991). See also Becker's formulation of illness as a dramatic rupture that seeks resolution through diagnostic order (1997). For a critique of this tendency to associate "order" with "healing," see Taussig (1987).

3. In an example particularly relevant to my analysis, Ewing characterizes her study of *pir*s in Pakistan in the following terms: "Though there are many living Sufi pirs in Pakistan with whom individuals interact in specific social relationships, I will focus here not [on] how these individuals actually interact with their pirs as people, but on how the Sufi pir functions as a kind of 'personal symbol' for Pakistanis of this particular socio-cultural background" (1993: 71). While approaching Hüsniye's relationship with Zöhre Ana in these terms would assuredly produce important insights, I am suggesting here that we are nonetheless missing a great deal by not attending more exhaustively to the broader fields of relatedness in which encounters with figures such as Zöhre Ana are embedded.

4. Csordas's discussion of "incremental efficacy" in relation to religious and ritual healing (1994) captures an important aspect of the temporally dispersed qualities of therapeutic processes.

5. While there is not space to adequately develop a comparative framework for thinking about the different ways relations of care form around healers, it is important to note that the organization of these relationships varied with the form of healing being used as well as the type of problem being addressed. For example, whereas the relationships that formed around Zöhre Ana were organized by the singularity of her presence and an enduring sense of obligation, relationships with *cinci hoca*s—although also marked by gratitude and indebtedness—were typically more transient. As the story of Fadime and her niece illustrated, relationships with *cinci hoca*s were generally forged not around the *hoca*'s exceptional divine qualities but by his ritual expertise and command of expert religious knowledge.

6. During one interview—after the interviewee explained in great detail that he had, for nearly a decade, taken his nephew to countless *cinci hoca*s, shrines, hospitals, and neurologists throughout the country; and after he gave two distinct accounts of the origins of his nephew's affliction (one neurological, the other involving *cin*s)—I

naively asked him which account he believed. Exasperated (with me), he responded: "Which one do I believe? Whichever one works. I'll keep trying everything."

7. In emphasizing the importance of relatedness for therapeutic experience, I am not arguing that the "Turkish self" is somehow distinctively "relational" or "sociocentric." For such an argument concerning the "relational self" within a Lebanese context, see Joseph (1999).

8. My aim here is not to dismiss the sizable literature in the study of religious healing that emphasizes the embodied and performative qualities of ritual in making sense of its capacity to provoke personal and social transformation. See, for instance, Csordas (1994), Desjarlais (1992), Kapferer (1991), Schieffelin (1985), Laderman (1991), Roseman (1991), and the edited volume by Laderman and Roseman (1996). To put my distinction crudely at this point, if phenomenological approaches to healing were intended to offer an "experience-near" account that "fleshed out" the cognitivist tendencies of "meaning-centered" analyses of healing and affliction, I am developing an approach to therapeutic processes that emphasizes the vital and complementary importance of relationality—an *emphasis*, critically, that does not dismiss the significance of meaning and bodily experience to therapeutic processes.

9. In emphasizing the significance of relatedness, I am attempting to say something different from arguments that locate therapeutic efficacy in "social support." For examples of this sort of argument within the study of ritual healing, see V. Turner (1967) and Katz (1982). My argument is distinct in that I am saying not simply that Hüsniye felt "supported" by Zöhre Ana and others, but that healing—as a project of world and subject making—unfolds through densely woven fields of social relatedness that are at once ambiguous in their effects and unstable in their intensities through time.

10. In a brief aside in an otherwise relentless reflection on the brutality of colonial violence, Taussig captures a related point concerning the therapeutic role of the mundane: "the situation in the shaman's house is one where patients and healers acquire a rather intimate knowledge of and understanding of each other's foibles, toilet habits, marital relations, and so forth. By and large I think it fair to say that the therapeutic efficacy of the shamanism with which I am acquainted owes as much to the rough-and-tumble of this everyday public intimacy as to the hallucinogenic rites that allow the shaman to weave together the mundane and the extraordinary" (1987: 344). Cheryl Mattingly, in discussing the work of occupational therapists in the U.S., makes a similarly persuasive observation concerning the therapeutic potential of casual banter (1998).

11. This is also the reason I have found the vocabulary of "charisma" and "charismatic authority" inadequate for my purposes (see Lindholm 1990). Especially in its classic Weberian formulation—where charisma is a "certain quality of an individual personality by virtue of which he is set apart from ordinary men and treated as endowed with supernatural, superhuman, or at least specifically exceptional powers or qualities" (Weber 1964: 358)—"charisma" is commonly conceptualized in terms that

are at once overly individualizing (as the possession of an individual) and dyadic (as the product of a relationship between leader and follower). Even the more sophisticated formulations of charisma, as in Bourdieu and Passeron's discussion of the "successful prophet"—"the one who formulates for the groups or classes he addresses a message which the objective conditions determining the material and symbolic interests of those groups have predisposed them to attend to and take in" (Bourdieu and Passeron 1990: 25–26)—rely on a dialecticism that dramatically simplifies, to the point of distortion, the complexity of interpersonal relationships and social lives through which a "charismatic" presence moves. Csordas's important reformulation of charisma comes closest to overcoming these limitations (1997). Building on Sapir's locating of culture in the interactions of individuals and the meanings they abstract from these interactions, Csordas argues that charisma should be located intersubjectively, as existing among participants in a religious movement. For a related argument, see Lindquist (2006).

12. Appreciating the dense and shifting complexity and indeterminacy of social ties through which something like healing occurs also humbles, in my estimation, the persistent scholarly desire to isolate discrete "mechanisms"—biological or otherwise— capable of explaining how such forms of healing work.

13. Biehl and Locke make a similar point when they argue that "It is not enough to simply observe that assemblages exist; we must attend . . . to the ways these configurations are constantly constructed, undone and redone by the desires and becomings of actual people—caught up in the messiness, the desperation and aspiration, of life in idiosyncratic milieus" (2010: 337).

14. Katherine Ewing makes a related argument in her wonderful study of *pirs* in Pakistan (1997). Ewing's principal concern is with the ways that the ideologies of Pakistani nationalism and modernity generate subject positions that *pirs* and their followers inhabit in divergent ways as speaking subjects. Although Ewing's analysis informed my consideration of the sorts of ideological labor being undertaken in everyday conversations about religious healing in Hürriyet and Aktepe, the present chapter marks an important shift from this approach. For instance, rather than examining the way that Hüsniye negotiates larger ideological structures and their accompanying subject positions and identities, I have considered the ways such large-scale forces and processes work their way through the intimacies of interpersonal ties, interpersonal ties that are at once the conditions of experience and the infrastructure of social lives.

Chapter 6. Healing Secular Life: Two Regimes of Loss

1. Following Fuat Keyman, "the making of Turkey was based upon both a war of independence against Western imperialism and an acceptance of its epistemic and moral dominance" (1995: 96–97).

2. For a critique of approaching issues of power and agency in Turkey in terms of a cultural politics of postcoloniality, see Silverstein (2003).

3. Novelist Orhan Pamuk describes a group of prominent Turkish writers working during the late Ottoman and early Republican periods as being engaged in a similar project. As Pamuk describes their intentions, "They were picking their way through the ruins [of Istanbul] looking for the signs of a new Turkish state, a new Turkish nationalism" (2004: 249).

4. Moreover, as this chapter demonstrates, drawing unambiguous distinctions between "patient stories" and "healer stories" can be difficult, being that over time patients can become healers, healers can become patients, and healers can treat themselves. This is certainly not unique to Hürriyet and Aktepe. One regularly finds in the anthropological literature on religious and ritual healing accounts of the careers of healers beginning with defining experiences of illness or affliction.

5. The Sivas Congress, which gathered the leaders of the Turkish nationalist movement and delegates from throughout the Anatolian provinces in the city of Sivas in September of 1919, is regarded as a pivotal moment in the history of Turkey's national liberation.

6. Adnan Menderes served as prime minister from 1950 to 1960.

7. The Hezbollah being mentioned here is unrelated to the Hezbollah of Lebanon. His reference to beheadings coincides with a series of media reports being aired at the time that revealed that members of the (Turkish) Hezbollah were being hired by members of the government to assassinate prominent Kurdish figures.

8. I regularly encountered stories that shared the same basic narrative arc of Aydın's account. A different resident of Hürriyet, for instance, told a nearly identical account that diverged only at the point of resolution. Where Aydın's account ends with his confronting the *hoca* about the veracity of the elders' stories about *cins*, this second account culminates with the person leaving the village for his mandatory military service. "There, I learned about science, about the organs in the body, about physiology. I acquired knowledge, and thus realized that what I was doing was stupid."

9. Readers may have already recognized in Aydın's account the basic outline of a story similarly told by Claude Lévi-Strauss, concerning a Kwakiutl shaman named Quesalid who became a well-regarded shaman despite his rejection of the shaman's claims (1963). Like Quesalid, Aydın comes to realize that the powers of the healer are based on deception, although the healer's rituals may still be effective in that they can, as the village *hoca* explained, "bolster one's morale." While a noteworthy similarity, I want to resist the set of analytic distinctions between "real" and "fraudulent," or "authentic" healers and "quacks," that further pursuing this resemblance would require—as is commonly the case when Lévi-Strauss's account of Quesalid is invoked. There are two reasons (among others) for why I reject an analytic approach grounded in the language of "fraudulence." First, what we see the *hoca* in Aydın's village doing— offering treatments whose validity he questions in an effort to bolster a person's morale—can just as easily be regarded as virtuous in a different (therapeutic) setting. Aktepe's neighborhood *imam*, for instance, was willing to engage in practices of questionable theological permissibility in an effort to appease those seeking his help, much

as the physicians and nurses of the neighborhood health clinics would offer treatments that they knew had no scientific justification. Beyond illustrating the situational qualities of accusations of "fraudulence" and their dependence, in this case, on structures of medical power that differentiate permissible from impermissible forms of therapeutic practice, these examples also suggest that we cannot presume that any therapeutic interaction is free of deception; indeed, one could argue that all forms of healing involve some form of deception. Second, my principal concern in this chapter is not a healer's status as either "authentic" (*gerçek*) or "fake" (*sahtekar*), but with the processes through which a healer's therapeutic abilities come to be recognized as diminished or absent, and how this recognition is narrated. In either case, the language of "fraudulence" and "authenticity" was inadequate in capturing the complexity and temporality of loss being narrated in these accounts. For insightful commentaries on Lévi-Strauss's account of Quesalid, see Michael Taussig's essay "Viscerality, Faith, and Skepticism" (2006). Langford (2002), also citing Lévi-Strauss, offers a compelling analysis of the underlying assumptions about "authenticity" that structure discourses of fraudulence and quackery, especially as they relate to colonial and post-colonial histories of Ayurvedic medicine in India.

10. For a phenomenological account of the importance of presence—or "kinesthetic attentiveness"—in ritual and religious healing, see Desjarlais (1996: 145).

11. For Bataille, the discontinuities of the world progressively intensify as humans develop from a societal condition exemplified by sacrifice, through those characterized by festival and warfare, and onto the advent of the military order and industrial growth (1989).

12. An analogous comparison between the sun and religious experience is made by Bataille: "The sacred is exactly comparable to the flame that destroys the wood by consuming it. It is that opposite of a thing which an unlimited fire is; it spreads, it radiates heat and light, it suddenly inflames and blinds in turn. Sacrifice burns like the sun that slowly dies of the prodigious radiation whose brilliance our eyes cannot bear, but it is never isolated and, in a world of individuals, it calls for the general negation of individuals as such" (1989: 53).

13. This approach also helps us avoid depicting Nihal's experience of disillusionment as a loss of "belief," a term that has been duly criticized on a number of grounds: as indicating error and falsehood, as connoting a definitive and fixed position in relation to an object or idea (which does not allow for the co-presence of mixed and shifting commitments), as oversimplifying a polyvalent set of commitments (that are not only multiple, but also varying over time and in relation to a given context), and as an overly cognitive formulation of the bodily, affective, and social dimensions of one's orientation toward religious authority (see Good 1994; Needham 1972; Asad 2011). When I do engage the language of belief—as when my interlocutors asked me if I "believed" (*inanmak*) in *cin*s (or magic, or *keramet*, or Zöhre Ana)—I am presuming that they meant by this question something more complicated than what William Cantwell Smith described as the modern sense of

(Christian) belief: "Given the uncertainty as to whether there be a God [or *cin*, or magic, or *keramet*] or not, as a fact of modern life, I announce that my opinion is 'yes.' I judge God [or *cin*, or magic, or *keramet*] to be existent" (Smith 1977: 44, quoted in Good 1994: 16).

14. Walter Benjamin famously distinguished his approach to "historical materialism" in the following terms: "To historians who wish to relive an era, Fustel de Coulanges recommends that they blot out everything they know about the later course of history. There is no better way of characterising the method with which historical materialism has broken. It is a process of empathy whose origin is the indolence of the heart, *acedia*, which despairs of grasping and holding the genuine historical image as it flares up briefly. Among medieval theologians it was regarded as the root cause of sadness. . . . The nature of this sadness stands out more clearly if one asks with whom the adherents of historicism actually empathize. The answer is inevitable: with the victor" (Benjamin 1968: 256).

Appendix: Genres of Healing

1. While the *ocaklı* may be popularly ascribed titles like *ana* (lit. "mother") or *dede* (lit. "grandfather")—terms commonly used to designate female and male spiritual leaders—we should be careful to distinguish this use of *dede* from the Alevi concept of *dede*. While some Alevi *dede*s are on occasion considered to have the ability to cure illnesses or fulfill wishes—in their association with their lineage, or *ocak*—they are distinct from the *ocaklı* described here. Among Turkey's Sunni Muslim majority, there is no figure that precisely resembles the *dede* as it is understood among the Alevi. In terms of the more general category of *ocaklı*, however, I encountered little discernible difference in how Alevi and Sunni *ocaklı* practiced.

2. The use of amulets containing written verses from the Qur'an for therapeutic or protective purposes is widespread and has a long history in the Muslim world. See Doumato (2000) and Flueckiger (2006). For a detailed discussion of the *muska* in Turkey, see Eyuboğlu (1987, 1998).

3. See, for instance, the popular book *Anadolu Evliyaları* (The Saints of Anatolia) (Araz 1966). For a discussion of tomb or shrine visitation in Turkey, see Tapper (1990), Olson ((1991, 1994) and Marcus (1992).

4. For a discussion of these healing traditions in a Black Sea village setting, see Önder (2005).

Glossary

ana	female spiritual leader; lit., "mother"; female equivalent of "*baba*," a term used to describe a male spiritual leader
ayet	verse of the Qur'an
büyü	magic
cem	or *âyîn-i cem*; principal communal ritual of the Alevi
cemevi	house of gathering; setting of the *cem*
cin	spirit
cinci hoca	practitioner of a form of healing that treats individuals who have been struck, harassed, or possessed by *cin*s; may also be referred to as *üfürükçü*, *muskacı*, or simply *hoca*
dede	lit., "grandfather"; title used to designate an Alevi religious leader
dergâh	the lodge or gathering place of a religious order
evliya	a person acknowledged as possessing extraordinary spiritual powers based on their possession of *keramet*, the God-given ability to perform miracles; commonly translated as "saint"; Arabic, *walī* (pl., *awliyā*)
gecekondu	a house built without legal permission; "squatter's house"; lit., "built or settled at night or overnight"
keramet	the God-given power to perform miracles; Arabic, *karama*
kurşuncu	practitioner of a form of healing that involves the pouring of molten lead (*kurşun*) into a basin of water and reading the resulting solidified piece of lead to discern the source the patient's problem
laiklik	secularism; laicism; French, *laïcité*
muska	curative amulet
muskacı	see "*cinci hoca*"
nefes	lit., "breath"; in the present context, it refers to either divinely inspired poetic speech or breath that has curative powers

tarikat	religious order
tılsım	talisman; amulet
nazar	"evil eye"
ocaklı	persons who (or, at times, places that) have special powers to heal based on their association with or descent from an ancestor to whom miraculous powers were attributed; lit., "with the *ocak*"
şifa ayetleri	Qur'anic verses regarded as having therapeutic effects
tarikat	religious order
türbe	tomb
üfürükçü	see "*cinci hoca*"
vakıf	charitable or pious foundation

References

Abrams, Philip. 1988. Notes on the Difficulty of Studying the State. *Journal of Historical Sociology* 1, 1: 58–89.

Abu-Lughod, Lila, ed. 1998. *Remaking Women: Feminism and Modernity in the Middle East*. Princeton, N.J.: Princeton University Press.

Agamben, Giorgio. 1998. *Homo Sacer: Sovereign Power and Bare Life*. Stanford, Calif.: Stanford University Press.

Alexander, Catherine. 2002. *Personal States: Making Connections Between People and Bureaucracy in Turkey*. Oxford: Oxford University Press.

Alloula, Malek. 1986. *The Colonial Harem*. Minneapolis: University of Minnesota Press.

Altınay, Ahmet Refik. 1927. *Samur Devri*. İstanbul: Kütüphane-i Hilmi.

Altınay, Ayşe Gül. 2004. *The Myth of the Military-Nation: Militarism, Gender, and Education in Turkey*. New York: Palgrave.

Anderson, Benedict. 1991. *Imagined Communities: Reflections on the Origin and Spread of Nationalism*. London: Verso.

Anderson, Warwick. 1998. Where Is the Postcolonial History of Medicine? *Bulletin of the History of Medicine* 72, 3: 522–30.

———. 2006. *Colonial Pathologies: American Tropical Medicine, Race, and Hygiene in the Philippines*. Durham, N.C.: Duke University Press.

Araz, Nezihe. 1966. *Anadolu Evliyaları* (The Saints of Anatolia). İstanbul: Atlas Kitabevi.

Aretxaga, Begoña. 2001. The Sexual Games of the Body Politic: Fantasy and State Violence in Northern Ireland. *Culture, Medicine and Psychiatry* 25, 1: 1–27.

Arı, Eyal. 2004. The People's Houses and the Theatre in Turkey. *Middle Eastern Studies* 40, 4: 32–58.

Arnold, David. 1993. *Colonizing the Body: State Medicine and Epidemic Disease in Nineteenth-Century India*. Berkeley: University of California Press.

Asad, Talal. 1993. *Genealogies of Religion: Discipline and Reasons of Power in Christianity and Islam*. Baltimore: Johns Hopkins University Press.

———. 2003. *Formations of the Secular: Christianity, Islam, Modernity*. Stanford, Calif.: Stanford University Press.

———. 2011. Thinking About Religious Beliefs and Politics. In *The Cambridge Companion to Religious Studies*, ed. Robert A. Orsi. Cambridge: Cambridge University Press.

Asad, Talal, Wendy Brown, Judith Butler, and Saba Mahmood. 2009. *Is Critique Secular? Blasphemy, Injury, and Free Speech.* Berkeley: University of California Press.

Atatürk, Mustafa Kemal. 1959. *TBMM Zabıt Ceridesi (Journal of Proceedings of the Turkish Grand National Assembly)* 18, 2.

————. 1981. *Atatürk'ün Sağlıkla İlgili Özdeyişleri ve Sözleri.* Ankara: Sağlık ve Sosyal Yardım Bakanlığı.

Aydın, Erdem. 1995. *Osmanlı İmparatorluğunda Halk Sağlığı Hizmetleri.* İstanbul: I. Uluslararası Türk Tababeti Tarihi Kongresi.

————. 1996a. Sosyalleştirmenin Tarihsel Yönü. In *Sağlık Hizmetleri.* Antalya: Akdeniz Üniversitesi Tıp Fakültesi Dergisi.

————. 1996b. Anadolu'daki Ticaret Yolları ve Selçuklu Sağlık Hizmetleri. *Yeni Tip Tarihi Araştırmaları* 2–3: 164–75.

————. 1997. Türkiye'de Tafira ve Kırsal Kesim Sağlık Hizmetleri Örgütlenmesi Tarihi. *Toplum ve Hekim* 12, 80: 21–44.

————. 1998. *Türkiye'de Sıtma Savaşı.* Ankara: Hacettepe Üniversitesi Tıp Fakültesi.

Aziz, Şevket. 1934. Biyosoyoloji. *Ülkü* 3, 16: 251–62.

Bakhtin, Mikhail. 1981. *The Dialogic Imagination: Four Essays.* Trans. Caryl Emerson and Michael Holquist. Austin: University of Texas Press.

Bal, Hüseyin. 1997a. *Alevi-Bektaşi Köylerinde Toplumsal Kurumlar: Burdur ve Isparta'nın İki Alevi Köyünde Yapılmış Köy Araştırması.* İstanbul: Ant Yayınları.

————. 1997b. *Sosyolojik Açıdan Alevi-Sünni Farklılaşması ve Bütünleşmesi: Isparta'nın Alevi-Sünni Ortak Yaşayan İki Köyü Üstüne Yapılmış Karşılaştırmalı bir Araştırma.* İstanbul: Ant Yayınları.

Barthes, Roland. 1972. *Mythologies.* New York: Hill and Wang.

Bashford, Alison. 2004. *Imperial Hygiene: A Critical History of Colonialism, Nationalism and Public Health.* London: Palgrave.

Basu, Helene, and Pnina Werbner, eds. 1998. *Embodying Charisma: Modernity, Locality and the Performance of Emotion in Sufi Cults.* New York: Routledge.

Bataille, Georges. 1988. *The Accursed Share: An Essay on General Economy.* New York: Zone Books.

————. 1989. *Theory of Religion.* New York: Zone Books.

Becker, Gay. 1997. *Disrupted Lives: How People Create Meaning in a Chaotic World.* Berkeley: University of California Press.

Benjamin, Walter. 1968. *Illuminations.* New York: Schocken Books.

Berkes, Niyazi. 1964. *The Development of Secularism in Turkey.* Montreal: McGill University Press.

Bhabha, Homi. 1994. Of Mimicry and Man: The Ambivalence of Colonial Discourse. In *The Location of Culture.* New York: Routledge.

Bhargava, Rajeev, ed. 1998. *Secularism and Its Critics.* Delhi: Oxford University Press.

Biehl, João. 2005. *Vita: Life in a Zone of Social Abandonment.* Berkeley: University of California Press.

Biehl, João, and Peter Locke. 2010. Deleuze and the Anthropology of Becoming. *Current Anthropology* 51, 3: 317–51.

Birge, John Kingsley. 1937. *The Bektashi Order of Dervishes.* London: Luzac Oriental.

Bloch, Maurice. 1989 [1974]. Symbols, Song, Dance, and Features of Articulation: Is Religion an Extreme Form of Traditional Authority? In *Ritual, History, and Power: Selected Papers in Anthropology.* London: Athlone.

Boddy, Janice. 1989. *Wombs and Alien Spirits: Women, Men, and the Zar Cult in Northern Sudan.* Madison: University of Wisconsin Press.

Bourdieu, Pierre. 1977. *Outline of a Theory of Practice.* Cambridge: Cambridge University Press.

Bourdieu, Pierre, and Jean-Claude Passeron. 1990. *Reproduction in Education, Society and Culture.* London: Sage.

Bowen, Roger. 2008. *Why the French Don't Like Headscarves: Islam, the State, and Public Space.* Princeton, N.J.: Princeton University Press.

Bozdoğan, Sibel. 2001. *Modernism and Nation Building: Turkish Architectural Culture in the Early Republic.* Seattle: University of Washington Press.

Bozdoğan, Sibel, and Reşat Kasaba. 1997. *Rethinking Modernity and National Identity in Turkey.* Seattle: University of Washington Press.

Brodwin, Paul. 1996. *Medicine and Morality in Haiti: The Contest for Healing Power.* Cambridge: Cambridge University Press.

Brown, Peter. 1981. *The Cult of the Saints: Its Rise and Function in Latin Christianity.* Chicago: University of Chicago Press.

Bryant, Rebecca. 2005. The Soul Danced into the Body: Nation and Improvisation in Istanbul. *American Ethnologist* 32, 2: 222–38.

Buyandelgeriyn, Manduhai. 2007. Dealing with Uncertainty: Shamans, Marginal Capitalism, and the Remaking of History in Postsocialist Mongolia. *American Ethnologist* 34, 1: 127–47.

Cannell, Fenella. 2010. The Anthropology of Secularism. *Annual Review of Anthropology* 39: 85–100.

Casanova, José. 1994. *Public Religions in the Modern World.* Chicago: University of Chicago Press.

Çelik, İsmail. 1974. Nazar, Nazarlık, ve İlgili Büyüsel İşlemler. *Boğaziçi Üniversitesi Halkbilim Yıllığı* 133: 155–84.

Chatterjee, Partha. 1993. *The Nation and Its Fragments: Colonial and Postcolonial Histories.* Princeton, N.J.: Princeton University Press.

———. 2006. Fasting for Bin Laden: The Politics of Secularization in Contemporary India. In *Powers of the Secular Modern: Talal Asad and His Interlocutors,* ed. David Scott and Charles Hirschkind. Stanford, Calif.: Stanford University Press.

Çınar, Alev. 2005. *Modernity, Islam, and Secularism in Turkey.* Minneapolis: University of Minnesota Press.

Comaroff, Jean. 1985. *Body of Power, Spirit of Resistance: The Culture and History of a South African People.* Chicago: University of Chicago Press.

————. 1993. The Diseased Heart of Africa: Medicine, Colonialism, and the Black Body. In *Knowledge, Power, and Practice: The Anthropology of Medicine and Everyday Life*, ed. Shirley Lindenbaum and Margaret M. Lock. Berkeley: University of California Press.

Comaroff, Jean, and John L. Comaroff, eds. 1993. *Modernity and Its Malcontents: Ritual and Power in Postcolonial Africa*. Chicago: University of Chicago Press.

————. 1999. Occult Economies and the Violence of Abstraction: Notes from the South African Postcolony. *American Ethnologist* 26, 2: 279–303.

————. 2002. Alien-Nation: Zombies, Immigrants, and Millennial Capitalism. *South Atlantic Quarterly* 101, 4: 779–805.

Connolly, William. 2000. *Why I Am Not a Secularist*. Minnesota: University of Minnesota Press.

Cornell, Vincent. 1998. *Realm of the Saint: Power and Authority in Moroccan Sufism*. Austin: University of Texas Press.

Crandon-Malamud, Libbet. 1991. *From the Fat of Our Souls: Social Change, Political Process, and Medical Pluralism in Bolivia*. Berkeley: University of California Press.

Crapanzano, Vincent. 1973. *The Hamadsha: A Study in Moroccan Ethnopsychiatry*. Berkeley: University of California Press.

Cruise O'Brien, Donald, and Christian Coulon, eds. 1988. *Charisma and Brotherhood in African Islam*. Oxford: Clarendon Press.

Csordas, Thomas. 1990. Embodiment as a Paradigm for Anthropology. *Ethos* 18, 1: 5–47.

————. *The Sacred Self: A Cultural Phenomenology of Charismatic Healing*. Berkeley: University of California Press.

————. 1995. *Embodiment and Experience: The Existential Ground of Culture and Self*. Cambridge: Cambridge University Press.

————. 1997. *Language, Charisma, and Creativity: The Ritual Life of a Religious Movement*. Berkeley: University of California Press.

————. 1999. Ritual Healing and the Politics of Identity in Contemporary Navajo Society. *American Ethnologist* 26, 1: 3–23.

————. 2002. The Rhetoric of Transformation in Ritual Healing. In *Body/Meaning/Healing*. New York: Palgrave Macmillan.

Csordas, Thomas, and Arthur Kleinman. 1996. The Therapeutic Process. In *Medical Anthropology: Contemporary Theory and Method*, ed. Carolyn Fishel Sargent and Thomas M. Johnson. London: Praeger.

Danforth, Loring. 1989. *Firewalking and Religious Healing*. Princeton, N.J.: Princeton University Press.

Das, Veena. 2007. *Life and Words: Violence and the Descent into the Ordinary*. Berkeley: University of California Press.

Das, Veena, and Deborah Poole. 2004. Introduction: State and Its Margins: Comparative Ethnographies. In *Anthropology in the Margins of the State*, ed. Veena Das and Deborah Poole. Santa Fe, N.M.: School of American Research Press.

Davison, Andrew. 1998. *Secularism and Revivalism in Turkey: A Hermeneutic Question.* New Haven, Conn.: Yale University Press.

———. 2003. Turkey, a "Secular" State? The Challenge of Description. *South Atlantic Quarterly* 102, 2: 333–50.

de Certeau, Michel. 1984. *The Practice of Everyday Life.* Berkeley: University of California Press.

———. 2000. *The Possession at Loudun.* Chicago: University of Chicago Press.

de Vries, Hent, ed. 2006. *Political Theologies: Public Religions in a Post-Secular Age.* New York: Fordham University Press.

Deeb, Lara. 2006. *An Enchanted Modern: Gender and Public Piety in Shi'i Lebanon.* Princeton, N.J.: Princeton University Press.

Deleuze, Gilles. 2007. *Two Regimes of Madness: Texts and Interviews, 1975–1995.* New York: Semiotext(e).

Deleuze, Gilles, and Félix Guattari. 1987. *A Thousand Plateaus: Capitalism and Schizophrenia.* Minneapolis: University of Minnesota Press.

Demirhan-Erdemir, Ayşegül, and Öztan Öncel. 2006. A Famous Turkish Physician from Military Medical School: Dr. Refik Saydam and His Public Health Works. *Journal of the International Society for the History of Islamic Medicine* 5, 9: 47–53.

Demirtaş, Neslihan. 2009. *Social Spatialization in a Turkish Squatter Settlement: The Dualism of Strategy and Tactic Reconsidered.* Frankfurt: Peter Lang.

Denny, Frederick. 1988. "God's Friends": The Sanctity of Persons in Islam. In *Sainthood: Its Manifestations in World Religions,* ed. Richard Kieckhefer and George Doherty Bond. Oxford: Oxford University Press.

Derrida, Jacques. 1998. Faith and Knowledge: The Two Sources of "Religion" at the Limits of Reason Alone. In *Religion,* ed. Jacques Derrida and Gianni Vattimo. Stanford, Calif.: Stanford University Press.

Desjarlais, Robert. 1992. *Body and Emotion: The Aesthetics of Illness and Healing in the Nepal Himalayas.* Philadelphia: University of Pennsylvania Press.

———. 1996. Presence. In *The Performance of Healing,* ed. C. Laderman and M. Roseman. New York: Routledge.

Devlet İstatistik Enstitüsü. 1974. *Türkiye İstatistik Yıllığı 1973.* Ankara: Devlet İstatistik Enstitüsü.

———. 1975. *Türkiye İstatistik Yıllığı 1974.* Ankara: Devlet İstatistik Enstitüsü.

Dole, Christopher. 2004. In the Shadows of Medicine and Modernity: Medical Integration and Secular Histories of Religious Healing in Turkey. *Culture, Medicine, and Psychiatry* 28, 3: 255–80.

———. 2006. Mass Media and the Repulsive Allure of Religious Healing: The Cinci Hoca in Turkish Modernity. *International Journal of Middle East Studies* 38, 1: 31–54.

Dols, Michael. 1992. *Majnun: The Madman in Medieval Islamic Society.* Oxford: Oxford University Press.

Doumato, Eleanor Abdella. 2000. *Getting God's Ear: Women, Islam, and Healing in Saudi Arabia and the Gulf.* New York: Columbia University Press.

Dow, James. 1986. Universal Aspects of Symbolic Healing: A Theoretical Synthesis. *American Anthropologist* 88, 1: 56–69.

Dressler, Markus. 2008. Religio-Secular Metamorphoses: The Re-Making of Turkish Alevism. *Journal of the American Academy of Religion* 76, 2: 280–311.

Dubetsky, Alan. 1977. Class and Community in Urban Turkey. In *Commoners, Climbers, and Notables: A Sampler of Studies on Social Ranking in the Middle East*, ed. C. A. O. Nieuwenhuijze. Leiden: Brill.

Duyar-Kienast, Umut. 2005. *The Formation of Gecekondu Settlements in Turkey*. New Brunswick, N.J.: Transaction Publishers.

Ege, Rıdvan. 1998. *Atatürk ve Cumhuriyet Dönemi Sağlık Hizmetleri, 1923–1998*. Ankara: Türk Hava Kurumu Basımevi.

Eickelman, Dale, and James Piscatori. 1996. *Muslim Politics*. Princeton, N.J.: Princeton University Press.

Eng, David, and David Kazanjian, eds. 2002. *Loss: The Politics of Mourning*. Berkeley: University of California Press.

Erdemir, Aykan. 2005. Tradition and Modernity: Alevis' Ambiguous Terms and Turkey's Ambivalent Subjects. *Middle East Studies* 41, 6: 937–51.

Erder, Sema. 1996. *İstanbul'a bir Kent Kondu: Ümraniye*. İstanbul: İletişim.

———. 1997. *Kentsel Gerilim: Enformel İlişki Ağları Alan Araştırması*. Ankara: Um: ag.

Eren, Nevzat, and Nuray Tanrıtanır. 1998. *Cumhuriyet ve Sağlık*. Ankara: Türk Tabipleri Birliği.

Erman, Tahire. 1996. Women and the Housing Environment: The Experiences of Turkish Migrant Women in Squatter (Gecekondu) and Apartment Housing. *Environment and Behavior* 28, 6: 764–98.

———. 1998. Becoming "Urban" or Remaining "Rural": The Views of Turkish Rural-to-Urban Migrants on the "Integration" Question. *International Journal of Middle East Studies* 30: 541–61.

Erman, Tahire, and Emrah Göker. 2000. Alevi Politics in Contemporary Turkey. *Middle East Studies* 36, 4: 99–118.

Ersoy, Melih. 1985. *Göç ve Kentsel Bütünleşme*. Ankara: Türkiye Gelişme Araştırmaları Vakfı Yayınları.

Evrenol, H. Malik. 1936. Zekâsi Yüksek Çocuklar Yetiştirmenin Yolları. *Ülkü* 6, 34: 256–258.

Ewing, Katherine. 1993. The Modern Businessman and the Pakistani Saint: The Interpenetration of Worlds. In *Manifestations of Sainthood in Islam*, ed. Grace Martin Smith and Carl W. Ernst. Istanbul: Isis.

———. 1997. *Arguing Sainthood: Modernity, Psychoanalysis, and Islam*. Durham, N.C.: Duke University Press.

Eyuboğlu, İsmet. 1987. *Anadolu Büyüleri*. İstanbul: Der Yayınları.

———. 1998. *Anadolu İlaçları*. İstanbul: Toplumsal Dönüşüm Yayınları.

Fanon, Frantz. 1965. *Studies in a Dying Colonialism*. Trans. Haakon Chevalier. New York: Monthly Review Press.

Faroquhi, Suraiya. 1979. The Life Story of an Urban Saint in the Ottoman Empire: Piri Baba of Merzifon. İstanbul Üniversite Fakültesi Tarih Dergisi 32: 651–76.

Favret-Saada, Jeanne. 1980. Deadly Words: Witchcraft in the Bocage. Cambridge: Cambridge University Press.

Ferguson, James. 1999. Expectations of Modernity: Myths and Meanings of Urban Life on the Zambian Copperbelt. Berkeley: University of California Press.

Fischer, Michael M. J. 2003. Emergent Forms of Life and the Anthropological Voice. Durham, N.C.: Duke University Press.

———. 2010. Comments (on Biehl and Locke's "Deleuze and the Anthropology of Becoming"). Current Anthropology 51, 3: 337–38.

Fişek, Nusret. 1981. Atatürkçülük ve Sağlık Politakamız. Cumhuriyet, 2 April 1981.

Fitzgerald, Timothy. 2007. Discourse on Civility and Barbarity: A Critical History of Religion and Other Categories. New York: Oxford University Press.

Flueckiger, Joyce. 2006. In Amma's Healing Room: Gender and Vernacular Islam in South India. Bloomington: Indiana University Press.

Fortun, Kim. 2001. Advocacy After Bhopal: Environmentalism, Disaster, New Global Orders. Chicago: University of Chicago Press.

Foucault, Michel. 1978. The History of Sexuality, Vol. 1, An Introduction. New York: Vintage.

———. 1980. Two Lectures. In Power/Knowledge: Selected Interviews and Other Writings 1972–1977, ed. Colin Gordon. New York: Pantheon Books.

———. 1986. The History of Sexuality. Vol. 3, The Care of the Self. New York: Pantheon.

———. 1991. Governmentality. In The Foucault Effect: Studies in Governmentality, ed. Graham Burchell, Colin Gordon, and Peter Miller. Chicago: University of Chicago Press.

———. 2006. Psychiatric Power: Lectures at the Collège de France, 1973–74. New York: Palgrave Macmillan.

Gaines, Atwood. 1991. Cultural Constructivism: Sickness Histories and the Understanding of Ethnomedicines Beyond Critical Medical Anthropology. In Anthropologies of Medicine: A Colloquium on West European and North American Perspectives, ed. Beatrix Pfleiderer and and Gilles Bibeau. Wiesbaden: Vieweg.

———. 1992. Ethnopsychiatry: The Cultural Construction of Psychiatries. In Ethnopsychiatry: The Cultural Construction of Professional and Folk Psychiatries, ed. Atwood D. Gaines. Albany: State University of New York Press.

Geertz, Clifford. 1968. Islam Observed: Religious Development in Morocco and Indonesia. New Haven, Conn.: Yale University Press.

Gellner, Ernest. 1969. Saints of the Atlas. London: Weidenfeld and Nicolson.

———. 1981. Muslim Society. Cambridge: Cambridge University Press.

Geschiere, Peter. 1997. The Modernity of Witchcraft: Politics and the Occult in Postcolonial Africa. Charlottesville: University of Virginia Press.

Gilsenan, Michael. 1973. Saint and Sufi in Modern Egypt: An Essay in the Sociology of Religion. Oxford: Clarendon Press.

Goffman, Erving. 1981. *Forms of Talk*. Philadelphia: University of Pennsylvania Press.

Gökay, Dr. Fahreddin Kerim. 1939a. Türkiye'nin Hijien Mental ve Psikiyatri Sahasındaki Hizmetleri. *Tıb Dünyası* 12, 7: 4185–86.

———. 1939b. Hastaneler Meselesi. *Tıb Dünyası* 12, 7: 4287–89.

Gökçe, Birsen, Feride Acar, Ayşe Ayata, Aytül Kasapoğlu, İnan Özer, and Hamza Uygun. 1993. *Gecekondularda Ailelerarası Geleneksel Dayanışmanın Çağdaş Organizasyonlara Dönüşümü*. Ankara: T. C. Başbakanlık Kadın ve Sosyal Hizmetler Müsteşarlığı Yayınları.

Goldziher, Ignaz. 1971. Veneration of Saints in Islam. In Goldhizer, *Muslim Studies*, trans. C. Renate Barber and Samuel Miklos Stern. London: Allen and Unwin.

Göle, Nilufer. 1996. *The Forbidden Modern: Civilization and Veiling*. Ann Arbor: University of Michigan Press.

Gönenç, Remzi. 1936. Sağlık Bahtiyarlıktır. *Ülkü* 7, 37: 48–51.

Good, Byron. 1977. The Heart of What's the Matter: The Semantics of Illness in Iran. *Culture, Medicine and Psychiatry* 1, 1: 25–55.

———. 1994. *Medicine, Rationality, and Experience: An Anthropological Perspective*. Cambridge: Cambridge University Press.

Good, Byron, and Mary-Jo DelVecchio Good. 1992. The Comparative Study of Greco-Islamic Medicine: The Integration of Medical Knowledge into Local Symbolic Contexts. In *Paths to Asian Medical Knowledge*, ed. Charles M. Leslie and Allan Young. Berkeley: University of California Press.

Gordon, Deborah. 1988. Tenacious Assumptions in Western Medicine. In *Biomedicine Examined*, ed. Margaret M. Lock and Deborah Gordon. Dordrecht: Kluwer Academic.

Güneş-Ayata, Ayşe. 1987. Migrants and Natives: Urban Basis of Social Conflict. In *Migrants, Workers, and the Social Order*, ed. Jeremy S. Eades. London: Tavistock.

———. 1992. The Turkish Alevi. *Innovation* 5, 3: 109–14.

Gür, Aslı. 2007. Stories in Three Dimensions: Narratives of Nation and the Anatolian Civilizations Museum. In *The Politics of Public Memory in Turkey*, ed. Esra Özyürek. Syracuse, N.Y.: Syracuse University Press.

Habermas, Jürgen. 1984. The French Path to Postmodernity: Bataille Between Eroticism and General Economics. *New German Critique* 33, 1: 79–102.

Hacettepe University Institute of Population Studies. 1999. *Turkish Demographic and Health Survey 1998*. Ankara: Hacettepe University Institute of Population Studies.

Halliburton, Murphy. 2003. The Importance of a Pleasant Process of Treatment: Lessons on Healing from South India. *Culture, Medicine and Psychiatry* 27, 2: 161–86.

Harding, Susan. 2001. *The Book of Jerry Faldwell: Fundamentalist Language and Politics*. Princeton, N.J.: Princeton University Press.

Harrison, Mark. 1994. *Public Health in British India: Anglo-Indian Preventive Medicine, 1859–1914*. Cambridge: Cambridge University Press.

Hart, Kimberly. 2009. The Orthodoxization of Ritual Practice in Western Anatolia. *American Ethnologist* 36, 4: 735–49.

Hefner, Robert. 1998. Multiple Modernities: Christianity, Islam, and Hinduism in a Globalizing Age. *Annual Review of Anthropology* 27: 83–104.

Henkel, Heiko. 2007. The Location of Islam: Inhabiting Istanbul in a Muslim Way. *American Ethnologist* 34, 1: 57–70.

Heper, Metin. 1978. *Gecekondu Policy in Turkey: An Evaluation with a Case Study of Rumelihisarüstü Squatter Area in Istanbul*. Istanbul: Boğaziçi University Publications.

Herzfeld, Michael. 1981. Meaning and Morality: A Semiotic Approach to Evil Eye Accusations in a Greek Village. *American Ethnologist* 8: 560–74.

Hirschkind, Charles. 2006. *The Ethical Soundscape: Cassette Sermons and Islamic Counterpublics*. New York: Columbia University Press.

Hoffman, Valerie. 1995. *Sufism, Mystics, and Saints in Modern Egypt*. Columbia: University of South Carolina Press.

Hunt, Nancy Rose. 1999. *A Colonial Lexicon: Of Birth Ritual, Medicalization, and Mobility in the Congo*. Durham, N.C.: Duke University Press.

Hüsnü, Niyazi. 1933. İlim ve İnkılâp. *Ülkü* 2, 8: 115–17.

Ibn Khaldun. 1967. *The Muqaddimah: An Introduction to History*. Trans. Franz Rosenthal. Princeton, N.J.: Princeton University Press.

Irvine, Judith. 1996. Shadow Conversations: The Indeterminacy of Participant Roles. In *Natural Histories of Discourse*, ed. Michael Silverstein and Greg Urban. Chicago: University of Chicago Press.

İzgü, Muzaffer. 1970. *Gecekondu*. Yenişehir: Yenişehir.

Jakobsen, Janet, and Ann Pellegrini, eds. 2008. *Secularisms*. Durham, N.C.: Duke University Press.

Joralemon, Donald. 1986. The Performing Patient in Ritual Healing. *Social Science and Medicine* 23: 841–45.

Joseph, Suad. 1999. Theories and Dynamics of Gender, Self, and Identity in Arab Families. In *Intimate Selving in Arab Families: Gender, Self, and Identity*, ed. Suad Joseph. Syracuse, N.Y.: Syracuse University Press.

Julien, Charles André. 1970. *History of North Africa: Tunisia, Algeria, Morocco, from the Arab Conquest to 1830*. New York: Praeger.

Kadıoğlu, Ayşe. 1995. Milletini Arıyan Devlet: Türk Milliyetçiliğinin Açmazları. *Türkiye Günlüğü* 33: 91–100.

———. 1998. Republican Epistemology and Islamic Discourses in Turkey in the 1990s. *Muslim World* 88, 1: 1–21.

———. 2010. The Pathologies of Turkish Republican Laicism. *Philosophy & Social Criticism* 36, 3–4: 489–504.

Kandiyoti, Deniz. 1989. Women and the Turkish State: Political Actors or Symbolic Pawns? In *Woman-Nation-State*, ed. N. Yuval-Davis and F. Anthias. London: Macmillan.

Kansu, Şevket Aziz. 1936. İnsan Beyninin Kaynakları ve Tekamülü (Müterakki Dimağlaşma). *Ülkü* 8, 44: 111–18.

————. 1939. Kız ve Erkek Türk Çocukları Üzerinde Antropometrik Araştırmalar. *Ülkü* 12, 71: 398–408.

Kapferer, Bruce. 1991. *A Celebration of Demons: Exorcism and the Aesthetics of Healing in Sri Lanka*. Providence, R.I.: Berg.

Karaömerlioğlu, M. Asim. 1998. The People's Houses and the Cult of the Peasant in Turkey. *Middle Eastern Studies* 34, 4: 67–91.

Karpat, Kemal. 1963. The People's Houses in Turkey: Establishment and Growth. *Middle East Journal* 17: 55–67.

————. 1976. *The Gecekondu: Rural Migration and Urbanisation*. Cambridge: Cambridge University Press.

Katz, Pearl. 1982. *Boiling Energy: Community Healing Among the Kalahari Kung*. Cambridge, Mass.: Harvard University Press.

Keane, Webb. 1997. Religious Language. *Annual Review of Anthropology* 25: 47–71.

Keçeli, Şakır, and Aziz Yalçın. 1996. *Alevîlik-Bektaşîlik Açısından Din Kültürü ve Ahlâk Bilgisi*. Ankara: Ardıç Yayınları.

Keddie, Nikki, ed. 1972. *Scholars, Saints, and Sufis: Muslim Religious Institutions Since 1500*. Berkeley: University of California Press.

Keleş, Ruşen. 1983. *100 Soruda Türkiye'de Kentleşme, Konut ve Gecekondu*. İstanbul: Gerçek Yayınevi.

————. 1996. *Kentleşme Politikası*. Ankara: İmge.

Kemal, Yaşar. 1963. *Iron Earth, Copper Sky*. Trans. Thilda Kemal. London: Harvill.

Kendall, Laurel. 2003. Gods, Markets, and the IMF in the Korean Spirit World. In *Transparency and Conspiracy: Ethnographies of Suspicion in the New World Order*, ed. Harry G. Sanders and Todd West. Durham, N.C.: Duke University Press.

————. 2008. Of Hungry Ghosts and Other Matters of Consumption in the Republic of Korea: The Commodity Becomes a Ritual Prop. *American Ethnologist* 35, 1: 154–70.

Keyman, E. Fuat. 1995. On the Relation Between Global Modernity and Nationalism: The Crisis of Hegemony and the Rise of (Islamic) Identity in Turkey. *New Perspectives on Turkey* 13: 93–120.

Kezer, Zeynep. 2000. Familiar Things in Strange Places: Ankara's Ethnography Museum and the Legacy of Islam in Republican Turkey. *Perspectives in Vernacular Architecture* 8: 101–16.

Kiev, Ari. 1964. *Magic, Faith, and Healing: Studies in Primitive Psychiatry Today*. New York: Free Press.

Kinross, Patrick Balfour. 1964. *Ataturk: The Rebirth of a Nation*. London: Weidenfeld and Nicolson.

Kleinman, Arthur. 1980. *Patients and Healers in the Context of Culture*. Berkeley: University of California Press.

————. 1988. *The Illness Narratives: Suffering, Healing, and the Human Condition*. New York: Basic Books.

———. 1995. *Writing at the Margin: Discourse Between Anthropology and Medicine.* Berkeley: University of California Press.

———. 2006. *What Really Matters: Living a Moral Life Amidst Uncertainty and Danger.* New York: Oxford University Press.

Kleinman, Arthur, and Joan Kleinman. 1991. Suffering and Its Professional Transformation: Toward an Ethnography of Interpersonal Experience. *Culture, Medicine and Psychiatry* 15, 3: 275–301.

Kongar, Emre. 1976. *A Survey of Familial Change in Two Turkish Gecekondu Areas.* In *Mediterranean Family Structures*, ed. John G. Peristiany. Cambridge: Cambridge University Press.

Kuriyama, Shigehisa. 1999. *The Expressiveness of the Body and the Divergence of Greek and Chinese Medicine.* New York: Zone Books.

Kuru, Ahmet. 2007. Passive and Assertive Secularism: Historical Conditions, Ideological Struggles, and State Policies towards Religion. *World Politics* 59, 4: 568–94.

Lacan, Jacques. 1988. *The Seminar of Jacques Lacan: Freud's Papers on Technique, 1953–1954.* New York: Norton.

Laderman, Carol. 1991. *Taming the Wind of Desire: Psychology, Medicine, and Aesthetics in Malay Shamanistic Performance.* Berkeley: University of California Press.

Laderman, Carol, and Marina Roseman, eds. 1996. *The Performance of Healing.* New York: Routledge.

Lambek, Michael. 2002. *The Weight of the Past: Living with History in Mahajanga, Madagascar.* New York: Palgrave Macmillan.

Langford, Jean. 2002. *Fluent Bodies: Ayurvedic Remedies for Postcolonial Imbalance.* Durham, N.C.: Duke University Press.

Laroui, Abdallah. 1982. *L'idéologie arabe ontemporaine: Essai critique.* Paris: Maspero.

Lefort, Claude. 1988. The Permanence of the Theologico-Political? In Lefort, *Democracy and Political Theory.* Cambridge: Polity Press.

Leslie, Charles M., and Allan Young, eds. 1992. *Paths to Asian Medical Knowledge.* Berkeley: University of California Press.

Levi, Jerome. 1999. The Embodiment of a Working Identity: Power and Process in Rarámuri Ritual Healing. *American Indian Culture and Research Journal* 23, 3: 13–46.

Lévi-Strauss, Claude. 1963. *Structural Anthropology.* New York: Basic Books.

Lewis, Raphaela. 1971. *Everyday Life in Ottoman Turkey.* New York: Putnam.

Lindholm, Charles. 1990. *Charisma.* Cambridge, Mass.: Blackwell.

Lindquist, Galina. 2006. *Conjuring Hope: Magic and Healing in Contemporary Russia.* New York: Berghahn.

Mahmood, Saba. 2005. *Politics of Piety: The Islamic Revival and the Feminist Subject.* Princeton, N.J.: Princeton University Press.

Makal, Mahmut. 1954. *A Village in Anatolia.* Trans. Sir Wyndham Deedes. London: Vallentine, Mitchell.

Maloney, Clarence. 1976. *The Evil Eye*. New York: Columbia University Press.

Mango, Andrew. 1999. *Atatürk: The Biography of the Founder of Modern Turkey*. Woodstock, N.Y.: Overlook Press.

Marcus, Julie. 1992. *A World of Difference: Islam and Gender Hierarchy in Turkey*. London: Zed.

Mardin, Şerif. 1989. *Religion and Social Change in Modern Turkey: The Case of Bediüzzaman Said Nursi*. Albany: State University of New York Press.

———. 1991. The Just and the Unjust. *Daedalus* 120, 3: 113–29.

Masquelier, Adeline. 2001. *Prayer Has Spoiled Everything: Possession, Power, and Identity in an Islamic Town of Niger*. Durham, N.C.: Duke University Press.

Mattingly, Cheryl. 1998. *Healing Dramas and Clinical Plots: The Narrative Structure of Experience*. Cambridge: Cambridge University Press.

Mbembé, Achille. 2001. *On the Postcolony*. Berkeley: University of California Press.

Meeker, Michael. 1991. The New Muslim Intellectuals in the Republic of Turkey. In *Islam in Modern Turkey: Religion, Politics and Literature in a Secular State*, ed. Richard Tapper. London: Tauris.

———. 2002. *A Nation of Empire: The Ottoman Legacy of Turkish Modernity*. Berkeley: University of California Press.

Mélikoff, Irène 1998. Bektashi/*Kızılbaş*: Historical Bipartition and Its Consequences. In *Alevi Identity: Cultural, Religious and Social Perspectives*, ed. Tord Olsson, Elisabeth Özdalga, and Catharina Raudvere. Istanbul: Swedish Research Institute in Istanbul.

Meyer, Birgit. 1998. Commodities and the Power of Prayer: Pentecostalist Attitudes Towards Consumption in Contemporary Ghana. *Development and Change* 29, 4: 751–76.

Meyer, Birgit, and Peter Pels, eds. 2003. *Magic and Modernity: Interfaces of Revelation and Concealment*. Stanford, Calif.: Stanford University Press.

Milli Gazetesi. 1999a. Mamak, Projelerimizle Kentleşecek. *Milli Gazetesi*, May 30.

———. 1999b. Mamak'ı Modernleştireceğiz. *Milli Gazetesi*, May 31.

Ministry of Culture, Republic of Turkey. 2005. *Folk Medicine*. http://www.kultur.gov.tr/EN/belge/2–16163/eski2yeni.html. Accessed October 2010.

Mishler, Elliot G. 1981. Critical Perspectives on the Biomedical Model. In *Social Contexts of Health, Illness, and Patient Care*, ed. Elliot G. Mishler, Lorna R. Singham, Samuel D. Hauser, Ramsay Liem, Stuart T. Osherson, and Nancy E. Waxler. Cambridge: Cambridge University Press.

Mitchell, Timothy. 2000. The Stage of Modernity. In *Questions of Modernity*, ed. Timothy Mitchell. Minneapolis: University of Minnesota Press.

Moore, Henrietta L., and Todd Sanders. 2001. *Magical Interpretations, Material Realities: Modernity, Witchcraft and the Occult in Postcolonial Africa*. New York: Routledge.

Morris, Rosalind. 2000. *In the Place of Origins: Modernity and Its Mediums in Northern Thailand*. Durham, N.C.: Duke University Press.

Mueggler, Erik. 2001. *The Age of Wild Ghosts: Memory, Violence, and Place in Southwest China*. Berkeley: University of California Press.

Murat, Salih. 1933. İlim ve Âlim. *Ülkü* 1, 4: 325–29.

Nâsır, Zeki. 1933a. Halk Sıhhati. *Ülkü* 1, 1: 73–75.

———. 1933b. Köylerimizin Sağlık İşleri. *Ülkü* 2, 7: 42–45.

———. 1934. Yürek Hastalıkları. *Ülkü* 4, 21: 210–14.

Navaro-Yashin, Yael. 2002. *Faces of the State: Secularism and Public Life in Turkey*. Princeton, N.J.: Princeton University Press.

Needham, Rodney. 1972. *Belief, Language, and Experience*. Chicago: University of Chicago Press.

Nguyen, Vinh-Kim, and Karine Peschard. 2003. Anthropology, Inequality, and Disease: A Review. *Annual Review of Anthropology* 32, 1: 447–74.

Noyan, Bedri. 1995. *Bektaşîlik Alevîlik Nedir?* İstanbul: ANT ve CAN Yayınları.

———. 1998. *Bütün Yönleriyle Bektaşilik ve Alevilik, I. Cilt*. Ankara: Ardıç Yayınları.

———. 1999. *Bütün Yönleriyle Bektaşilik ve Alevilik, II. Cilt*. Ankara: Ardıç Yayınları.

Nuri, İbnerrefik Ahmet. 1933. Katil Bebek. *Ülkü* 1, 2: 166–70.

Obeyesekere, Gananath. 1981. *Medusa's Hair: An Essay on Personal Symbols and Religious Experience*. Chicago: University of Chicago Press.

Olson, Emelie. 1991. Of Türbe and Evliya: Saints' Shrines as Environments That Facilitate Communication and Innovation. In *Structural Change in Turkish Society*, ed. Mübeccel Belik Kıray. Bloomington: Indiana University Press.

———. 1994. The Use of Religious Symbol Systems and Ritual in Turkey: Women's Activities at Muslim Saints' Shrines. *Muslim World* 84, 2–3: 202–16.

Olsson, Tord, Elisabeth Özdalga, and Catharina Raudvere, eds. 1998. *Alevi Identity: Cultural, Religious and Social Perspectives*. Istanbul: Swedish Research Institute.

Ömer, Kerim. 1933. Hangi Suları İçmeli. *Ülkü* 1, 3: 246–49.

Önder, Sylvia Wing. 2007. *We Have No Microbes Here: Healing Practices in a Turkish Black Sea Village*. Durham, N.C.: Carolina Academic Press.

Ong, Aihwa. 1987. *Spirits of Resistance and Capitalist Discipline: Factory Women in Malaysia*. Albany: State University of New York Press.

Orsi, Robert. 2005. *Between Heaven and Earth: The Religious Worlds People Make and the Scholars Who Study Them*. Princeton, N.J.: Princeton University Press.

Öztek, Zafer, and Nevzat Eren. 1996. *Sağlık Ocağı Yönetimi*. Ankara: Palme Yayınları.

Öztürkmen, Arzu. 1994. The Role of People's Houses in the Making of National Culture in Turkey. *New Perspectives on Turkey* 11 (Fall): 159–81.

Ozyegin, Gul. 2001. *Untidy Gender: Domestic Service in Turkey*. Philadelphia: Temple University Press.

Özyürek, Esra. 2004. Miniaturizing Atatürk: Privatization of State Imagery and Ideology in Turkey. *American Ethnologist* 31, 3: 371–91.

———. 2006. *Nostalgia for the Modern: State Secularism and Everyday Politics in Turkey*. Durham, N.C.: Duke University Press.

Pamuk, Orhan. 2004. *Istanbul: Memories and the City*. New York: Knopf.

Pandolfo, Stefania. 2000. The Thin Line of Modernity: Some Moroccan Debates on Subjectivity. In *Questions of Modernity*, ed. Timothy Mitchell. Minneapolis: University of Minnesota Press.

Parla, Taha. 1985. *The Social and Political Thought of Ziya Gökalp, 1876–1924*. Leiden: Brill.

Parla, Taha, and Andrew Davison. 2008. Secularism and Laicism in Turkey. In *Secularisms*, ed. Janet R. Jakobsen and Ann Pellegrini. Durham, N.C.: Duke University Press.

Pérouse, Jean-François. 2004. Deconstructing the Gecekondu. *European Journal of Turkish Studies* 1. http: //www.ejts.org/document195.html.

Pigg, Stacey. 1996. The Credible and the Credulous: The Question of "Villagers' Beliefs" in Nepal. *Cultural Anthropology* 11, 2: 160–201.

Prakash, Gyan. 1999. *Another Reason: Science and the Imagination of Modern India*. Princeton, N.J.: Princeton University Press.

Rancière, Jacques. 1999. *Dis-agreement: Politics and Philosophy*. Trans. Julie Rose. Minneapolis: University of Minnesota Press.

———. 2004. *The Politics of Aesthetics: The Distribution of the Sensible*. Trans. Gabriel Rockhill. London: Continuum.

———. 2009. The Aesthetic Dimension: Aesthetics, Politics, Knowledge. *Critical Inquiry* 36, 1: 1–19.

Recep. 1933. Ülkü Niçin Çıkıyor. *Ülkü* 1, 1: 1–2.

Rhodes, Lorna A. 1996. Studying Biomedicine as a Cultural System. In *Medical Anthropology: Contemporary Theory and Method*, ed. Carolyn Fishel Sargent and Thomas M. Johnson. Westport, Conn.: Praeger.

Rifat, Hikmet. 1934. Zehirli Gazlardan Fosgen. *Ülkü* 3, 13: 59–62.

Rose, Nikolas. 1999. *Powers of Freedom: Reframing Political Thought*. Cambridge: Cambridge University Press.

Roseman, Marina. 1993. *Healing Sounds from the Malaysian Rainforest: Temiar Music and Medicine*. Berkeley: University of California Press.

Roy, Olivier. 2004. *Globalized Islam: The Search for a New Ummah*. New York: Columbia University Press.

Rudnyckyj, Daromir. 2009. Spiritual Economies: Islam and Neoliberalism in Contemporary Indonesia. *Cultural Anthropology* 24, 1: 104–41.

Sabah. 1999. Zöhre Ana Yolun Sonunda. *Sabah*, February 5.

Sachs, Lisbeth. 1983. *Evil Eye or Bacteria: Turkish Migrant Women and Swedish Health Care*. Stockholm Studies in Social Anthropology. Stockholm: University of Stockholm.

Sağlık Bakanlığı. 1996. *Sağlık İstatistikler 1995*. Ankara: Sağlık Bakanlığı.

———. 2002. *Sağlık İstatistikler 2000*. Ankara: Sağlık Bakanlığı.

Sağlık ve Sosyal Yardım Bakanlığı. 1973. *Sağlık Hizmetlerinde 50 Yıl*. Ankara: Sağlık ve Sosyal Yardım Bakanlığı.

Şahin, Sehriban. 2005. The Rise of Alevism as a Public Religion. *Current Sociology* 53, 3: 465–85.

Said, Edward W. 1979. *Orientalism*. New York: Vintage.

Saktanber, Ayşe. 2002. *Living Islam: Women, Religion and the Politicization of Culture in Turkey*. London: Tauris.

Sanal, Aslihan. 2011. *New Organs Within Us: Transplants and the Moral Economy*. Durham, N.C.: Duke University Press.

Sayyid, Bobby S. 1997. *A Fundamental Fear: Eurocentrism and the Emergence of Islamism*. London: Zed Books.

Scheper-Hughes, Nancy. 1993. *Death Without Weeping: The Violence of Everyday Life in Brazil*. Berkeley: University of California Press.

Scheper-Hughes, Nancy, and Margaret Lock. 1987. The Mindful Body: A Prolegomenon to Future Work in Medical Anthropology. *Medical Anthropology Quarterly* 1, 1: 6–41.

Schieffelin, Edward. 1985. Performance and the Cultural Construction of Reality. *American Ethnologist* 12, 4: 707–24.

Schmitt, Carl. 1985. *Political Theology: Four Chapters on the Concept of Sovereignty*. Cambridge, Mass.: MIT Press.

Scott, David, and Charles Hirschkind. 2006. *Powers of the Secular Modern: Talal Asad and His Interlocutors*. Stanford, Calif.: Stanford University Press.

Scott, Joan. 2007. *The Politics of the Veil*. Princeton, N.J.: Princeton University Press.

Şenyapılı, Tansı. 1992. A New Stage of Gecekondu Housing in Istanbul. In *Development of Istanbul Metropolitan Area and Low-Cost Housing*, ed. Ilhan Tekeli, Tansı Şenyapılı, Ali Türel, Murat Güvenç and Erhan Acar. Istanbul: Turkish Social Science Association.

Shankland, David. 1990. Alevi and Sunni in Rural Turkey: Diverse Paths of Change. In *Culture and Economy: Changes in Turkish Villages*, ed. Paul Stirling. Huntingdon, UK: Eothen.

———. 1999. *Islam and Society in Turkey: Progress, Development, Change*. Huntingdon, UK: Eothen.

———. 2003. *The Alevis in Turkey: The Emergence of a Secular Islamic Tradition*. London: RoutledgeCurzon.

Sharp, Lesley. 1993. *The Possessed and the Dispossessed: Spirits, Identity, and Power in a Madagascar Migrant Town*. Berkeley: University of California Press.

Shefer-Mossensohn, Miri. 2009. *Ottoman Medicine: Healing and Medical Institutions, 1500–1700*. Albany: State University of New York Press.

Silverstein, Brian. 2003. Islam and Modernity in Turkey: Power, Tradition and Historicity in the European Provinces of the Muslim World. *Anthropology Quarterly* 76, 3: 497–517.

———. 2008. Disciplines of Presence in Modern Turkey: Discourse, Companionship, and the Mass Mediation of Islamic Practice. *Cultural Anthropology* 23, 1: 118–53.

———. 2011. *Islam and Modernity in Turkey*. New York: Palgrave Macmillan.

Sirman, Nükhet. 1989. Feminism in Turkey: A Short History. *New Perspective on Turkey* 3, 1: 1–34.

———. 1990. State, Village and Gender in Western Turkey. In *Turkish State, Turkish Society*, ed. Andrew Finkel and Nükhet Sirman. London: Routledge.

Sıhhat ve İçtimai Muavenet Vekâleti. 1957. *Halk Sağlığı Bilgileri*. Ankara: Akın Matabaası and T. C. Sıhhat ve İçtimai Muavenet Vekâleti Neşriyatı.

Sıhhıye Mecmuası. 1937. Atatürk'ün Etimesgut İçtimai Hıfzıssıhha Dispanseri. *Sıhhıye Mecmuası* 13, 89: 482.

Smith, Grace Martin, and Carl W. Ernst, eds. 1993. *Manifestations of Sainthood in Islam*. Istanbul: Isis Press.

Smith, Wilfred Cantwell. 1977. *Belief and History*. Charlottesville: University of Virginia Press.

Soekfeld, Martin. 2008. *Struggling for Recognition: The Alevi Movement in Germany and in Transnational Space*. Oxford: Berghahn.

Soileau, Mark. 2006. Humanist Mystics: Nationalism and the Commemoration of Saints in Turkey. Ph.D. dissertation, Religious Studies, University of California, Santa Barbara.

———. Forthcoming. Spreading the Sofra: Sharing and Partaking in the Bektashi Ritual Meal. *History of Religions*.

Solak, İsmet. 1991. *Cemden Gelen Nefesler*. Ankara: Zöhre Ana-Ali (VA) Sosyal Hizmet Vakfı.

Stewart, Kathleen. 2007. *Ordinary Affects*. Durham, N.C.: Duke University Press.

Stoller, Paul. 1989. *The Taste of Ethnographic Things: The Senses in Anthropology*. Philadelphia: University of Pennsylvania Press.

Swartz, Leslie, and Hayley MacGregor. 2002. Integrating Services, Marginalizing Patients: Psychiatric Patients and Primary Health Care in South Africa. *Transcultural Psychiatry* 39, 2: 155–72.

Tambar, Kabir. 2010. The Aesthetics of Public Visibility: Alevi *Semah* and the Paradoxes of Pluralism in Turkey. *Comparative Studies in Society and History* 52, 3: 652–79.

Tambiah, Stanley. 1977. The Cosmological and Performative Significance of a Thai Cult of Healing Through Meditation. *Culture, Medicine and Psychiatry* 1: 97–132.

———. 1984. *The Buddhist Saints of the Forest and the Cult of Amulets*. Cambridge: Cambridge University Press.

Tan, M. Turhan. 1938. *Osmanlı Rasputini Cinci Hoca*. İstanbul: SLE Sühulet Kitabevi.

Tapper, Nancy. 1990. Ziyaret: Gender, Movement, and Exchange in a Turkish Community. In *Muslim Travelers: Pilgrimage, Migration, and the Religious Imagination*, ed. Dale Eickelman and James Piscatori. Berkeley: University of California Press.

Tapper, Richard, and Nancy Tapper. 1987. "Thank God We're Secular!": Aspects of Fundamentalism in a Turkish Town. In *Studies in Religious Fundamentalism*, ed. Lionel Caplan. Albany: State University of New York Press.

Taussig, Michael. 1983. *The Devil and Commodity Fetishism*. Chapel Hill: University of North Carolina Press.

———. 1987. *Shamanism, Colonialism, and the Wild Man: A Study in Terror and Healing*. Chicago: University of Chicago Press.

———. 1997. *The Magic of the State*. New York: Routledge.

———. 2006. Viscerality, Faith and Skepticism. In *Walter Benjamin's Grave*. Chicago: University of Chicago Press.

Taylor, Charles. 2007. *A Secular Age*. Cambridge, Mass.: Harvard University Press.

Tsing, Anna. 1990. Gender and Performance in Meratus Dispute Settlement. In *Power and Difference: Gender in Island Southeast Asia*, ed. Jane Monnig Atkinson and Shelly Errington. Stanford, Calif.: Stanford University Press.

———. 1993. *In the Realm of the Diamond Queen: Marginality in an Out-of-the-Way Place*. Princeton, N.J.: Princeton University Press.

Turam, Berna. 2007. *Between Islam and the State: The Politics of Engagement*. Stanford, Calif.: Stanford University Press.

———. 2008. Turkish Women Divided by Politics: Secularist Activism Versus Pious Non-Resistance. *International Feminist Journal of Politics* 10, 4: 475–94.

Turner, Bryan S. 1974. *Weber and Islam: A Critical Study*. London: Routledge.

Turner, Victor. 1967. A Ndembu Doctor in Practice. In *The Forest of Symbols: Aspects of Ndembu Ritual*. Ithaca, N.Y.: Cornell University Press.

Uğurlu, M. 1994. Türkiye'de Öncü Bir Toplum Hekimi Dr. Mehmet Cemalettin Or. *Ankara Üniversitesi Tıp Fakültesi Mecmuası* 47, 1: 1–50.

Ülkü. 1933. Cümhüriyetin Sağlık, Bakım, ve Yardım İşleri. *Ülkü* 2, 9: 253–59.

van der Veer, Peter. 2001. *Imperial Encounters: Religion and Modernity in India and Britain*. Princeton, N.J.: Princeton University Press.

Veysel, Aşık. 1985. *Dostlar Beni Hatırlasın: Bütün Şiirleri, Sanatı, Hayatı*. Ankara: Özgür Yayınları.

Vryonis, Speros. 1991. *The Turkish State and History: Clio Meets the Grey Wolf*. Thessaloniki: Institute for Balkan Studies.

Warner, Michael, Jonathan VanAntwerpen, and Craig Calhoun, eds. 2010. *Varieties of Secularism in a Secular Age*. Cambridge, Mass.: Harvard University Press.

Weber, Max. 1958 [1905]. *The Protestant Ethic and the Spirit of Capitalism*. Trans. Talcott Parsons. New York: Scribner.

———. 1964. *The Theory of Social and Economic Organization*. New York: Free Press.

White, Jenny B. 1994. *Money Makes Us Relatives: Women's Labor in Urban Turkey*. Austin: University of Texas Press.

———. 2002. *Islamist Mobilization in Turkey: A Study in Vernacular Politics*. Seattle: University of Washington Press.

Yavuz, M. Hakan. 2003. *Islamic Political Identity in Turkey*. New York: Oxford University Press.

———. 2009. *Secularism and Muslim Democracy in Turkey*. Cambridge: Cambridge University Press.

Yörükan, Turhan. 1968. *Gecekondular ve Gecekondu Bölgelerinin Sosyo-Kültürel Özellikleri*. Ankara: İ mar ve Iskân Bakanlığı.

Yürür-Kutlay, Nükhet. 1998. Refik Saydam'ın Sağlık Politikası ve Hıfzıssıhha Merkezi'nin Bu Politikadaki Yeri. *Yeni Tip Tarihi Araştırmaları* 4: 187–206.

Žižek, Slavoj. 1997. *The Plague of Fantasies*. London: Verso.

———. 1999. *The Ticklish Subject: The Absent Centre of Political Ontology*. London: Verso.

Zürcher, Erik Jan. 1997. *Turkey: A Modern History*. London: Tauris.

Index

Acknowledgments

This book has been with me for so long, and taken part in so many relationships, that it is impossible to name individually all those to whom I am indebted. It is the generosity that this debt represents, and the impetus to think further that it has inspired, which, ultimately, made this book possible. In singling out but a few people who have lent particular support to me over the course of this project, it is unfortunate that I cannot name those to whom I have the most profound debt. The kindness, patience, and hospitality of my neighbors and collaborators in the neighborhoods where I conducted research continue to inspire me. I am honored to have been welcomed into their lives and entrusted with their stories.

Of those who can be named, I would like to extend particular thanks to Thomas Csordas for his encouragement, company, and clarity during the earliest stages of this project. The project similarly benefited during this period from extended conversations with Jonathan Sadowsky, Atwood Gaines, and Charlotte Ikels. I am also deeply indebted to Micah Parzen, who has been an ongoing source of support and inspiration since the beginning. Dan Kerr has likewise been a committed and intrepid co-conspirator. Beyond his continuous support, his commitment to the ability of those at the margins to critically analyze their own lives and, by extension, the conditions of society that make such lives possible has left an indelible mark on this book.

This book bears the traces of numerous conversations and relationships that took shape while I was a fellow in the Department of Social Medicine at Harvard Medical School, especially in the Medical Anthropology and Cultural Psychiatry Research Seminar. I would particularly like to thank Sarah Pinto, Michael Fischer, Angela Garcia, Clara Han, Erica James, Aslihan Sanal, Sadeq Rahimi, Everett Zhang, Sarah Horton, Michael Nathan, Alastair Donald, and Tony Robben. I want to express special gratitude to Byron Good and Mary-Jo DelVecchio Good, for their encouragement to pursue research in Turkey and, more important, the years of support, conversation, and generosity that followed. Arthur Kleinman's support has been similarly inspiring and humbling; signs of his passionate commitment to the care of others run throughout the pages to follow. Steve Caton, Engseng Ho, Omar al-Dewachi, Aykan Erdemir, Tuğba Tanyeri-Erdemir, and other participants in the Harvard Middle East Anthropology Workshop provided both a welcoming environment and discerning comments on critical aspects of this project. This book also benefited from Cemal Kafadar's kind inclusion of me into the Seminar on Turkey in the Modern World, as well as several remarks—assuredly insignificant to him—that proved incredibly helpful.

In Turkey, I want to offer special thanks to Akile Gürsoy who provided tremendous support during the early stages of fieldwork. Thanks as well to Nalan Şahin for her gracious hospitality and introducing me to the unique challenges and possibilities of public health in Turkey. Tayfun Atay went out of his way to assist me with the field research and his help is greatly appreciated. I would also like to thank Ozkul Çobanoğlu for many stimulating conversations and his endless wealth of humorous and always edifying stories. Likewise, the numerous engaging conversations with Tahire Erman and Fuat Keyman kept me on track during fieldwork. Sibel Kalaycıoğlu and Helga Rittersberger-Tılıç were of great assistance in providing much needed insights into conducting research in the sorts of neighborhoods where this project would be based. Dr. Yaman Ors and his colleagues in the Department of Deontology at Hacettepe University were likewise supportive in my efforts to navigate Turkey's history of medical reform. I would also like to thank Neslihan Demirtaş, Nurdan Atalay, and Ülviye Demirci for their help during fieldwork.

This book could not have been possible without the help of Mark Soileau. From this project's initial conceptualization to the reading of draft chapters, I have learned an incredible amount from Mark and benefited tremendously from his and Dilek's hospitality. My debt is truly profound. It is through Mark that I would also meet Bilal Topluk, whose uncontainable curiosity and incredible generosity provided important respite over the course of this project. Conversations, meals, and drinks with Kubilay Atılan over the years, spanning the U.S. and Turkey, were a similarly welcoming and always enlightening respite.

There are those who read individual chapters, and even the more daring who read nearly the entire manuscript. Here, I would like to thank Susan

Shaw, Amy Stamm, Caroline Melly, Britt Halvorson, Johan Lindquist, Maple Razsa, and Robert Desjarlais. I want to extend particular thanks to Johan Lindquist and his colleagues at Stockholm University for their patience with a very early formulation of what would become one of the book's central arguments. This project also benefited from many conversations with colleagues, past and present, including Deborah Gewertz, Alan Babb, Mitzi Goheen, Ron Lembo, Lynn Morgan, Jamal Elias, Monica Ringer, Debbora Battaglia, Tom Dumm, Adam Sitze, Jeffers Engelhardt, Marisa Parham, Nadia Guessous, Yogesh Chandrani, and Michael Kasper. I am incredibly indebted to Berna Turam, and I look forward to collaborating in the future. Most of all, I want to thank John Drabinski for both keeping me on task and bringing remarkable clarity at critical moments of this project. Considering that our friendship has spanned the most challenging period of this project, it seems only fitting that we share the birth of both new books and new babies.

Funding for this project was provided by the National Institute of Mental Health (1R03 MH059993) and the American Research Institute in Turkey. I am very grateful to these agencies for their support. I would also like to express my gratitude to the Institute of Turkish Studies, Andrew W. Mellon Foundation, and the Miner D. Crary Fellowship at Amherst College for financial assistance during the writing stages of this project. Chapter 1 is a revised version of "In the Shadows of Medicine and Modernity: Medical Integration and Secular Histories of Religious Healing in Turkey," *Culture, Medicine and Psychiatry* 28, 3 (2004): 255–80; reprinted by permission of Springer Science + Business Media. I thank the editors, editorial staff, and reviewers at *CMP* for their assistance. I am fortunate to have had the opportunity to work with University of Pennsylvania Press. I want to thank Peter Agree and Kirin Narayan in particular, for both their discerning editorial comments and their commitment to seeing this project through.

Finally, I want to express my deepest gratitude to Joy, Andiyah, Inez, and Zadie. In addition to my many absences, my obsession with the care of relations certainly strained our own at times. It is through you, both individually and together, that I was able to truly appreciate the richness, possibility, and vitality of the everyday. Joy, your brilliance, and patience with me, continues to astound me. Andiyah, Inez, and Zadie, I hope to be able to teach you as much about life and care as I was able to learn from all those I met during the course of my fieldwork. None of this could have been done without you. Thank you.